ORDINARY FAMILIES, SPECIAL CHILDREN

Ordinary Families, Special Children

A Systems Approach to Childhood Disability

Milton Seligman, PhD
Rosalyn Benjamin Darling, PhD

The Guilford Press
New York   London

© 1989 The Guilford Press
A Division of Guilford Publications, Inc.
72 Spring Street, New York, NY 10012

Printed in the United States of America

Last digit is print number: 9 8 7 6 5 4 3 2

Library of Congress Cataloging-in-Publication Data

Seligman, Milton, 1937–
    Ordinary families, special children : a systems approach to
childhood disability / by Milton Seligman, Rosalyn Benjamin Darling.
        p.   cm.
    Includes bibliographies and index.
    ISBN 0-89862-742-7
    1. Handicapped children—United States—Family relationship.
2. Parents of handicapped children—United States.   3. Family social
work—United States.   I. Darling, Rosalyn Benjamin.   II. Title.
HV888.5.S45 1989
362.4′088054—dc 19   88-24460
                                                                    CIP

To the memories of our fathers—
  Edgar Seligman
  Sidney Benjamin

Preface

The birth of a child with a disability is an unanticipated event. No family—regardless of race, ethnicity, or socioeconomic status—is immune to childhood disability; yet almost all are poorly prepared to cope with its occurrence. Childhood disability makes demands on families in terms of time, social stigma, psychological well-being, family relationships, economic resources, and freedom of movement. American society does not always provide sufficient support in the form of financial aid, respite care, or other assistance to allow these families to maintain an ordinary lifestyle. Some are able to achieve such a lifestyle through supports available in the family or community. The response of ordinary families to this extraordinary event, then, will be shaped by the social world within which the family resides.

As the title of the book suggests, families with children who have a disability are just like other families. However, the crisis of giving birth to a child with a disability thrusts family members into a situation that may make their lives different from those of other families. Childhood disability is typically life-long and may have many implications for how family members adapt and cope. Our purpose in writing this book is to examine the many intertwined family, child, and social system variables that contribute to the response of families to childhood disability. We hope to shed light on those elements of family and community life that facilitate or detract from the family members' ability to cope. An additional goal is to describe relevant intervention strategies for these families. The book has thus been organized to consider both family systems and larger social systems in defining the contextual world of the family and to describe useful system-based therapeutic modalities for professionals to consider in their work with these families.

Ordinary families take many forms. Like other families in society, families with disabled children are of various socioeconomic and ethnic backgrounds; they may have one or two parents; they may include grandparents or other relatives; they may have parents who work or who are unemployed. Vincent and Salisbury (1988) note that 20% of American families with children were headed by a single parent in 1984 and that 57% of black families with children were headed by a single parent. They write, "Combining the incidence of divorce, widowhood, and single parenthood, 67% of the children born in America today will be raised by a single parent for part of their lives" (p. 49). They note further that by 1990 perhaps 75% of all children under the age of six will receive day care while their parents work. Old models of family structure and function may be inadequate to explain changing patterns of family life. Intervention strategies must acknowledge the diversity of the American family today, and programs must design helping models that are effective because they are responsive to family composition and lifestyle.

Our discussion of families with children who have disabilities comes mainly from two sources: empirical investigations and personal accounts from family members. We believe that one source without the other is insufficient for a complete understanding of family strengths and needs. The research provides valuable broad-based scientific information; yet, without the inclusion of a more phenomenological perspective, any understanding of the experience of disability in the family is bereft of the richness of personal experience. Through quotes from family members, we hope to convey to the reader a qualitative sense of families' daily lives.

Professionals who work with families of children with disabilities must strive to understand both the social worlds of families in general and the special needs imposed by disability. The goal of this book is to increase such understanding by documenting the impact of childhood disability on the roles and lifestyles of various family members and on the family as a whole. We hope that the reader will come away from the book with a deeper appreciation of the difficulties faced by families—as well as the strengths that families demonstrate and acquire—as a result of the experience of living with a special child.

A number of people helped make this book possible. We wish to thank Sharon Panulla, Pearl Weisinger, and Karen Osborne—our editor, production editor, and copyeditor, respectively—at The Guilford Press for their assistance, and Roberta Allen for typing parts of the manuscript. Jon, Eric, and Seth Darling also contributed their support, patience, and word processing skills. Lisa and Lori Seligman provided important insights regarding disability and sibling relationships. Nancy Elman and Karen Compomizzi read certain chapters and shared their considerable insights about family issues. We are grateful for their help. Finally, we wish to acknowledge the contribution of the many families of children with disabilities who are quoted and whose experiences are related throughout the book. Their lives are the basis and the reason for our work, and we hope that this book will add in some small way to the quality of their lives.

M. S.
R. B. D.

REFERENCE

Vincent, L. J. & Salisbury, C. L. (1988). Changing economic and social influences on family involvement. *Topics in Early Childhood Special Education, 8*, 48–59.

Contents

ORDINARY FAMILIES, SPECIAL CHILDREN

1

Introduction and Conceptual Framework: Social Systems and Family Systems

It is only in recent years that conceptions of family functioning have been taken seriously by professionals who work with families with a chronically disabled member. The singular focus on the disabled individual has, as its major drawback, neglect of other family members. In some instances, the nonafflicted family member may be coping poorly. The concentrated focus on the disabled family member is also shortsighted in that it neglects the dynamic nature of family functioning. A deficiency in one family member affects the entire system (and, in turn, affects the disabled family member), thus forcing the family to reconceptualize how it plans to continue functioning effectively in the present and the future.

The reluctance to embrace a broader, or ecological, perspective may have been partially caused by the reign of psychoanalysis, which focuses on intrapsychic rather than interpersonal processes. Related to this is psychoanalytic theory's almost exclusive focus on the mother, with a particular focus on the mother–child relationship. Parke (1981) notes that fathers, for example, are ignored purposely because of the assumption that they are less important than mothers in influencing the developing child. Extant theories reflect the traditional conception of the remote father. Bowlby (1951) also stresses that the mother is the first and most important object of infant attachment and that fathers play only a supporting role.

With few exceptions (Minuchin, 1978), family theorists and family therapists have not studied or shown a particular interest in chronically disabled persons within the context of the family. Whatever the reasons for this heretofore narrow perspective, there is presently considerable interest in integrating theories of family systems with the available information about chronically disabled persons and their families (see, e.g., Berger & Foster, 1986; Blacher, 1984; Crnic, Friedrich & Greenberg, 1983; Seligman, 1983; Turk & Kerns, 1985; Turnbull & Turnbull, 1986; Imber-Black, 1988).

The purpose of this chapter is briefly to trace the history of family-centered health care and to provide a few conceptual frameworks for understanding family functioning in general as well as family functioning when a disabled child is present.

HISTORY OF FAMILY-CENTERED HEALTH CARE

Doherty (1985) provides a useful review of early family intervention programs, beginning with the first organized effort to provide family-based care, the Peckham Experiment. Southeast London was the site for this project, which began in 1926 and ended in 1939. The Peckham Experiment consisted of interdisciplinary teams, led by physicians, whose unit of intervention was the family. The primary goal was to study and promote health by strengthening the family. The team engaged in social and recreational activities as well as physical evaluations. The Peckham Experiment ended with World War II.

In the same year that the Peckham Experiment ended, the Cornell Project began in New York City. The project was a 2-year study of 15 families that examined the relationship between health and family patterns and ways to treat families in interdisciplinary teams. Like the Peckham Experiment, this project ended with World War II (when the United States entered the war in 1941).

Motivated by the Peckham Experiment, the Montefiore Medical group conducted a study and service project from 1950 to 1959, studying 100 families and controls. The study families were seen by a team consisting of an internist, a pediatrician, a public health nurse, and a social worker. By working with the family unit, the work group focused on disease prevention. Due to difficulties of team coordination and the reluctance of professionals to try out new roles, the project never fulfilled its potential.

Doherty (1985) concludes that none of these innovative, multidisciplinary family intervention projects had an effect on health care services in North America during the first half of this century. Post–World War II medicine continued to emphasize specialization and the biomedical aspects of patient care. The new speciality of family medicine, initiated in 1969, brought the idea of family-centered care nominally to the surface.

But only in the 1980s has this discipline explored and utilized models for integrating families into patient care.

According to Doherty, nursing and social work have evidenced a resurgence in family interventions during this past decade. Historically, nursing has been sensitive to patients' physical and social environments (Newman, 1983). In many health care settings, the nurse is the primary provider of health education to the family. The study of the family system is presently integrated into the nursing curriculum in many programs.

Social work was founded with a family emphasis but lost it during the discipline's middle years (Hartman & Laird, 1983). Social work in the 1920s was marked by an interest in mental hygiene and psychoanalysis. The emergence of family systems theory in the 1970s motivated social work to regain a family emphasis.

The Peckham Experiment, the Cornell Project, and the Montefiore Medical Group had seemingly modest impacts on family treatment as it presently exists. The conceptual and treatment bases of family interventions in health care did not begin to develop systematically until family systems theory and family therapy emerged in the 1950s, although Richardson's 1945 book, *Patients Have Families*, inspired a new medical subspecialty—family medicine (Doherty, 1985). The focus then, which has continued through the decades, has been the treatment of families experiencing psychosocial problems. In concert with the emerging research literature pointing to family factors in health and illness, family intervention has brought the issue of the family in health care to the forefront of interest in social work, psychology, psychiatry, and rehabilitation (Doherty, 1985).

According to Turk and Kerns (1985), however, the large body of research on the impact of illness on the family and the role of the family in the maintenance of health and the response to illness has not been integrated into developing disciplines. Furthermore, Turk and Kerns assert that this knowledge remains the domain of such areas as public health, psychosomatic medicine, and medical sociology, while at the same time the conceptualizations of family theorists have received little attention in behavioral medicine and health psychology. Turk and Kerns seem, however, to concur to some degree with Doherty (1985) that the family perspective is presently gaining more acceptance in applied fields.

We are at the threshold of significantly increased interest in the family and its reciprocal impact on family members with chronic conditions. The particular focus of this book, and hence this chapter, is on families with a disabled child or adolescent. To further our understanding of these families we ought to be better informed about family dynamics generally and especially about the dynamics of families with a disabled child.

Earlier we noted that, in recent years, there has been some effort to join the concepts of family systems with knowledge about families with a disabled child. Contributors to the professional literature have made attempts to promote a better understanding of such important concepts as stress as it affects family functioning (Crnic, Friedrich, & Greenberg, 1983; Wikler, 1981) and the effects of social support and social networks on the family (Holroyd, 1974; Kazak & Marvin, 1984). These important issues will be addressed later in this chapter, building on the work of family systems theorists. But Ann Turnbull and her associates have developed a useful conceptual framework, marrying family systems constructs with information about families with exceptional children. We now turn our attention to the contribution of Turnbull and colleagues.

FAMILY SYSTEMS THEORY

Some years ago, Minuchin (1974), in a brief paragraph, captured the essence of the interactive nature of the family:

> The individual influences his context and is influenced by it in constantly recurring sequences of interaction. The individual who lives within a family is a member of a social system to which he must adapt. His actions are governed by the characteristics of the system and these characteristics include the effects of his own past actions. The individual responds to stresses in other parts of the system to which he adapts; and he may contribute significantly to stressing other members of the system. The individual can be approached as a subsystem, or part of the system, but the whole must be taken into account. (p. 9)

Minuchin makes it clear that the family operates as an interactive unit and that what affects one member affects all members. Earlier, Von Bertalanffy (1968) had observed that all living systems are composed of interdependent parts and that the interaction of these parts creates characteristics not contained in the separate entities. As Carter and McGoldrick (1980) note, the family is more than the sum of its parts. Therefore, family life can best be understood by studying the relationship among its members. McGoldrick and Gerson (1985) are unequivocal in their view that the family is the primary and most powerful system to which a person ever belongs. They agree with other theorists when they assert that:

> The physical, social and emotional functioning of family members is profoundly interdependent, with changes in one part of the system reverberat-

ing in others parts of the system. In addition, family interactions and relationships tend to be highly reciprocal, patterned and repetitive. (p. 5)

However, before one can grasp the dynamic nature of family functioning, it is imperative to have an understanding of the characteristics, both static and dynamic, that comprise most family units. We turn, then, to Turnbull, Summers, and Brotherson's (1986) and to Turnbull and Turnbull's (1986) conceptualization of the family. These authors have made a noteworthy effort to apply family systems theory to the study of families with a disabled child.

Family Structure

Family structure speaks to the variety of membership characteristics that serve to make families unique. This "input" factor includes membership characteristics, cultural style, and ideological style.

Membership Characteristics

As Turnbull and colleagues (1986) note, much of the literature on families with disabled members is based on the assumption of family homogeneity. Families differ with regard to numerous membership characteristics: extended family members who may or may not reside in the household; single-parent families; families with an unemployed bread winner; or families in which there is a major psychological disorder, such as substance abuse, mental illness, or the continuing influence on family ideology of a deceased family member.

Although membership characteristics of families with disabled members have been studied, little has been done to investigate the relationship of these attributes to either successful or unsuccessful family interaction. Turnbull and Turnbull (1986) remind us that membership characteristics change over time. For example, the exiting of a family member will precipitate different communication and relationship patterns.

Cultural Style

Turnbull and colleagues (1986) state that a family's cultural beliefs are possibly the most static component of the family and can play an important role in shaping its ideological style, interactional patterns, and functional priorities. Cultural style may be influenced by ethnic, racial, or religious factors or by socioeconomic status. In her review of the literature, Schorr-Ribera (1987) points out that culturally based beliefs affect the manner in which families adapt to a child with a disability and also can influence their usage of and level of trust in caregivers and caregiving institutions.

Ideological Style

Ideological style is based on a family's beliefs, values, and coping behaviors and is also influenced by subcultural beliefs. McGoldrick, Pearce, and Giordano (1982) note, for example, that Jewish families place a great deal of importance on intellectual achievement. Such academic achievement may be sought, in part, to enable one to pursue professional opportunities designed to escape the repercussions of discrimination; therefore, college attendance is strongly urged. Italian families, which tend to emphasize family closeness and affection, may view college attendance as a threat to family cohesiveness. Other beliefs and values may be handed down from generation to generation and influence how family members interact with one another and with other families and other systems (such as schools and governmental agencies). It is important to be reminded here that families from the same subculture differ, as noted in Chapter 8.

While a family's responses to a disabled child may be influenced by ideological style, the reverse may also be true, namely, that such a child may influence a family's values. For example, when a disabled child is born a family must not only respond to the event itself but must also confront its beliefs about people who have disabilities. Since chronic afflictions do not discriminate on racial, subcultural, or socioeconomic grounds, a child with a disability may be born to a family that is very dogmatic and prejudiced. In such an instance, the family must grapple with what the child means to them psychologically and practically. In addition, family members must also examine their beliefs about persons with a minority-group status, namely, persons with disabilities. The birth of a disabled child thus results in a double shock to the family.

Ideological style influences the coping mechanisms of families. Turnbull and colleagues (1986) define coping as any response designed to reduce stress. Coping behaviors can motivate the family to change the situation or change the perceived meaning of the situation. An illustration of a potentially dysfunctional coping strategy comes from a recent study revealing that fathers of mentally retarded adolescents, compared to a matched control group of fathers of nondisabled adolescents, employed significantly more withdrawal and avoidance behaviors to cope with their anxiety (Houser, 1987).

McCubbin and Patterson (1981) classify coping styles into internal and external strategies; *internal* strategies include passive appraisal (problems will resolve themselves over time) and reframing (making attitudinal adjustments to live with the situation constructively), while *external* strategies include social support (ability to use familial and extrafamilial resources), spiritual support (use of spiritual interpretations, advice from clergymen), and formal support (use of community and professional resources).

Family Interaction

As Turnbull and Turnbull (1986) argue, it is important for professionals to realize that disabled children do not function in isolation. This reafirms the notion that persons live within a context—the family—and that when something happens to one member of the family, everyone is affected.

To say that a family is a unit comprised of a certain number of individuals and that they function in a dynamic interrelationship is to provide only a partial picture of how a family operates. Turnbull and colleagues (1986) elaborate on the four components of the interactional system: subsystems, cohesion, adaptability, and communication.

Subsystems

Within a family there are four subsystems:

1. marital—husband and wife,
2. parental—parent and child,
3. sibling—child and child,
4. extrafamilial—extended family, friends, professionals, and so forth.

The makeup of subsystems is affected by the structural characteristics of families (e.g., size of extrafamilial network, single mother or father, number of children) and by the current life-cycle stage.

Professionals need to be cautious when they intervene in a subsystem. An intervention designed to strengthen the bond between a mother and her disabled child, for example, can have implications for the mother's relationship with her husband and other children. Strategies need to be considered within the context of the other subsystems so that the resolution of one problem does not bring about the emergence of others. Perhaps such difficulties can be minimized by including (rather than excluding) family members when problems arise and by communicating the purpose and expected outcome of a particular intervention.

Cohesion and Adaptability

The subsystems describe *who* in the family will interact, whereas cohesion and adaptability describe *how* family members interact.

Cohesion can best be characterized by the concepts of enmeshment and disengagement. Minuchin (1974) says that highly enmeshed families have weak boundaries between subsystems and can be characterized as overinvolved and overprotective. Such families have difficulty allowing for a sense of individuality. Overprotective families can have deleterious effects on their disabled children. Such families experience considerable anxiety in "letting go" of their disabled children and hence may keep them from participating in growth-promoting activities.

Conversely, disengaged families have rigid subsystem boundaries (Minuchin, 1974). In regard to a family with a disabled child, interactions may be characterized by underinvolvement. Turnbull and Turnbull (1986) describe two situations that illustrate disengagement: one where a father denies the disability and withdraws from both marital and parental interactions; the other where grandparents reject the disabled child to the point of not allowing the child to join the family during holiday meals, thus creating considerable tension in the family.

Well-functioning families are characterized by a balance between enmeshment and disengagement. Boundaries between subsystems are clearly defined, and family members feel both a close bonding and a sense of autonomy. Enmeshment and disengagement, then, represent the outer boundaries of a continuum; the approximate middle of the continuum is where one finds well-functioning families.

Adaptability refers to the family's ability to change in response to a stressful situation (Olson, Russell, & Sprenkle, 1980). Rigid families do not change in response to stress, and chaotic families are characterized by instability and inconsistent change. A rigid family would have difficulty adjusting to the demands of caring for a significantly impaired child. The father's rigid breadwinner role, for example, would not allow him to help with domestic chores or to assist with the child ("woman's work"), thereby placing an inordinate burden on the mother. The mother, thus, must put all of her energies into caretaking responsibilities, which leaves little time for the other children in the family or for interacting with other people. This family is in jeopardy of becoming isolated and dysfunctional.

A chaotic family has few rules to live by, and those that do exist are often changed. There is no family leader, and there may be endless negotiations and frequent role changes (Turnbull & Turnbull, 1986). Chaotic families seem to move frequently from a sense of closeness or enmeshment to one of distance and hostility/disengagement. According to Turnbull and colleagues (1986), families who interact in a functional way maintain a balance—when change occurs—between emotional unity and autonomy, between reacting to change and a sense of stability, and between closed and random communication.

Communication

From a family systems perspective, communication breakdowns reflect a problematic system rather than faulty people. Communication problems reside in the interactions between people, not within people (Turnbull & Turbull, 1986). When working with families from a system point of view the emphasis is on changing patterns of interaction and not on changing individuals. There is an avoidance of placing blame on one family member or another and instead efforts are made to explore the factors that contribute to problematic communication patterns. Families sometimes believe that a particular family member is responsible for the problems they are experiencing but they usually discover that difficulties often reside in faulty communication. Often blaming a family member is less anxiety-provoking than examining dysfunctional communication patterns for which all family members bear a responsibility.

Family Functions

Turnbull and colleagues (1986) conceptualize family functions as products, or outputs, of family interaction. They reflect the *results* of interaction in terms of the ability to meet the needs of the family's members. To carry out functions successfully requires considerable interdependence between the family and its extrafamilial network. Also, families differ in regard to the priorities they attach to different functions and in regard to who is expected to carry out certain functions.

According to Turnbull and Turnbull (1986), the following reflect typical family functions:

1. economic (e.g., generating income, paying bills, and banking);
2. domestic/health care (e.g., transportation, purchasing and preparing food, medical visits);
3. recreation (e.g., hobbies, recreation for the family and for the individual);
4. socialization (e.g., developing social skills, interpersonal relationships);
5. self-identity (e.g., recognizing strengths and weaknesses, sense of belonging);

6. affection (e.g., intimacy, nurturing);
7. educational/vocational (e.g., career choice, development of work ethic, homework).

A disabled child residing with the family, especially a severely impaired child, can increase consumptive demands without proportionately increasing the family's productive capability (Turnbull et al., 1986). As a result, a disabled child residing in the least restrictive environment— namely, the family—may unintentionally generate a restrictive environment for all family members.

Furthermore, it is conceivable that a disabled child can change the family's self-identity, reduce its earning capacity, constrict its recreational and social activities, and affect career decisions. One can see in fairly concrete terms how a disabled child can affect the family by reflecting on the family functions noted above. This discussion also puts into perspective the notion that well-functioning families need to be flexible and open to change.

The discussion thus far has reflected on potential family problems. It is just as conceivable that children with disabilities can have a positive effect on family functions (e.g., Featherstone, 1980; Grossman, 1972; Seligman, 1979). For example, in one study Turnbull, Brotherson, and Summers (1985) report that families perceive a major positive contribution of a retarded member to be related to guidance, affection, and self-definition. In their study, parents and siblings describe positive attitudinal and value changes that they attribute to the retarded family members. In Turnbull and Turnbull's (1985) *Parents Speak Out*, contributors identify numerous positive benefits a disabled child has had on parental and sibling values.

Some authors question the emphasis placed on the role of parents as teachers of their child (Seligman, 1979; Turnbull et al., 1986). It is important to remember that the educational function is only one of several functions. Parents have many roles to play and many functions to perform, and one needs to be concerned about how the overburdening of one role or function affects the others. Also, in asking parents to assume an educational function it is useful to inquire about the parents' wish to take on that role, whether they are comfortable with it or feel prepared to assume it. Families are sometimes asked to do more at home with their child than the family system can tolerate. Too much stress can be placed on the family when professionals fail to coordinate the activities they ask the family to assume. With certain types of childhood impairments, a family may be given "homework" by the teacher, speech therapist, and physical therapist, among others. There needs to be some monitoring of the functions professionals ask a family to assume and a recognition of how the overburdening of one family function can affect the successful performance of the others. (For a further discussion of parents as teachers, see Chapter 9.) Professionals belonging to other social systems can help alleviate stress but they can also contribute to it. Therefore, professionals "must appreciate the requirement for ongoing interaction with larger systems, the stress generated thereby, and the need to intervene in ways that promote autonomy, enhance family resources, and facilitate empowerment of the family on behalf of their handicapped member" (Imber-Black, 1988, p. 105).

Family Life Cycle

The family, as defined by systems theorists, surely seems complex enough when one considers family structure, family interaction, and family functions. To these concepts is added the dynamic element of the family system, the family life cycle. As a family progresses over time, changes occur in its structure and function. These changes, in turn, affect the way the family interacts.

The family life cycle is a series of developmental stages in which, during a particular stage, the family's lifestyle is relatively stable and each member is engaged in developmental tasks related to that period of life (Duvall, 1957). For example, a family with two late-adolescent children is coping with the usual intensity and ambivalence of adolescent life in addition to the concerns that characterize adult (the parents') mid-life. Change occurs for this family when one of the children leaves home, which affects the family structure (i.e., a reduction from four to three persons at home) and may affect other aspects of family life, such as family interaction and communication.

Theorists have identified from 6 to 24 developmental stages (Carter & McGoldrick, 1980). Olson and colleagues (1984) identify seven stages, which are discussed here and include couple, childbearing, school age, adolescence, launching, postparental, and aging.

Each stage has its own developmental tasks; for example, parenting is important during the childbearing stage and nonexistent during the aging stage. Such functions are highly age related; for example, physical care by parents is essential during infancy, and educational and vocational guidance is important when children are in high school and college. Whereas bonding and attachment are vital in infancy, letting go is important when children reach late adolescence. Thus a key aspect of life-cycle stages is the change in function required of families over time.

Developmental transitions (moving from one stage to another) can be a major source of stress and possibly even family dysfunction. According to a study by Olson and colleagues (1984), "launching" creates the greatest amount of family stress.

Turnbull and colleagues (1986) relate the developmental stages derived from systems theorists to the stress families with disabled children experience. Below, for each pertinent stage identified by Olson and colleagues (1984), are listed some illustrative stress factors:

1. Childbearing: Getting an accurate diagnosis; making emotional adjustments; informing other family members
2. School age: Clarifying personal views regarding mainstreaming versus segregated placements; dealing with reactions of child's peer group; arranging for childcare and extracurricular activities
3. Adolescence: Adjusting for chronicity of child's disability; dealing with issues of sexuality; coping with peer isolation and rejection; planning for the child's vocational future
4. Launching: Recognizing and adjusting to the family's continuing responsibility; deciding on appropriate residential placement; dealing with the lack of socialization opportunities for disabled members
5. Postparental: Reestablishing relationship with spouse (that is, if child has been successful launched); interacting with disabled member's residential service providers

THE SOCIAL ECOLOGY MODEL

Early studies of childhood behavior were often conducted in laboratory settings where the many variables that affect human subjects could be controlled. In studying childhood behavior, Vasta (1982) questions whether relationships demonstrated under laboratory conditions hold true in the natural environment. One of the leading critics of traditional laboratory research, Bronfenbrenner (1979), argues that; "The emphasis on rigor has led to experiments that are elegantly designed but are often limited in scope. This limitation derives from the fact that many of these experiments involve situations that are unfamiliar, artificial, and short-lived, and call for unusual behaviors that are difficult to generalize to other settings" (p. 18).

In the early studies of families with disabled children, researchers fell prey to a somewhat similar problem by defining the unit of study or intervention in very specific terms, focusing only on the child and neglecting the family as a legitimate unit of study. Later studies focused on the mother, with a particular emphasis on mother–child bonding. The consideration of the family as a dynamic, interdependent unit was a major step forward, and yet there continued to be a flaw in the conceptualization of the family. We know that young disabled children with disabilities do not live in isolation. Likewise, the family lives in a broader context. The formulation of the family within a social ecology framework has been discussed extensively by Bronfenbrenner (1979) and has more recently been discussed in relation to families with a disabled child (Bubolz & Whiren, 1984; Mitchell, 1983).

Bubolz and Whiren (1984) characterize a social ecology approach as incorporating the biological and physical dimensions of the organism and environment as well as their psychosocial characteristics and interactions. Similar to the interaction component in the family systems model, the basic tenet of the social ecology paradigm is that a change in any part of the ecological system affects subparts of the system, creating the need for system adaptation (equilibrium). The ecological environments of the family furnish the resources necessary for life and make up the life support and social support systems.

Similar to boundary concerns in the family systems model, the social ecology model is also concerned with the permeability of the family in interacting with environmental systems; for example, whether a family with a disabled child is open to the supportive influences of other similarly situated families (e.g., support groups) or whether it is amenable to assistance from social agencies or other sources of help.

Bronfenbrenner (1979) describes an elaborate theory in which the family is viewed as a system nested within a number of other societal systems (see Figure 1-1). A key tenet of the social ecology point of view is that if one wishes to change behavior (perhaps, in this instance, the behavior of the family), one needs to change environments. The social ecology view further asserts that a child or family can be affected by events occurring in settings in which the person is not even present. An example of this phenomenon is the possible effect on a young child of the conditions of parental employment. Employment conditions can be the consequence of the health of the economy. And the health of a local economy can, in turn, be affected by events occurring on a national or even international scale (e.g., a war). Thus the behavior of a child or a family unit can be influenced by a variety of external and remote events. This view encourages a broad conceptualization of the forces that impinge on the family. Such a framework incorporates contributions to the literature that focus on the social policies that affect families of disabled children.

As shown in Figure 1-1, Bronfenbrenner's subsystems include the microsystem, mesosystem, exosystem, and macrosystem. Mitchell (1983) has applied Bronfenbrenner's concepts to the study of families with disabled children. A discussion of Mitchell's adaptation is presented below.

The *microsystem* constitutes the pattern of activities, roles, and interpersonal relations experienced by the family. In it one finds the following components: mother–father, mother–disabled child, mother–nondisabled

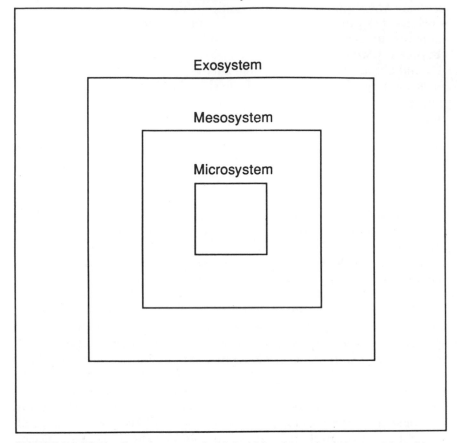

FIGURE 1-1. The family as a system embedded within other societal systems. Adapted from
Bonfenbrenner (1979).

child, father–disabled child, father–nondisabled child, disabled child–nondisabled child. This pattern of subsystems resembles the family systems
theory already explored. Some of the potential problems of families with a
disabled child that parallel the subsections of the microsystem include:

1. Mother–father: How well parents cope individually and as a couple before the birth of a disabled child; how well they accept the
   child's disabilities
2. Mother–disabled child: Mother's depression, guilt, and self blame;
   how enmeshed or disengaged she may be with the child

3. Mother–nondisabled child: How much attention the nondisabled child receives; using sibling in compensatory way; giving non-disabled child excessive caretaking responsibility for disabled sibling
4. Father–disabled child: Whether father withdraws or is psychologically and instrumentally present
5. Father–nondisabled child: Same as #3 above
6. Disabled child–nondisabled child: Feelings of guilt, shame; fear of catching the disability; disabled sibling's enslaving nondisabled brother/sister; nondisabled sibling's feelings of ambivalance toward disabled brother/sister.

The microsystem functions in a *mesosystem* comprising a wide range of settings in which a family actively participates. The following combine to comprise the mesosystem:

1. Medical and health care workers: How diagnosis is handled; professionals' availability and depth of knowledge; attitudes of professionals toward families with chronically disabled children; professionals' skill in being honest with parents but also kind, humane, and helpful
2. Extended family: Grandparents' degree of acceptance/rejection of disabled grandchild; grandparents' and other extended family members' willingness to relieve parental stress by helping with certain family functions
3. Friends/neighbors: Level of community acceptance and support, which can help parents cope with their feelings of shame and embarrassment
4. Work/recreation associates: Whether family members are treated as normal and equal, without child's disabilities projected onto them
5. Early intervention programs: There has been high praise for early intervention programs, but due to various factors they may not be available for some families
6. Other parents: Much social, psychological, and practical help is available from support groups for parents and siblings; they can collectively effect social policy through legislative initiatives
7. Local community: Availability of services tends to differ markedly in urban and rural communities and in poor versus affluent communities

In the *exosystem* there are settings in which the family is not actively involved, yet they can affect the family, such as:

1. Mass media: The mass media can affect attitudes about disabled persons, for example, by portraying them as poor souls, incapable and undesirable, or as able, likeable, and reliable.
2. Health: Families of severely impaired children in particular are dependent on health care systems.
3. Social welfare: For some families, financial and other governmental supports are essential for family well-being; SSI disability payments also help maintain living standards for needy families.
4. Education: The existence of the Education for All Handicapped Children Act insures certain rights; and while an adversarial relationship sometimes exists between parents and schools, schools can help families achieve respite from disabled children.

And, finally, there is the *macrosystem*, which is the ideological or belief systems inherent in the social institutions of society. It includes:

1. Ethnic/cultural, religious, and socioeconomic elements: Ethnic/cultural and religious values can affect how disability is viewed by family members and can also play a role in how a family chooses to interact with the service delivery system; socioeconomic status may determine or reflect a family's instrumental resources.
2. Economic and political elements: The health of the economy and the political atmosphere can have important impacts on programs for disabled persons and their families.

Bronfenbrenner (1979) asserts that the core of a social ecology orientation, distinguishing it from other models, is the concern with the progressive accommodation between a growing organism and its immediate environment and the way this relationship is mediated by forces from more remote regions in the larger social and physical milieu. Thus a major shift in the government's philosophy can, when the philosophy is translated into legislation, affect the availability of funds for social programs designed to help families with disabled children. Likewise, an impasse between parents and the school over a child's proper educational placement affects not only the family, which feels frustrated, angry, and powerless, but also school personnel, who are distraught about the parents' resistance and defensiveness.

To understand families with disabled children it simply is not sufficient to study only the child, nor the child and his/her mother, nor the dynamics occurring within the family; it is also necessary to examine the family within the context of larger social, economic, and political realities.

RELATED CONCEPTS

A number of theorists and investigators have concentrated on a particular aspect or component of family adaptation. Several of these contributors formulate concepts that are similar or interrelated and, therefore, do not constitute clearly separate entities. Nevertheless, the following discussion will center on several key concepts that are often cited in the literature and relate directly to families with disabled children.

Stress

The notion of stress has been touched on earlier in this chapter. Stress has been mentioned in relation to life-cycle changes and is also implicated in events occurring within the family's social ecology.

Hill (1949) developed a theoretical model of stress that is often cited in the family literature (McCubbin & Patterson, 1983; Wikler, 1981) and has been designated as the *ABCX* family crises model: *A* (the stressor event) interacts with *B* (the family's crisis-meeting resources) which interacts with *C* (the definition the family makes of the event) to produce *X* (the crisis).

The *A* factor (the stressor) is a life event or transition that can produce change in the family system. The family's boundaries, goals, patterns of interaction, roles, or values may be threatened by change caused by a stressor (McCubbin & Patterson, 1983). A stressor event, for example, may be the family's need to generate more income due to the economic burdens visited on them by a disabled child. This hardship can place demands on the roles and functions of family members, alter their collective goals, and affect the family's interaction.

The *B* factor (family resources) has been described as the family's ability to prevent an event or change in the family from causing a crisis (McCubbin & Patterson, 1983). The *B* factor is the family's capacity to meet obstacles and shift its course of action. This factor relates directly to the notion that the family's flexibility and quality of relationship prior to the presence of a disabled child may be an important predictor of its ability to adapt.

The *C* factor is the definition the family makes of the seriousness of the experienced stressor. The *C* factor reflects the family's values and their previous experience in dealing with change and meeting crises. This factor resembles a key component of Ellis's (1958) theory of neurosis. He asserts that it is not the event itself, but the meaning attributed to the event, that constitutes the source of neurotic thinking and behavior.

Taken together the three factors all influence the family's ability to prevent the stressor event from creating a crisis (the X factor). A crisis reflects the family's inability to restore balance and stability. It is important to note that stress may never become a crisis if the family is able to use existing resources and defines the situation as a manageable event.

Social Support

Social support is often viewed as a mediating or buffering factor in meeting the demands of a stressful event (Cobb, 1976; Crnic, Greenberg, Ragozin, Robinson, & Basham, 1983). The presence of a disabled child is considered a stressful event (Crnic, Greenberg, Ragozin, Robinson, & Basham, 1983) and one that is considered chronic in nature (Olshansky, 1962).

Researchers such as Crnic, Greenberg, Ragozin, Robinson, & Basham (1983) have examined social support in terms of three ecological levels: (1) intimate relationships (e.g., spousal), (2) friendships, and (3) neighborhood or community support. For example, in their study designed to assess the relationship of maternal stress and social support, these authors found that mothers with greater social support were more positive in their behavior and attitudes toward their infants. Intimate (spousal) support proved to have the most positive effects.

Kazak and Marvin (1984) and Kazak and Wilcox (1984) have developed an innovative conceptualization of social support networks and applied this model to the study of families with disabled children. Kazak and Marvin (1984) elaborate on three components of social networks: network size, network density, and boundary density.

Kazak and Marvin (1984) define *network size* as the number of persons perceived as offering different types of support, such as spiritual, medical, psychological, or instrumental support. These authors contend that, in general, the larger the social network, the greater the possibility of successful adaptation.

Network density refers to the extent to which members of an individual's social network know each other, independent of the focal person. Density provides an indication of the interrelatedness of the social network. In their study of families with spina bifida children, Kazak and Wilcox (1984) found that the social networks of families with spina bifida children were fairly dense, suggesting that the people from whom help was sought knew and interacted with one another. These authors state that high-density networks are associated with higher levels of parental stress. Kazak (in press b) argues that this conclusion has certain implications for formal helpers (as opposed to family, extended family, and friends): if fewer friends are available to families, the role of formal helpers may be crucial; formal helpers could augment the assistance friends may be providing; the best way to integrate professional helpers into a family's dense network to maximize social support needs to be determined.

The third characteristic of social networks is *boundary density*, which is a measure of that portion of the network membership that is shared by the individuals involved. That is, the boundary density is determined by the number of network members whom both parents know and utilize. One method of determining boundary density is to ascertain to what extent spouses list the same network members. Kazak and Wilcox (1984) report that network overlap (high boundary density) tends to be associated with marital stability.

Two other characteristics of social networks are discussed by Kazak and Wilcox (1984): network reciprocity and network dimensionality.

Network reciprocity is the degree to which affective and instrumental aid is both given and received. Kazak and Wilcox (1984) provide an illustration of this concept: "Asking a friend to watch a child requiring specialized care may contribute to network drain and may not be matched by requests of a similar magnitude from the network" (p. 649).

Network dimensionality is the number of functions served by a relationship. Network members who are able to provide multiple types of help are viewed as being supportive and contributing to positive adaptation (Kazak & Wilcox, 1984).

These authors assert that there are three areas of concern relevant to understanding the ecological context of families with disabled children. These points relate directly to the notion of social networks. First, it is important to specify the precise nature of existing stresses and to integrate this knowledge into a family model. Implied here is that an examination of the social support network needs to be undertaken by professionals and factored into existing models of family functioning. Second, although these families are sometimes characterized as socially isolated from their support networks, greater specification is needed in terms of the nature, extent, and consequences of this isolation. Third, the dissatisfaction families express regarding their relationships with professional personnel (Seligman, 1979; Chapter 9, this volume), on whom they are often dependent, underscores the importance of examining more closely the availability of informal sources of support.

Kazak and colleagues have continued to engage in research on the social network model and stress with families of disabled children. The interested reader may wish to consult her other publications in this area (Kazak, in press a; Kazak, in press b; Kazak, 1986; Kazak & Clark, 1986).

Developmental Transitions

The family life cycle was discussed earlier as a component of family systems theory. To briefly review, the family life cycle refers to seven life stages described by Olson and colleagues (1984): couple, childbearing, school age, adolescence, launching, postparental, and aging. Due to the nature and severity of a child's disability and the family's response to it, families with disabled children must concern themselves with a series of stages that, at least to some extent, are unique to such families. For some families it is not possible to apply any type of developmental or stage theory model because of new major events that continue to occur throughout the child's lifetime. This may be true, for example, in a family with a hemophilic child, where periodic "bleeds" can cause considerable ongoing stress. Such events trigger a new cycle of upset, changing demands, and new adaptations.

Farber (1975) and Fewell (1986) remind us that children with disabilities will be slower in reaching certain life-cycle or developmental milestones and some may never achieve them. As a disabled child approaches critical periods, parents may experience renewed anxiety or sadness. Fewell (1986) describes six periods that are particularly stressful to parents of disabled child.

Encountering the Disability

The nature of a child's disability generally determines when the parents learn about it. Genetic disabilities, such as Down syndrome, are apparent soon after birth. Conditions such as deafness or language and learning disabilities may not be discovered until the child is older. Also, families may be confronted with disability due to accident or illness when the child is older. The confirmation of a serious and chronic problem generally precipitates a crisis and affects the entire family. Immediate reactions may be those of shock, disappointment, and depression, with the family often following a fairly predictable series of stages of adjustment (Seligman, 1979; Chapter 2, this volume). Contact with physicians and health care workers is particularly intense at this stage.

Early Childhood

The early childhood years can be difficult ones for the family, as they anxiously watch for their child to achieve certain developmental milestones. The chronicity of a child's disabilities and what it means to the family are major parts of the early childhood years. The nature and severity of the disability may play a key role in the family's perception and behavior (Fewell & Gelb, 1983; Lyon & Preis, 1983). In regard to a child's developmental delay, Fewell (1986) observes that:

> The task of diapering a three-year old is simply not as easy as it was when the child was one year old. The larger and heavier child requires more energy to lift and carry. The emotional burden is also great: parents anticipate the end of diapers and two o'clock bottles, and when these things don't end, it can shatter dreams and invite questions about the future. (pp. 16–17)

A parent's concern about the future is vividly portrayed by educator and parent Helen Featherstone (1980)*:

> I remember, during the early months of Jody's life, the anguish with which I contemplated the distant future. Jody cried constantly, not irritable, hungry cries, but heartrending shrieks of pain. Vain efforts to comfort him filled my nights and days. One evening when nothing seemed to help, I went outside, intending to escape his misery for a moment, hoping that without me he might finally fall asleep. Walking in summer darkness, I imagined myself at seventy, bent and wrinkled, hobbling up the stairs to minister to Jody, now over forty, but still crying and helpless. (p. 19)

Although early intervention programs are generally welcomed, Fewell (1986) notes that a crisis may develop when a child enters an early intervention program, because:

1. families see older children with a similar condition and wonder whether their children will resemble them as they develop;
2. families become aware that the services needed by their children can represent a significant financial drain on them as well as a burden on their available time;
3. families who share their experiences with other families realize that they may need to "fight" for the services their children need, further draining the family's resources;
4. families learn that they are often expected to be their children's primary caregivers and teachers.

Professionals may treat parents as patients who need treatment rather than as parental and caregiving experts. Perhaps most discouraging at this stage is the realization of the chronic burden a child might be for parents and siblings as they view the future with some degree of uncertainty and anxiety.

*Excerpts from Featherstone (1980) are copyright by Basic Books, Inc. Reprinted by permission.

School Entry

Parents may experience another setback or period of adjustment when they realize that their child fails to fit into the mainstream of the traditional educational system. A child may require special-education classes and a separate transportation system. As more of their schoolmates learn that they have a disabled brother or sister, siblings may find this a particularly difficult period. This stage can be characterized as the period when the family "goes public," when they venture beyond the boundaries of the family. And finally, parents, if they have not done so already, must adjust the educational and vocational goals they had envisioned for their child.

It is important to note that the difficulties parents experience depends on the nature of the child's disability (e.g., there may be relatively few adjustments if the child is moderately physically disabled) and the preparedness of the school system to provide adequate educational and adjunct services for children with special needs. Also, during this period parents may debate the merits of a segregated versus mainstreamed educational setting for their child.

Adolescence

Adolescence marks the period when children begin to separate from their parents. This period also reflects the time when adolescent children experience considerable change, turmoil, and ambivalence (Marshak, 1982). For families of disabled children, who continue to remain dependent, this stage can be a painful reminder of their child's failure to traverse this life-cycle stage successfully.

Peer acceptance or the lack of it may be particularly painful for the entire family during the adolescent years. Peer acceptance may determine the extent to which the child may feel rejected and isolated, which in turn may contribute to the stress parents and siblings experience.

Beginning Adult Life

Public education offers both children and parents several benefits. It helps the child gain important educational and vocational skills, as well as independence; it provides respite for the parents. But as a child's education draws to an end, parents must make some difficult choices. Because of limited vocational possibilities and inadequate community living arrangements, some families may be left with few choices. This is a stressful period in that the specter of the child's future looms and can cause considerable concern and anxiety.

Maintaining Adult Life

Where a disabled person will live and the level of care needed characterize the family's concerns at this stage. A major concern is the future care of their adult child as parents worry about the ensuing years when they may not be able to be active overseers of when they have died. Mental health professionals are particularly important here in helping families plan for their child's future in terms of vocational and leisure-time activities as well as living arrangements. Adult siblings, as well as other extended family members, may be useful resources and should be explored as potential helpers during this period. Although community support services are always needed, their availability and accessibility can be particularly acute at this time.

In a fitting conclusion to her discussion of the aforementioned stages, Fewell (1986) notes that:

> When a family has a disabled child, all the actors in this support network must adapt to the extended needs of the disabled member. The adaptations family members make are often significant, and individual destinies may be determined by the experience. Family adaptations change as the child matures; the stress at various periods may affect family members differently, for much depends on the familial and environmental contributions to the dynamic interactions of adaptation at a given point in time. (p. 19)

SUMMARY

This chapter presents several conceptual perspectives of the family with a disabled child. Perhaps key to this chapter are the notions that families are remarkably complex and dynamic and that there are many factors that make up and impinge on family life. The family does not remain static but changes as new events occur; also, families change as they progress through the life cycle and as they experience their child's developmental milestones. In our interventions with families with disabled children we must be well grounded in the static and dynamic features of families if we are to be successful with them.

The approach to be taken in the following chapters, then, will be a systems approach. Derived from both the psychological and sociological literature, this approach views the child as part of a family system of interacting units and a social system of interacting families, individuals, and social institutions. Chapters 2 and 3 look at how family reactions to the birth and rearing of a disabled child are socially shaped. Chapter 4, 5, and 6 explore the effects of childhood disability on various members of the family system and on the family as a whole. Chapter 7 describes family-based intervention practices. In Chapter 8 and 9, we return to the larger social system perspective and look at interactions between families and others, both within and outside their social worlds. Finally, Chapter 10 illustrates the application of a social system perspective to the assessment of family needs. By combining the systems literature from two fields, we hope to provide the reader with a broader and deeper understanding of families of children with special needs.

REFERENCES

Berger, M., & Foster, M. (1986). Applications of family therapy theory to research and interventions with families with mentally retarded children. In J. J. Gallagher & P. M. Vietze (Eds.), *Families of handicapped persons* (pp. 251–260). Baltimore: Brooks.

Blacher, J. (Ed.). (1984). *Severely handicapped young children and their families: Research in review*. Orlando, FL: Academic.

Bowlby, J. (1951). *Maternal care and mental health*. Geneva: World Health Organization.

Bronfenbrenner, U. (1979). *The ecology of human development*. Cambridge, MA: Harvard University Press.

Bubolz, M. M., & Whiren, A. P. (1984). The family of the handicapped: An ecological model for policy and practice. *Family Relations, 33,* 5–12.

Carter, E., & McGoldrick, M. (Eds.). (1980). *The family life cycle: A framework for family therapy*. New York: Gardner.

Cobb, S. (1976). Social support as a moderator of life stress. *Psychosomatic Medicine, 38,* 300–314.

Crnic, K. A., Friedrich, W. N., & Greenberg, M. T. (1983). Adaptation of families with mentally retarded children: A model of stress, coping and family ecology. *American Journal of Mental Deficiency, 88,* 125–138.

Crnic, K. A., Greenberg, M. T., Ragozin, A. S., Robinson, N. M., & Basham, R. B. (1983). Effects of stress and social support on mothers and premature and full-term infants. *Child Development, 54,* 209–217.

Doherty, W. J. (1985). Family intervention in health care. *Family Relations, 34,* 129–137.

Duvall, E. (1957). *Family development*. Philadelphia: Lippincott.

Ellis, A. (1958). Rational psychotherapy. *Journal of General Psychology, 59,* 34–49.

Farber, B. (1975). Family adaptations to severely mentally retarded children. In M. J. Begab & S. A. Richardson (Eds.), *The mentally retarded child and society: A social science perspective* (pp. 247–266). Baltimore, MD.: University Park Press.

Featherstone, H. (1980). *A difference in the family*. New York: Basic Books.

Fewell, R. (1986). A handicapped child in the family. In R. R. Fewell & P. F. Vadasy (Eds.), *Families of handicapped children* (pp. 3–34). Austin, TX: Pro-Ed.

Fewell, R. R., & Gelb, S. A. (1983). Parenting moderately handicapped persons. In M. Seligman (Ed.). *The family with a handicapped child* (pp. 175–202). New York: Grune & Stratton.

Grossman, F. K. (1972). *Brothers and sisters of retarded children*. Syracuse, NY: Syracuse University Press.

Hartman, A., & Laird, J. (1983). *Family-centered social work practice*. New York: Free Press.

Hill, R. (1949). *Families under stress*. New York: Free Press.

Holroyd, J. (1974). The questionnaire on resources and stress: An instrument to measure family response to a handicapped family member. *Journal of Community Psychology, 2*, 92-94.

Houser, R. (1987). *A comparison of stress and coping by fathers of mentally retarded and non-retarded adolescents.* Unpublished doctoral dissertation, University of Pittsburgh.

Imber-Black, E. (1988) *Families and larger systems: A family therapist's guide through the labyrinth.* New York: Guilford.

Kazak, A. E. (in press a). Professional helpers and families with disabled children: A social network perspective. *Marriage and Family Review.*

Kazak, A. E. (in press b). Families with disabled children: Stress and social networks in the samples. *Journal of Abnormal Child Psychology.*

Kazak, A. E. (1986). *Stress and social network in families with older institutionalized retarded children.* Unpublished manuscript, University of Pennsylvania, Philadelphia.

Kazak, A. E., & Clark, M. W. (1986). Stress in families of children with myelomeningocele. *Developmental Medicine and Child Neurology, 28*, 220-228.

Kazak, A. E., & Marvin, R. S. (1984). Differences, difficulties and adaptation: Stress and social networks in families with a handicapped child. *Family Relations, 33*, 67-77.

Kazak, A. E., & Wilcox, B. L. (1984). The structure and function of social support networks in families with handicapped children. *American Journal of Community Psychology, 12*, 645-661.

Lyon, S., & Preis, A. (1983). Working with families with severely handicapped persons. In M. Seligman (Ed.), *The family with a handicapped child* (pp. 203-234). New York: Grune & Stratton.

Marshak, L. (1982). Group therapy with adolescents. In M. Seligman (Ed.), *Group psychotherapy and counseling with special populations* (pp. 185-214). Baltimore: University Park Press.

McCubbin, H. I., & Patterson, J. M. (1981). *Systematic assessment of family stress, resources, and coping: Tools for research, education and clinical intervention.* St. Paul: University of Minnesota, Department of Family Social Science, Family Stress and Coping Project.

McCubbin, H. I., & Patterson, J. M. (1983). The family stress process: The double ABCX model of adjustment and adaptation. *Marriage and Family Review, 6*, 7-37.

McGoldrick, M., & Gerson, R. (1985). *Genograms in family assessment.* New York: Norton.

McGoldrick, M., Pearce, J. K., & Giordano, J. (1982). *Ethnicity and family therapy.* New York: Guilford.

Minuchin, S. (1974). *Families and family therapy.* Cambridge, MA: Harvard University Press.

Minuchin, S. (1978). *Psychosomatic families.* Cambridge, MA: Harvard University Press.

Mitchell, D. (1983). Guidance needs and counseling of parents of mentally retarded persons. In N. N. Singh & K. M. Wilton (Eds.), *Mental retardation: Research and services in New Zealand.* Christchurch, New Zealand: Whitoulls.

Newman, M. A. (1983). A continuing evolution: A history of nursing science. In N. L. Chaska (Ed.), *Time to speak* (pp. 385-393). New York: McGraw-Hill.

Olshansky, S. (1962). Chronic sorrow: A response to having a mentally defective child. *Social Casework, 43*, 191-194.

Olson, D. H., McCubbin, H. I., Barnes, H., Larsen, A., Muxen, M., & Wilson, M. (1984). *One thousand families: A national survey.* Beverly Hills, CA: Sage.

Olson, D. H., Russell, C. S., & Sprenkle, D. H. (1980). Circumplex model of marital and family systems II: Empirical studies and clinical intervention. In J. P. Vincent (Ed.),

26 Social Systems and Family Systems

Advances in family intervention assessment and theory (Vol. 1) (pp. 129–179). Greenwich, CT: JAI Press.

Parke, R. D. (1981). *Fathers.* Cambridge, MA: Harvard University Press.

Richardson, H. B. (1945). *Patients have families.* New York: Commonwealth Fund.

Schorr-Ribera, H. K. (1987). *Ethnicity and culture as relevant rehabilitation factors in families with children with disabilities.* Unpublished manuscript, University of Pittsburgh.

Seligman, M. (1979). *Strategies for helping parents of exceptional children: A guide for teachers.* New York: Free Press.

Seligman, M. (Ed.). (1983). *The family with a handicapped child: Understanding and treatment.* Orlando, FL: Grune & Stratton.

Seligman, M. (1985). Handicapped children and their families. *Journal of Counseling and Development, 64,* 274–277.

Turk, D. C., & Kerns, R. D. (1985). *Health, illness and families: A life-span perspective.* New York: Wiley.

Turnbull, A. P., Brotherson, M. J., and Summers, J. A. (1985). The impact of deinstitutionalization on families: A family systems approach. In R. H. Bruininks (Ed.), *Living and learning in the least restrictive environment* (pp. 115–152). Baltimore: Brookes.

Turnbull, A. P., Summers, J. A., & Brotherson, M. J. (1986). Family life cycle: Theoretical and empirical implications and future directions for families with mentally retarded members. In J. J. Gallagher & P. M. Vietze (Eds.), *Families of handicapped persons* (pp. 45–65). Baltimore, MD: Brooks.

Turnbull, A. P., & Turnbull, H. R. (1986). *Families, professionals, and exceptionality.* Columbus, OH: Merrill.

Turnbull, H. R., & Turnbull, A. P. (Eds.). (1985). *Parents speak out: Then and now.* Columbus, OH: Merrill.

Vasta, R. (1982). *Strategies and techniques of child study.* New York: Academic.

Von Bertalanffy, L. (1968). *General systems theory.* New York: Braziller.

Wikler, L. (1981). Chronic stresses of families of mentally retarded children. *Family Relations, 30,* 281–288.

2

Becoming the Parent of a Disabled Child: Reactions to First Information

The father of a disabled child (Abraham, 1958) has written:

> No event in your entire babyhood could rival the despair of its first day. That, in itself, is consolation for parents who find out the worst right at the start. There is no lower depression than the day of being told. (p. 64)

Various writers have suggested that certain crisis periods are especially traumatic for parents of children with disabilities (see, e.g., MacKeith, 1973), including when parents first learn or suspect that their child has a disability, school-entry age, time of leaving school, and when parents become older. Of these, the crisis of first information or suspicion is probably the most difficult, and families' needs for support are greatest at that time. In this chapter, we review some popular theories about family reactions to news of their child's disability and suggest a model of family reactions during the infancy period using an interactionist perspective.

APPROACHES TO UNDERSTANDING FAMILY REACTIONS

Stage Theory

Many writers have suggested that parents pass through a series of stages before they accept a diagnosis of disability in their child. Blacher (1984a) lists 24 studies that present some variant of stage theory as part of their

27

conclusions about parent reactions. Many writers have suggested a similarity between the sequence of stages in the acceptance of death and dying and the sequence found in parents of children with disabilities. Solnit and Stark (1961) have argued that parents must mourn the loss of their wished-for normal child before they can accept their real defective child.

In a typical study concluding with a stage model, Drotar, Baskiewicz, Irvin, Kennell, and Klaus (1975) looked at the parents of 20 children with congenital malformations and found a common sequence of reactions:

1. Shock: Most parents' initial reaction to their child's diagnosis was overwhelming shock, because they had anticipated a normal baby.
2. Denial: Parents tried to escape from reality by disbelieving the diagnosis.
3. Sadness, anger, anxiety: The most common reaction was intense sadness, which accompanied or followed denial.
4. Adaptation: Eventually, intense feelings subsided and parents were able to care for their children.
5. Reorganization: Positive, long-term acceptance finally developed. Guilt also tended to lessen with time.

One composite of a number of studies (Gargiulo, 1985) identified three stages:

1. Primary phase, characterized by shock, then denial, and finally grief and depression;
2. Secondary phase, marked by ambivalence, followed by guilt, then anger, shame, and embarrassment;
3. Tertiary phase, beginning with bargaining, then adaptation and reorganization, and finally acceptance and adjustment.

The following quote, from one of the parents of a deaf child (Allen & Allen, 1979), lends support to these stage theories:

> At first I had a feeling of numbness, of unreality and depression. The "pain" gradually overcame me during the next few days . . . an all-consuming pain. . . . I hid [the hearing aid] for about two weeks. . . . Then, one day I remember thinking, "I can't hide it forever." . . . At that point I took my first steps toward adjustment. . . . The terrible pain was still present, but I was better able to cope with it. . . . Now I cry mostly because I'm so proud of Jeffrey and what he has become. At 14, he's okay. . . . I still hate the deafness, but we've all learned to live with it. (pp. 280–282)

Chronic Sorrow and Nonsequential "Stage" Theories

A number of studies (see, e.g., Wikler, Wasow, & Hatfield, 1981) have suggested that, although the reactions described by the stage theorists may be present in parents of disabled children, these reactions are not necessarily experienced sequentially. The reactions may, in fact, occur repeatedly, precipitated by various life crises and turning points. The parent whose earlier quote supported stage theory has also written:

> I still carry some pain around that occasionally surfaces. With each major change in Jeffrey's development, I have found myself going through the same emotional adjustments I did in the very beginning. (Allen & Allen, 1979, p. 282)

Olshansky (1962) has argued that parents of mentally retarded children do not ever competely abandon the grief process. Rather, he suggests the *normal* reaction to the birth of a child with a disability is *chronic sorrow*. He writes:

> The permanent, day-by-day dependence of the child, the interminable frustrations resulting from the child's relative changelessness, the unesthetic quality of mental defectiveness, the deep symbolism buried in the process of giving birth to a defective child, all these join together to produce the parent's chronic sorrow. (p. 192)

In this view, chronic sorrow is a natural reaction, and its continued presence many years after a child's birth is not pathological. In fact, chronic sorrow and acceptance of a child's disability may coexist as part of the normal, long-term process of parental adjustment. In one well-adjusted family, for example, the father remarked that "retardation is not number one around here. It's just something that Karen has." Yet, the mother related these feelings about a recent experience*:

> I had a friend who had a daughter who was born a week after Karen. . . . This year . . . I kind of compared. I said, "Oh look at Jackie. You know, so much different. She's going to be a young lady, and Karen, you know, she's still really a baby compared to that." (Darling, 1979, p. 167)

"Kinds of Families/Kinds of Children" Theories

"Kinds of families/kinds of children" theorists do not necessarily reject stage theory or any of its variants. Rather, they suggest that whether a

---

* Excerpts from Darling (1979) are copyright by Sage Publications, Inc. Reprinted by permission.

family will pass through certain stages or have specific reactions will vary according to a number of factors:

- socioeconomic status
- support services (or lack of them)
- physician attitude
- presence of other children and spouse in the home
- prior information
- availability of support persons in the community
- single- versus two-parent homes
- religiosity
- previous births of nondisabled children
- actual physical appearance of the child

In addition, Schell and Marion (reported in Mori, 1983) include the severity and social acceptability of the child's disability. Mori (1983) adds the manner in which parents are informed of the diagnosis, the child's age at onset or diagnosis, and the sex of the parent involved. Other factors, noted by Collins-Moore (1984), include:

- general emotional maturity of the parent
- cultural attitudes
- education
- parent's age
- birth order
- child's sex
- child's ability to respond to the parent
- etiology of the disability
- prognosis

Because of the great diversity among families, no single reaction or sequence of reactions can be found in all parents of children with disabilities. (The effects of subcultural diversity are explored further in Chapter 8). In addition to predisposing characteristics that shape parental reactions, situational contingencies play an important role in parental response. These contingencies are discussed in the next section.

Interactionist Perspective

Symbolic interactionism is a sociological approach to social psychology that derives from the work of George Herbert Mead, Charles Horton Cooley, and others. This approach suggests that beliefs, values, and knowledge are socially determined through interaction and the ability of individuals to "take the role of the other," or understand the meanings attached to situations by other people. The symbolic interactionist view of human behavior focuses on social process rather than on static characteristics of individuals, such as sex, ethnicity, or personality type. When applied to families of children with disabilities, parental reactions would be interpreted within the context of the parents' interactional histories prior to their child's birth and their experiences afterward. Parents attach meanings to their experiences as a result of definitions they have encountered in their interactions with others.

Not all interactions are equally important. Among the most important are those with *significant others*, usually close family members and friends. When significant others define their situation positively, parents are likely to define it positively as well. The effects of interactions with significant others, along with the broader interactional context, will be explored in the next section, as we trace the development of parental reactions from the prenatal through the postpartum periods.

AN INTERACTIONIST APPROACH TO UNDERSTANDING PARENTS' INITIAL REACTIONS

The Prenatal Period

Prior Knowledge About Disability

Prior to their child's birth, most parents have had only limited experience with individuals with disabilities. In general, they have been exposed primarily to the stereotypes and stigmatizing attitudes toward the disabled that pervade our culture. Richardson (1970) and others have shown that almost all groups in the population have negative attitudes toward the physically disabled, and Gottlieb (1975) and others have shown that the mentally disabled are also negatively labeled in our society.

During the prenatal period, then, most parents dread the possibility of giving birth to a disabled child. As one mother of a Down syndrome child said, "I remember thinking, before I got married, it would be the worst thing that could ever happen to me" (Darling, 1979, p. 124). Parents' concerns are sometimes even greater when they know of other families who have had children with disabilities: "I've always been worried about having a child who was handicapped—one of our friends has a terribly retarded child, terribly retarded. We were concerned. We just wanted a healthy child" (Parent of a nondisabled child, reported in Darling, 1979, p. 127).

In some cases, parents claim to have had premonitions that something was wrong with their baby:

> I always said if it wasn't a girl, there was something wrong [this mother
> already had two nondisabled boys]. It just felt different from my other
> pregnancies, and my sister-in-law had just lost a baby at seven months.

> I felt very strongly that she was deformed. . . . She didn't kick as much as I
> thought she should.

> I thought something might be wrong because I was sick all the time and I
> wasn't sick at all during my first pregnancy. (Darling, 1979, pp. 125–126)

In these cases, concerns seem to be based on experience. These parents'
definitions of "what pregnancy should be like" did not fit their actual
experience of pregnancy. Such parents are not typical, however, and most
anticipate the birth of a healthy baby.

When parents express concerns about the health of their unborn
child, these concerns are usually discounted by friends, relatives, and
others. Even a mother who had *four* children with the same genetic
disorder managed to rationalize her fears during each successive pregnancy with the help of physicians who assured her that her bad luck was
not likely to recur. With regard to her third pregnancy, she said: "I was
unrealistic. I said, 'He's going to be a Christmas baby. There won't be
anything wrong with him'" (Darling, 1979, p. 143). In general, then,
parents' fears about the health of their unborn baby are usually neutral-
ized through interactions with others, and most approach the birth situation anticipating a healthy child.

Expectations that a baby will be normal are also promoted by prepared childbirth classes. Although these classes typically cover the possibility of unexpected events during labor and delivery, the end product of
the birth process that is presented to prospective parents is generally a
normal, healthy baby. The possibility of birth defects is usually not
mentioned at all.

Most parents, then, are poorly prepared for the birth of child with a
disability. In some cases, parents are not even aware of the existence of
their child's disability prior to the baby's birth. As one parent said, "I
never heard of Down's. . . . Mental retardation wasn't something you
talked about in the house. . . . There wasn't much exposure" (Darling,
1979, p. 124). Similarly, the parent of a dwarf recalled this initial reaction:

> I heard Dr. Z use the word dwarf outside the room when he was talking to a
> resident. When he came in, I said, "Dwarf? Are you saying my child's a

dwarf?" What dwarf meant to me was a leprechaun. Whatever would *that* mean? Would you have to send them to a circus? (Ablon, 1982, p. 36)

In other cases, parents can recall having heard of a defect, but only in a limited, and typically negative, way: "I'd heard of it from a book. It was just a terrible picture on a certain page of an abnormal psych book that I can still sort of picture" (Darling, 1979, p. 125).

With the advent of modern technology, some childhood disabilities are being diagnosed prenatally. Through techniques such as amniocentesis, ultrasound, and maternal serum testing, parents are able to learn of problems prior to their child's birth. In cases of prenatal diagnosis, anticipatory grieving may be tempered by the hope that "maybe they made a mistake" and the baby will be all right after all. One mother, who was told after an ultrasound screening late in her pregnancy that her baby had hydrocephalus, said she was "shocked, sad, and depressed" after hearing the news but "hoped they were wrong" at the same time (Darling & Darling, 1982, p. 98). After she saw the baby's enlarged head in the delivery room, she no longer doubted the diagnosis.

Pregnancy as a Social Role: Expectations and Dreams

Attitudes toward pregnancy and birth vary among cultural and subcultural groups. Rosengren (1962) has shown, for example, that lower-class women are more likely than upper-class women to engage in "sick-role" behavior during pregnancy. The value placed on pregnancy is also likely to vary according to the value placed on children or large families in different groups. Within a context in which families are highly valued, as among some Italian-Americans, for example, pregnancy is also likely to be highly valued and the pregnant woman is likely to occupy an esteemed status. Within other cultural contexts, such as that segment of the urban American middle class in which one-child or two-child families are the norm, some pregnancies may even be disvalued. Certainly, whether a pregnancy is planned or unplanned, whether the parents are married or not, and other circumstances surrounding the pregnancy and birth situations will shape parental reactions, regardless of whether the child is born with a disability.

LaRossa (1977) has argued that a couple's first pregnancy creates a crisis that is a potential strain on the marital relationship. Similarly, Doering, Entwisle, and Quinlan (1980) claim that a first pregnancy is a progressively developing crisis. The threat is generally not serious enough to destroy an otherwise strong marriage, but we should keep in mind that pregnancy and birth are stress-producing situations, even when a baby is perfectly healthy.

Expectant parents also typically fantasize about their unborn baby. They may imagine the baby's sex, appearance, personality, or other attributes. Interactions with friends and relatives help to shape parents' fantasies. Folk wisdom sometimes plays a role, interpreting the pregnant woman's shape or size or the baby's prenatal movements as indicative of the child's sex, size, or temperament.

Parents enter the birth situation, then, with a particular base of knowledge, attitudes, expectations, and hopes. They possess varying degrees of knowledge about disabilities, various attitudes toward people with disabilities and toward their status as expectant parents, differing expectations about the birth situation, parenthood, and the attributes of their unborn child as well as hopes and wishes relating to those attributes.

The Birth Situation

A number of studies (see, e.g., Doering, Entwisle, & Quinlan, 1980; Norr, Block, Charles, Meyering, & Meyers, 1977) have suggested that parents who have taken prepared childbirth classes are more likely to define the birth situation in a positive manner. More prepared parents, however, are also likely to be more aware of deviations from normal delivery room routine that may occur in the case of a baby with a problem.

Rothman (1978) has argued that although prepared childbirth might seem more meaningful to the parents, it in fact places them in a situation as powerless as that of parents in the traditional, medically controlled birth situation. She suggests that hospital births are always medical events and the care of the mother and child are scheduled to fit institutional rhythms. Mothers' feelings of powerlessness are increased by admission procedures, such as stripping the woman of her clothing and jewelry, shaving the pubic area, and administering an enema. Danziger (1979) argues that medical control is also expressed through stimulation of labor and intervention in delivery. In the delivery room, then, even prepared parents may be intimidated by the professionally controlled setting. Feelings of powerlessness are likely to be magnified when a baby's problems are detected immediately after birth. As this mother's report shows, the parent has little control over events in the delivery room:

> When Billy was born I heard the nurse say, "Is it a boy or a girl?" and I knew right away something was wrong. . . . They wrapped him up so I could just see his head and they said, "We're going to bring him to the nursery now." I let him go because I knew something was wrong and I wanted him to be taken to where he would get attention. (Darling, 1979, p. 132)

Typically, concerns about a baby are not revealed directly to parents in the delivery room. Rather, parents become suspicious as a result of unintentional clues given by physicians and nurses:

> I remember very vividly. The doctor did not say anything at all when the baby was born. Then he said, "It's a boy," and the way he hesitated, I immediately said, "Is he all right?" And he said, "He has ten fingers and ten toes," so in the back of my mind I knew there was something wrong. (Darling, 1979, p. 129)

D'Arcy (1968) and Walker (1971) note clues, such as "the look on the nurse's face," consultations between nurses in hushed voices, and nurses who "looked at each other and pointed at something."

In rarer cases, the clues are not so subtle:

> When the baby was born, they said, "Oh my God, put her out." That's the first thing they said, "Oh my God, put her out" . . . and the next thing I remember was waking up in the recovery room. . . . I had my priest on my left hand and my pediatrician on my right hand . . . and they were trying to get me to sign a piece of paper. . . . I just couldn't believe that this was happening to me and I said to my priest, "Father, what's the matter?" and he said, "You have to sign this release. Your daughter is very sick," and I said to the pediatrician, "What's the matter with her?," and he said . . . she had something that was too much to talk about, that I shouldn't worry myself. . . . Nobody was telling me what this was. . . . I was very depressed. (Darling, 1979, p. 130)

Parental reactions in the immediate postpartum situation, then, may be characterized in many cases by the sociological concept of *anomie*, or normlessness. Because even prepared parents are unable to make sense of atypical events in the delivery room, the birth experience is stressful for almost all parents of children whose disabilities can be detected immediately by medical personnel. McHugh (1968) has shown that the components of anomie are *meaninglessness* and *powerlessness*, and both are commonly experienced by parents of disabled newborns.

As Chapter 9 shows, physicians may *deliberately* create meaninglessness and powerlessness in the belief that they are protecting the parents, who are "not ready to hear the truth" so soon after birth. Yet, as Chapter 9 also reveals, studies show that most parents *do* want to know their child's diagnosis right from the beginning; uncertainty and suspicion may be more stressful than bad news. Although most physicians do suggest a diagnosis before a baby leaves the hospital, occasionally the period of suspicion is protracted:

> He was born on Tuesday, and by Thursday, I was suspicious. Nurses would come in and ask to see pictures of my first child; then they would leave quickly. . . . The baby wasn't eating well, and once when a nurse came in after a feeding, I told her I was worried. She said, "It's all due to his condition." I asked, "What condition?" but she just walked out. . . . Then, the doctor asked me when I was going home. When I said, "Tomorrow," he said, "Good. That will give us more time to observe the baby." . . . The obstetricians kept asking if I noticed any difference between Joey and my first baby. . . . I asked to see the house pediatrician. . . . Then my husband arrived to take me home and he said to the doctor, "She doesn't know yet. I'll tell her later." [He had just been told himself.] (Darling, 1979, p. 129)

Parents' immediate reactions to the birth of a child with a disability, then, may involve suspicions created by interactions with professionals. The birth situation generally occurs in medically controlled settings in our society, placing parents in a state of submission to professional authority. As a result, they are likely to feel powerless and to experience stress when events do not proceed according to their expectations. As the next section shows, anomie may be a continuing reaction even after a diagnosis has been established.

The Postpartum Period

The Establishment of Parent–Child Bonding and Attachment

As many studies have shown, parents' initial reaction to the news that their child has a disability is likely to be negative. Rejection of the baby during the early postpartum period is common, as these statements illustrate:

> I was kind of turned off. I didn't want to go near her. It was like she had a disease or something, and I didn't want to catch it. I didn't want to touch her. (Mother of a child with Down syndrome)

> I saw her for the first time when she was 10 days old. . . . She was much more deformed than I had been told. At the time, I thought, "Oh my God, what have I done?" (Mother of a child with spina bifida) (Darling, 1979, pp. 135, 136)

The fact that parents have chosen to deny life-saving treatment to such children in the well-publicized "Baby Doe" cases is not surprising. Attachment to the baby is probably lowest during the first few hours after birth. Parents are also very vulnerable during the immediate postpartum period and likely to be highly susceptible to suggestions by professionals that their children not be treated. Lorber (1971), a British physician who advocated "selective treatment" for children born with spina bifida, has in fact written that he preferred to present his case for nontreatment to parents immediately after birth, before bonding had occurred.

Even when a baby has no disability, however, bonding between parent and child is not always an immediate reaction. LeMasters (1957) found that most of the parents of normal infants in his study had little effective preparation for parental roles and had romanticized parenthood. Shereshefsky, Liebenberg, and Lockman (1973) quote a new mother: "I don't think I was prepared at all because you read in books and you talk with people and you think that all of a sudden there is going to be this motherly surge of love, which is not true. . . . I had this colicky baby that spit up, and we had to stay home. It took me a long time" (p. 175). Dyer (1963) has noted that 80% of the parents he studied "admitted that things were not as they expected them after the child was born" (p. 200).

With any baby, disabled or not, attachment grows out of the process of parent–child interaction. When babies respond to parental attempts to feed and cuddle them, parents feel rewarded. Attachment is further enhanced when babies begin smiling and making sounds in response to parental gestures. Infants with disabilities, however, may not be able to respond to their parents' efforts. Blacher (1984b) summarizes the Bowlby-Ainsworth thesis: "Attachment formation is not an inevitable phenomenon . . . but is produced through dyadic interaction of the child and the care provider. Such interaction, involving reciprocal communication of feeling and meaning presupposes some cognitive development and sensory intactness in the child" (p. 10).

Bailey and Wolery (1984), Blacher (1984b), Collins-Moore (1984), Robson and Moss (1970), Waechter (1977), and others have suggested that the following characteristics of some childhood disabilities may impede the formation of parent–child attachment:

- the child's appearance, especially facial disfigurement
- negative response to being handled (stiffening, tenseness, limpness, lack of responsiveness)
- unpleasant crying
- atypical activity level—either lowered activity or hyperactivity
- high threshold for arousal
- no response to communication
- delayed smiling
- feeding difficulties
- medical fragility
- presence of medical equipment, such as feeding tubes or oxygen supplies

- life-threatening conditions
- prolonged hospitalization and consequent separation
- impaired ability to vocalize
- inability to maintain eye contact
- unpleasant behaviors, such as frequent seizures

Abnormal response patterns in infants may result in withdrawal by parents. As Stone and Chesney (1978) have written: "The failure of the handicapped infant to stimulate the mother leads to failure of the mother to interact with the infant" (p. 11). Frodi (1981) has shown, further, that child abuse is disproportionately high in the instance of premature, disabled, and otherwise deviant infants.

The tremendous adaptive capacity of families is evidenced by the fact that, given all the obstacles to parent–child attachment present in the case of childhood disability, the vast majority of parents *do* form strong attachments to their disabled infants. In general, all but the most severely disabled children are able to respond to their parents to some extent—by sound, gesture, or other indication of recognition. In addition, attachment is usually encouraged by supportive interactions with other people.

The mother of the Down syndrome infant quoted earlier explained:

> I talked to a nurse and then I felt less resentment. I said I was afraid, and she helped me feed the baby. . . . Then my girfriend came to see me. She had just lost her husband, and we sort of supported each other. . . . By the time she came home I loved her. When I held her the first time I felt love and I worried if she'd live. (Darling, 1979, p. 136)

Similarly, the mother of the child with spina bifida reported:

> As time goes on, you fall in love. You think, "This kid's mine, and nobody's gonna take her away from me." I think by the time she was two weeks old I wasn't appalled by her anymore. (Darling, 1979, p. 136)

Waisbren (1980) and others have reported the important role of social support in promoting parents' positive feelings about their children. One father of a child with Down syndrome said that, at first, he and his wife had decided not to send birth announcements, but then "everybody was saying he was so lucky to have *us* as parents." The parents then printed announcements that looked like theater tickets for a hypothetical play entitled "A Very Special Person" (Darling, 1979, p. 136). Minde (reported in Collins-Moore, 1984) also found that parents in a support group interacted more with their infants than other parents.

Various situational contingencies may also affect attachment. As Waechter (1977) and others have noted, the timing of the baby's birth in relation to other family events is important. Another member of the family may be ill, the family may be experiencing financial difficulties, or the parents may be having marital problems. The amount of time and energy available to parents for the new baby will depend on these contingencies. Professionals need to be aware of the family's situation when they look at parenting practices and parent–child relationships, so that expectations are not unrealistic.

Irvin, Kennell, and Klaus (1982) make a number of recommendations to professionals in order to encourage parent–child bonding, including the following:

1. Initial contact: Bring the baby to the parents as soon after birth as possible.
2. Positive emphasis: Show the baby's positive features to the parents.
3. Medication: Avoid tranquilizers.
4. Special caretaking: Assign a specific nurse who has time to listen.
5. Prolonged contact: Leave the child with the parents for as long as possible.
6. Visiting: Allow the father to remain on the maternity unit.
7. Questions: Encourage parents to ask questions.
8. Adaptation: Give the parents time to adapt.
9. Explaining findings: Professionals may need to repeat explanations several times.
10. Pace: Progress at the parents' pace.

The Case of Delayed Diagnosis

Not all disabilities are diagnosed in the immediate postpartum period. Some developmental disabilities, such as cerebral palsy or mental retardation, may not be readily apparent shortly after birth. Other disabilities occur as a result of accidents or illness later in infancy or childhood. In still other cases, professionals delay in communicating a known diagnosis to parents for a variety of reasons (these are discussed in greater detail in Chapter 9). In general, parents have said that they were better able to adjust when they were aware of their child's diagnosis from the beginning. The process of redefining as disabled a child once defined as "normal" appears to be a very difficult one for parents.

Most of the time, however, parents suspect that a problem exists before they receive a diagnosis, and diagnostic delay only protracts the period of suspicion and its attendant stress. The experience of one family is illustrative:

> The mother, who was a nurse and had an older child, felt from the time of birth that something was wrong with the baby. Her daughter would not nurse, her eyes were crossing, "and she always seemed to be looking at her right side." The mother asked her pediatrician about the baby's vision and hearing but was told that nothing was wrong. When the baby was three months old, she kept falling asleep, [and the mother suspected that a photographer who took her picture at that time knew that something was wrong]. The mother again questioned her pediatrician and was told that nothing was wrong. At five months, the baby began to have seizurelike periods, and the mother became increasingly concerned. Both her husband and her pediatrician continued to deny the problem. Her husband said, "I thought she was a little paranoid about it. . . . When you're not home all day you don't see the [baby's] lack of activity or anything like that." As a result, the mother tried harder to rationalize and began blaming herself, feeling that perhaps she had been neglecting the baby in favor of her older child. Finally, when the baby was six months old, the mother "broke down and started crying" in the pediatrician's office. [The child was finally diagnosed as mentally retarded.] (Darling, 1983, p. 127)

In such cases, parents tend to be relieved rather than shocked when they finally receive a diagnosis. This reaction is apparent in these families of mentally retarded children quoted by Dickman and Gordon (1985):

> When the doctor told us, he couldn't believe how well we accepted the diagnosis. All I can say is that it was such a relief to have someone finally just come out and say what we had feared for so long! We felt that now we could move ahead and do the best we could for Timmy.

> When James turned six months old, my husband and I decided to change pediatricians. The second doctor was an angel in disguise. She spotted the problem immediately. . . . The reason I called her an angel was that she finally put an end to the unknown. The not knowing exactly what was wrong was driving me crazy. (pp. 31, 32)

Similarly, in a study of 131 families with mentally retarded children, Baxter (1986) found that most parents who experienced little or no worry after a diagnostic encounter had gradually become aware of their child's "differentness" or had sought a diagnosis to confirm their own suspicions.

The Post-Diagnosis Experience

Although a diagnosis may relieve the stress associated with meaning-lessness and the suspicion that something is wrong, parents generally continue to experience anomie to some extent until issues of prognosis have been resolved and until the child is enrolled in a treatment program.

The Need for Prognostic Information

A father who had been told that his son would be "a slow learner" expressed the following concerns:

> [I was most worried about] how he would develop. It was the uncertainty of not knowing whether he'd be able to go to school and get a job or whether he'd always be dependent on us. It was just not knowing what was likely to happen and what the future held for him and for us. (Baxter, 1986, p. 85)

Similarly, a mother whose child had been diagnosed as having Down syndrome reported:

> The whole first year we didn't see anyone or go anywhere. I was worried what she would be like when she grew up. Would she be toilet trained? Would she walk or talk or do things like that? Who would take care of her if anything happened to us? . . . Our pediatrician kept putting us off, saying, "She's still too young." . . . I went down to the Visiting Nurse Association just to get some information, a pamphlet, anything, about Mongolism. (Darling, 1979, p. 148)

When parents receive only a diagnostic label or limited information from professionals, they generally continue to wonder—and worry —about what their child will be like in the future. Most parents are especially concerned about whether the child will be able to walk and talk, go to school, or play normal adult occupational and marital roles. Baxter (1986) has noted that the basic underlying factor in all expressions of parental worry is uncertainty. Parents of disabled children experience an ongoing need for information about the meaning of their child's condition—a need that professionals must meet. The parents in Baxter's study indicated that the most important type of help they had received from professionals was *information*, and that this help was more important than sympathy and emotional support.

The Quest for Treatment

In addition to providing information, professionals are also able to provide therapeutic intervention that will minimize the effects of a child's disability. (Some treatment issues are discussed in Chapter 7.) Once they learn that their child has a disability, virtually all parents are eager to begin a program of treatment. When they receive diagnostic information, parents are relieved of the stress of meaninglessness; until they begin to *do* something about their child's condition, however, they may continue to experience anomie in the form of powerlessness.

Some of the early literature in this field suggested that parents sought treatment because they unrealistically wanted their children to be cured. Numerous studies refer to parents' "shopping around" for a professional or program that would make their child "normal." When parents are questioned about such "shopping" behavior, however, most do not report curing as their goal. Rather, like parents of nondisabled children in our society, they are simply trying to be "good" parents and to do whatever they can to improve their children's quality of life. This mother's explanation of her motivation for seeking treatment is typical:

> Because nothing was happening, and I was just sitting there with this baby, we got involved with the patterning program. . . . We were never told he would be cured. They were the first people who reacted to Billy as a person or called him by name. Up to that time he had done nothing. My pediatrician said, "You're just looking for hopes." I said, "No, I'm just looking to *do* something for him. I'm sitting at home doing nothing." (Darling, 1979, p. 153)

Similarly, the mother of a profoundly retarded child in one of our (R.B.D.) programs said, after her baby had died, that she was grateful for the program. She felt no guilt at the baby's death because she had done everything she could for him while he was alive.

As early intervention programs have become more widespread and publicity about them has increased, parents' quests for services have become shorter. Yet most continue to search until they are satisfied with their children's medical care and have secured needed services, such as physical therapy or special stimulation programs. The extent of parents' quests for services will be based largely on the resources available to them. Most families have geographic and financial limitations that prevent them from searching endlessly for the "best" program for their child. Competing needs, such as other children at home or ill parents, may also prevent parents from enrolling their child in a time-consuming program or one far from home.

During the early months, then, parents are typically motivated by a strong need to reduce their anomie, their meaninglessness and powerlessness. As one mother said, "we wanted to get *us* in control instead of everybody else" (Darling, 1979, p. 147). Professionals can be most helpful to parents at this time by providing as much information as possible about diagnosis, prognosis, and the availability of treatment programs and other resources in the community—in as humane a manner as they can.

The Need for Emotional Support

One mother said:

> I met other parents of the retarded after we moved here. I felt that made the biggest difference in my life. . . . Down there [where we lived before], with my husband working so much and no other families with retarded children, I felt that I was just singled out for something, that I was weird. I felt a lot of isolation and bitterness. (Darling, 1979, pp. 162–163)

The parental need that professionals are probably least able to fill is the need for social support. The importance of social support in alleviating stress in families with disabled children has been well documented (see, e.g., Dyson & Fewell, 1986; Trivette & Dunst, in press). Trivette and Dunst (in press) have recently shown that parents' personal well-being, perceptions of child functioning, and family integration are positively influenced by a family's informal social support network. They conclude that "the negative consequences often associated with the birth and rearing of a child with developmental problems can be lessened or even alleviated to the extent that the members of a family's informal support network are mobilized to strengthen personal and familial well-being and buffer negative effects." In some cases the birth of a disabled child creates a rift in a family's relationship with former friends and family members. In other cases, even though friends and family are supportive, parents still need the special kind of support offered by others with children like their own.

Support within the Family and Other Existing Networks. One of the most difficult tasks facing new parents of children with disabilities is telling other family members and friends about their child's problem for the first time. Many have said that they "just didn't want to explain." In some cases, parents are afraid of upsetting elderly relatives or family members who are anticipating the birth of their own child.

Negative reactions from extended family members (see Chapter 6, which discusses grandparents) and friends range from denial of the child's problem to rejection of the child:

[My in-laws] to this day will not accept her as retarded. They will not say the word. They don't like us to talk about retardation. . . . She's their only grandchild.

My mother thought that if she prayed hard enough, Susan would be O.K.

People think that retardation is a contagious disease. . . . I don't understand how it threatens them . . . the fact that a van pulls up in our driveway, picks up our daughter, and takes her to a program.

When she was little, people were afraid to say anything. They would ask how [her nondisabled brother] was doing, but just asking about Julie was like a personal question. (Darling, 1979, pp. 145, 159, 160)

On the other hand, many families report that friends and relatives have been very supportive and helpful:

I called my mother as soon as I knew, and she came over. She was very supportive.

My father said, "What's the difference? She's yours."

The thing that surprised me was that everyone accepted it right off. (Darling, 1979, p. 146)

Receiving the support of family members may be more important among rural and small-town families, where extended family members tend to live in close proximity and serve as significant others and resources for one another. Heller, Quesada, Harvey, and Warner (1981) found, for example, that among families living in the Blue Ridge Mountains of Virginia, the identities of nuclear and extended families were fused. Kin were the major source of social support, and involvement with relatives was obligatory. Urban "middle-American" families, on the other hand, were more "primary-kin oriented," and the opinions of extended family members were not as important to them. The relative importance of the extended family in various subcultures is discussed further in Chapter 8.

Support Groups. When friends and family react negatively or are unavailable, parents must look elsewhere for support. Even when members of existing social networks try to be helpful, parents may still feel that they do not *really* understand the parents' situation. Meeting other parents of disabled children thus becomes very important to many parents after they learn about their child's disability.

Support groups composed of parents of disabled children and disabled adults serve a number of functions, including (1) alleviating loneliness and isolation, (2) providing information, (3) providing role models, and (4) providing a basis for comparison.

As the mother quoted earlier said, before she became involved with a support group, she felt as though she was "singled out for something." Another mother said: "I was in a once-a-week mothers' group, and it was very helpful. You find out you're not the only person with this problem" (Darling, 1979, p. 161). This function appears to be served equally well by groups of parents with similarly disabled children and parents of children with diverse disabilities. The fact of having a child who is "different" provides a common bond among these families.

Support groups also serve as sources of practical information. As the parent of a dwarf explained:

> The technical aspect is the easiest thing. The doctors can tell you all about that. What makes it so difficult is what you do every day and how you raise the child. And no one can tell you that except right here at this meeting. (Ablon, 1982, p. 43)

Similarly, the mother of a child with cerebral palsy said, "Meeting other parents you get practical hints—like how someone got their child to chew—that normal parents take for granted" (Darling, 1979, p. 163).

At meetings, too, parents have an opportunity to see others who are coping successfully with their situation. These others provide a model for them to emulate. Sometimes parents who have been too timid to change physicians or seek additional services for their child may have the courage to do so after hearing how other parents have successfully challenged the system. The positive effect of encountering successful models among disabled adults is apparent in this statement by the parent of a dwarf:

> At first we could not bring ourselves to go (to the meeting). Maybe we didn't want to see what she was going to look like. . . . We . . . did go to the next meeting. . . . That was the turning point, because at that meeting we began talking to a number of dwarfs. That's when we found out it was going to be O.K.: that dwarfs live like other people—they married, they drove cars, they took vacations, they held jobs—they could be like other people. (Ablon, 1982, p. 38)

Finally, when they meet other families, parents discover not only those who are coping successfully but also those whose children's problems are worse than theirs. Most develop a greater appreciation of their own situation as a result:

> You don't feel sorry for yourself when you see some children that are just vegetables.

> We went to a couples' group where we saw that other children were a lot
> worse than Peter.

> I was active in the parents' association at the beginning. I needed the help
> more then. . . . Some had much more severe children than I did. I felt lucky
> to have Elizabeth. . . . Now I don't feel so sorry for myself. (Darling, 1979,
> pp. 161–162)

These parents are typically surrounded by friends and relatives with
nondisabled children, who may achieve developmental milestones much
more quickly than their children. Many have difficulty watching their
disabled children's slow progress in comparison with the accomplishments of their friends' and relatives' children. Comparisons with other
disabled children, on the other hand, may be much more favorable. The
support group thus becomes an important reference group for these
families.

Although professionals may not be able to serve as a reference group
for parents, they can play an important role by helping parents locate
existing support groups—or starting new groups where none exists. A
number of parents have reported difficulty in finding other parents like
themselves. These stories are illustrative:

> We were walking on the beach and we saw four little people. I decided I'd
> follow them. I had to talk to them. I followed them for a long way and then I
> went up to the woman and said, "Excuse me, but I think my son is a little
> person"—I don't know what word I used, maybe 'dwarf'—"like you are.
> . . ." The woman told us about Little People of America. I had read about
> LPA in *Life* magazine before, but I didn't know how to contact them. When
> we got back, we wrote to B, and she had a mother call us in a few days.
> (Ablon, 1982, p. 37)

> A friend of mine called and said she thought she saw a girlfriend of ours
> that we'd gone to school with in the doctor's office, and she said that her
> daughter said there was a little girl there that looked like Michelle. I thought
> about it . . . I hadn't talked to this girl since we graduated from high school.
> I called her up and said, "You have a daughter, right? . . . I want to ask
> you a question. I don't want you to feel offended," I said, "if I'm wrong,
> I'm sorry." I said, "Is your daughter a Mongoloid?" She said, "Yes she is.
> How did you know?". . . She was our first exposure to other retarded people.
> (She told us about . . . the Association for the Retarded). (Darling, 1979,
> p. 148)

Professionals who inform parents about the existence of support groups
early in a child's life can be very helpful in avoiding the need for
protracted and often stressful searches.

When no support groups exist in an area, the professional should consider starting one. Linder (1970) has suggested that a professionally controlled parent group moves through three stages of development. In the first stage, parents describe the circumstances surrounding their child's diagnosis. During this stage parents express considerable anger and anguish over the manner in which these diagnoses were made. In the second stage, emotional reactions are replaced by an exchange of concrete information about treatment. In the third stage, parents engage in a more informal, conversational exchange involving aspects of one another's families apart from or in addition to the disabled child.

In guiding a parent group, then, the professional should be aware of parents' changing needs and concerns over time. Talking about feelings might be most appropriate in the first stage, whereas offering concrete suggestions and guidance for action is more appropriate in the second stage. The failure of some professionals to meet this second-stage need is reflected in these observations by Moersch (1978):

> Parents need the understanding of professionals, but they also need concrete services to help them in managing and living with the handicapped child. Some parents of older handicapped children have reported that they always had plenty of people to talk with them about their feelings of having a handicapped child, but it was very hard to find someone who could tell them what to do with feeding, toileting, or behavior problems. (p. 4)

In the third stage, if not before, professionals should be able to relinquish their leadership role and allow the group to become peer controlled.

Providing support during infancy and early childhood is important. Suelzle and Keenan (1981) found that reliance on personal support networks tended to decline over the life cycle, as did "rap sessions" with other parents. As the next chapter will show, parents tend to become involved in more "normalized" routines as their children grow out of infancy, and interests shift from involvement in segregated peer groups to immersion in the more integrated structures of the larger society. On the other hand, professionals should not insist on support group involvement during the infancy period. As Chapter 10 shows, some parents may not be ready for such involvement early in their children's lives. (Support groups are further discussed in Chapter 7.)

Interactions with Strangers

After they have told friends and family members about their child's problem, parents must face having to explain to strangers on the street, in restaurants, and in shopping malls. Most parents have said that taking their child out in public was very difficult for them at the beginning. These reports are illustrative:

> We took her to a store downtown, and she had a hat. . . . I wanted to make sure that hat would stay on so no one would see her ears. . . . We didn't want people to look at her. We didn't want to explain.

> I used to go to the laundromat . . . and so many people would say, "Your little girl is *so* good to sit there so quietly in the stroller." . . . I would just like, sit there, and my insides were like knots, and I would think, "Oh no, do I have to tell them about the cerebral palsy? Should I or shouldn't I? Should I just let it pass? . . ." All this is going through my mind. . . . I never told anybody. (Darling, 1979, pp. 155, 156)

Because children with disabilities sometimes look younger than their age, parents commonly avoid explanations by lying to strangers:

> He just looked like a little baby, even at two or three. People would ask how old he was—especially waitresses—and then they were embarrassed. So I started lying, and waitresses would say, "Oh, he's so cute!"

> We bought a car last February. Joey was 15 or 16 months old, and the salesman asked, "Is the baby eight or nine months old?" I said, "Yes." [My daughter] said, "He's one." I said, "Sh." I've been a little too hesitant about telling people. (Darling, 1979, p. 157)

Eventually, most parents become more comfortable explaining to strangers about their children's disabilities. Professionals can help them develop explanations they can use in these situations; support groups can also be helpful in sharing explanations that other parents have used.

Leaving Infancy: Moving toward Normalization

Parents' reactions to the news that their child has a disability, then, will vary according to their interactions with other people—before, during, and after the time that the news is received. The meanings they attach to their child's disability will continue to change as the child grows and they encounter new interaction situations.

The ability of individuals to cope with any situation depends on how they define the situation. Definition of the situation is one of the most difficult tasks facing new parents because of the degree of meaninglessness and powerlessness usually present. Because the birth of a child with a disability is generally an unanticipated event, parents must rely on other people to establish meaning for them. Professionals play an important role by providing parents with diagnostic, prognostic, and treatment information.

By the end of the infancy period, most parents have resolved their anomie. They may still be angry or disappointed by their children's disabilities, but they are beginning to understand them. If their search for a treatment program has been successful, they are also beginning to feel in control of their situation. At this point, their child's disability may decline in relative importance in their lives; the all-consuming need to make sense of an unexpected and painful event will eventually be replaced by the resumption of concerns with other family members, careers, and leisure activities.

The extent to which families will be able to return to a "normalized" lifestyle after the infancy period will vary according to the nature of a child's disability, available social supports, and other factors. These are discussed in the next chapter.

REFERENCES

Ablon, J. (1982). The parents' auxiliary of Little People of America: A self-help model for social support for families of short-statured children. In L. D. Borman (Ed.), *Helping people to help themselves* (pp. 31–46). New York: Haworth.

Abraham, W. (1958). *Barbara: A prologue*. New York: Rinehart.

Allen, J. C., & Allen, M. L. (1979). Discovering and accepting hearing impairment: Initial reactions of parents. *Volta Review, 81*, 279–285.

Bailey, D. B., & Wolery, M. R. (1984). *Teaching infants and preschoolers with handicaps*, Columbus, OH: Merrill.

Baxter, C. (1986). *Intellectual disability: Parental perceptions and stigma as stress*. Unpublished doctoral dissertation, Monash University, Victoria, Australia.

Blacher, J. (1984a). Sequential stages of parental adjustment to the birth of a child with handicaps: Fact or artifact? *Mental Retardation, 22*, 55–68.

Blacher, J. (1984b). *Severely handicapped young children and their families: Research in review*. Orlando, FL: Academic.

Collins-Moore, M. S. (1984). Birth and diagnosis: A family crisis. In M. G. Eisenberg, L. C. Sutkin, & M. A. Jansen (Eds.), *Chronic illness and disability through the life span: Effects on self and family* (pp. 39–46). New York: Springer.

Danziger, S. K. (1979). Treatment of women in childbirth: Implications for family beginnings. *American Journal of Public Health, 69*, 895–901.

D'Arcy, E. (1968). Congenital defects: Mothers' reactions to first information. *British Medical Journal, 3*, 796–798.

Darling, R. B. (1979). *Families against society: A study of reactions to children with birth defects*. Beverly Hills: Sage.

Darling, R. B. (1983). The birth defective child and the crisis of parenthood: Redefining the situation. In E. Callahan & K. McCluskey (Eds.), *Lifespan developmental psychology: Nonnormative life events* (pp. 115–143). New York: Academic.

Darling, R. B., & Darling, J. (1982). *Children who are different: Meeting the challenges of birth defects in society*. St. Louis: Mosby.

Dickman, I., & Gordon, S. (1985). *One miracle at a time: How to get help for your disabled child—From the experience of other parents*. New York: Simon & Schuster.

Doering, S. G., Entwisle, D. R., & Quinlan, D. (1980). Modeling the quality of women's birth experience. *Journal of Health and Social Behavior, 21*, 12–21.

Drotar, D., Baskiewicz, A., Irvin, A., Kennell, J., & Klaus, M. (1975). The adaptation of parents to the birth of an infant with a congenital malformation: A hypothetical model. *Pediatrics, 56*, 710–717.

Dyer, E. D. (1963). Parenthood as crisis: A re-study. *Marriage and Family Living, 25*, 196–201.

Dyson, L., & Fewell, R. R. (1986). Stress and adaptation in parents of young handicapped and nonhandicapped children: A comparative study. *Journal of the Division for Early Childhood, 10*, 25–35.

Frodi, A. M. (1981). Contributions of infant characteristics to child abuse. *American Journal of Mental Deficiency, 85*, 341–349.

Gargiulo, R. M. (1985). *Working with parents of exceptional children: A guide for professionals*. Boston: Houghton Mifflin.

Gottlieb, J. (1975). Public, peer, and professional attitudes toward mentally retarded persons. In M. J. Begab & S. A. Richardson (Eds.), *The mentally retarded and society: A social science perspective* (pp. 99–125). Baltimore: University Park Press.

Heller, P. G., Quesada, G. M., Harvey, D. L., & Warner, L. G. (1981). Familism in rural and urban America: Critique and reformulation of a construct. *Rural Sociology, 46*, 446–464.

Irvin, M. A., Kennell, J. H., & Klaus, M. H. (1982). Caring for the parents of an infant with a congenital malformation. In M. H. Klaus & J. H. Kennell (Eds.), *Parent–infant bonding* (2nd edition) (pp. 227–258). St. Louis: Mosby.

LaRossa, R. (1977). *Conflict and power in marriage: Expecting the first child*. Beverly Hills: Sage.

LeMasters, E. E. (1957). Parenthood as crisis. *Marriage and Family Living, 19*, 352–355.

Linder, R. (1970). Mothers of disabled children—The value of weekly group meetings. *Developmental Medicine and Child Neurology, 12*, 202–206.

Lorber, J. (1971). Results of treatment of myelomeningocele. *Developmental Medicine and Child Neurology, 13*, 279–303.

MacKeith, R. (1973). The feelings and behaviour of parents of handicapped children. *Developmental Medicine and Child Neurology, 15*, 524–527.

McHugh, P. (1968). *Defining the situation*. Indianapolis: Bobbs-Merrill.

Moersch, M. S. (1978). History and rationale for parent involvement. In S. L. Brown & M. S. Moersch (Eds.), *Parents on the team* (pp. 1–10). Ann Arbor: University of Michigan Press.

Mori, A. A. (1983). *Families of children with special needs: Early intervention techniques for the practitioner*. Rockville, MD: Aspen Systems Corporation.

Norr, K. L., Block, C. R., Charles, A., Meyering, S., & Meyers, E. (1977). Explaining pain and enjoyment in childbirth. *Journal of Health and Social Behavior, 18*, 260–275.

Olshansky, S. (1962). Chronic sorrow: A response to having a mentally defective child. *Social Casework, 43*, 190–193.

Richardson, S. A. (1970). Age and sex differences in values toward physical handicaps. *Journal of Health and Social Behavior, 11*, 207–214.

Robson, K. S., & Moss, H. A. (1970). Patterns and determinants of maternal attachment. *Journal of Pediatrics, 77*, 976–985.

Rosengren, W. R. (1962). The sick role during pregnancy: A note on research in progress. *Journal of Health and Human Behavior, 3*, 213–218.

Rothman, B. K. (1978). Childbirth as negotiated reality. *Symbolic Interaction, 1*, 124–137.

Shereshefsky, P. M., Liebenberg, B., & Lockman, R. F. (1973). Maternal adaptation. In P. M. Shereshefsky & L. J. Yarrow (Eds.), *Psychological aspects of a first pregnancy and early postnatal adaptation.* New York: Raven.

Solnit, A. J., & Stark, M. H. (1961). Mourning and the birth of a defective child. *The Psychoanalytic Study of the Child, 16,* 523–537.

Stone, N. W., & Chesney, B. H. (1978). Attachment behaviors in handicapped infants. *Mental Retardation, 16,* 8–12.

Suelzle, M., & Keenan, V. (1981). Changes in family support networks over the life cycle of mentally retarded persons. *American Journal of Mental Deficiency, 86,* 267–274.

Trivette, C. M., & Dunst, C. J. (in press). Proactive influences of social support in families of handicapped children. In N. Stinnet et al. (Eds.), *Family strengths (Vol. B): Positive and preventive measures.* Lincoln: University of Nebraska Press.

Waechter, E. H. (1977). Bonding problems of infants with congenital anomalies. *Nursing Forum, 16,* 299–318.

Waisbren, E. (1980). Parents' reactions after the birth of a developmentally disabled child. *American Journal of Mental Deficiency, 84,* 345–351.

Walker, J. H. (1971). Spina bifida—and the parents. *Developmental Medicine and Child Neurology, 13,* 462–476.

Wikler, L., Wasow, M., & Hatfield, E. (1981). Chronic sorrow revisited: Parent vs. professional depiction of the adjustment of parents of mentally retarded children. *American Journal of Orthopsychiatry, 51,* 63–70.

3

Childhood and Adolescence: Continuing Adaptation

> Parenthood of a retarded person . . . is a kaleidoscope of
> feeling and experience.
> It has its beauty, but it is always changing. It is
> irritation at ineffectual hands plucking endlessly at a knotted
> shoe-lace. . . .
> It is guilt at the irritation. . . .
> It is a surge of love for this person who needs your
> protection; and a surge of horror that he will always need it. . . .
> It is a glowing admiration for his learning achievements,
> against such odds.
> It is horror at the inexorable ticking of the
> developmental clock.
> It is a prayer that he will painlessly cease to live.
> It is the desperate rush to the doctor because he's
> looking ill. . . .
> It is 365 days a year.
>
> —Max (1985, pp. 261, 262)

NORMALIZATION: GOAL OF THE CHILDHOOD YEARS

By the end of the infancy period, the resolution of anomie is complete for most families. As their children move through the preschool years, parents generally try to resume activities that were disrupted by their child's birth and the period of anomie that followed. The mother who has left a job may wish to return to work; the parents may resume social activities; the family may want to take a vacation or pursue other recreational activities.

Parents are encouraged to maintain a "normal-appearing round of life" (Birenbaum, 1970, 1971) by other parents, friends, and professionals. Voysey (1975) argues that parents have a normality perspective because they are *expected* to be normal by other agents in society: parents' associations, magazine articles, clergy, and various helping professionals. These agents help parents rationalize their situation and teach them that they are *supposed* to be "coping splendidly" with their child's disability.

Voysey states that families develop an ideology of normalization, which contains the following elements: (1) acceptance of the inevitable ("it could happen to anyone"); (2) partial loss of the taken-for-granted ("taking it day-to-day"); (3) redefinition of good and evil ("there's always someone worse off"); (4) discovery of true values ("you appreciate your child's progress more when you don't just take it for granted"); (5) positive value of suffering ("it brings you closer together"); and (6) positive value of differentness ("it's for his own good").

Although the components of normalization vary by social class and other subcultural factors, in general, a normalized lifestyle for families with school-aged children in American society includes:

- employment for either or both parents
- appropriate educational placement for children
- access to appropriate medical care
- adequate housing
- social relationships with family and friends
- leisure time
- freedom of movement in public places
- sufficient financial resources to maintain their basic lifestyle

The presence of a child with a disability in the home can prevent a family from attaining any or all of these components.

The ability of families to achieve a normalized lifestyle will be determined by their opportunity structure, that is, their access to resources. Society provides a variety of resources, ranging from financial aid to respite care for disabled children. These resources are not equally distributed in the population, however, and for many families, life is a constant struggle. We suggest in this chapter that, regardless of the nature of a child's disability or of the personality or coping ability of the parents, the most important determinant of normalization for most families of disabled children is the availability of supportive resources in the community.

OBSTACLES TO NORMALIZATION

In a study of 330 parents of retarded children, Suelzle and Keenan (1981) found that perceptions of unmet needs varied over the life cycle. Perceived needs for family support, respite care, and counseling services were highest among parents of preschoolers and young adults and lowest among parents of school-aged children. In a study of families with autistic children, DeMyer and Goldberg (1983) found that the need for respite remained relatively constant during childhood and adolescence. In general, practical problems seem to replace coping difficulties as parents' primary concern as their children get older. These include (Moroney, reported in Mori, 1983): additional financial hardships, stigma, extraordinary demands on time, difficulties in such caregiver tasks as feeding, diminished time for sleeping, social isolation, less time for recreational pursuits, difficulties managing behavior, and difficulties performing routine household chores, among others. These and other problems, which serve as barriers to normalization, will be discussed in greater detail below.

Continuing Medical Needs

Children with disabilities generally require more specialized medical care and more frequent hospitalizations than others. In addition, these children may need medically related services, such as physical, occupational, and speech therapy. The availability of these services varies from one geographic location to another. Butler, Rosenbaum, and Palfrey (1987) have written that "where a child lives has become more than ever a predictor of the affordability and accessibility of care" (p. 163). They note a study showing that 12% of low-income children among the most severely disabled third of special-education students in Rochester, New York, did not have a regular physician and 7% did not have insurance coverage; in Charlotte, North Carolina, on the other hand, 34% of the same group had no regular physician and 32% had no insurance coverage. The study showed further that use of health care services was related to access: "Even for the most severely impaired group, the likelihood of seeing a physician was 3.5 times higher if the child had insurance coverage" (p. 163).

Even in areas where health care is readily available, parents may have difficulty locating a physician who is interested in treating children with disabilities. Pediatricians especially tend to prefer treating nondisabled children with acute, curable diseases. As a result, parents of children with disabilities may engage in lengthy searches before they find a physician with whom they are satisfied. As one disgruntled father of a severely disabled youngster commented, "It's like when you take your dog to the vet. . . . Not many doctors pick him up and try to communicate with him as a child" (Darling, 1979, p. 151).

Eventually, most parents do obtain satisfactory health care for their child. After their search is ended, parents may be reluctant to move to a new location, where they would have to begin to search once again. Opportunities for career advancement may be limited as a result. Families' freedom of movement may also be limited in other ways by their children's special medical needs:

> There are things we'd like to do with [our two nondisabled children]. We'd like to take some trips before [our daughter] goes to college. . . . But we can't do that now. . . . It's hard to travel with Billy now. . . . Because of his medical problems, I'm fearful to leave. I don't want to end up in a strange hospital somewhere. Everyone knows Billy at University Hospital now, and that's very relieving. (Darling, 1979, p. 182)

Special Educational Needs

Although the quest for medical services may become less of a priority as children approach school age, the search for appropriate educational programs often becomes more important at that time.

Preschool Education

For the disabled child, formal education may begin shortly after birth. With the proliferation of early intervention programs in recent years, many children have begun receiving services soon after they are diagnosed. These programs may be either home based or center based, although the best programs typically involve parents as teachers for their own children. Some programs include specialists, such as physical or speech therapists, in addition to specially trained teachers.

In some cases, however, parents do not discover early intervention programs until well into their children's preschool years. As one mother said:

> [The doctor] said, "Just take him home and love him." . . . I wondered, "Isn't there anything more?" . . . When he was 2½, I read in the newspaper about a preschool program for retarded children. (Darling & Darling, 1982, p. 133)

Parents may engage in extensive searches to find a preschool program that is appropriate for their child:

We were in the _____ Regional Center area. They said when he was three years old, they would take him in a program. . . . There was a bus that would have taken him but it would have been two hours one way and three hours the other, because we were at the very end of the line. . . . That's when we decided, "If he's going to have school, we're going to have to move." . . .

It was very difficult to get information. I called the state agencies, but they didn't give me anything. I finally had to go to every single town, every director of special ed, in the . . . area, and I visited just about every preschool they had. . . . Just about everyone I went to, there were some little kids sitting nicely, learning about their colors and shapes and everything . . . and there was this one little kid crawling around in the corner playing with the wastebasket, . . . and I knew that was Brian. . . .

If you live in _____ and have a handicapped child, you move, because they don't have any programs. . . . I wasn't going to be the one that fought the system. . . .

At _____ Program, the profoundly retarded were being shown books. . . . They weren't just left in a corner. . . . We could have afforded to live elsewhere more easily, but we moved to _____, because that's where the _____ program was. (Darling, 1979, pp. 174–175)

Such stories are not as common today. Public Law 99-457 (which is discussed further in Chapter 10), and other funding sources have made preschool education more available, and physicians and other professionals are better informed about the existence of local programs. Some gaps in the quantity and quality of these programs remain, however. Generally, by the end of the preschool years, parents have found a satisfactory program for their children. However, concerns about the quality of available educational programs are likely to arise again when children reach school age. Parents of nondisabled children may take for granted the fact that the school system will provide an appropriate education for their children; parents of children with special needs who have similar assumptions often learn that local programs do not meet those needs.

The School Years

Prior to the passage of Public Law 94-142, the Education for All Handicapped Children Act, in 1975, guidelines for the education of children with disabilities were vague, and parents' rights were not clearly stated. Because of difficulties they had in obtaining an appropriate education for their children, many parents of teenage and young adult children feel bitter and resentful toward the school system and, in some cases, even toward parents of younger children who have benefited from newer legislation and programs. The following stories, related by parents of older children, illustrate some of the difficulties they have faced:

In her old school, Karen had been in the same [trainable] class for three or four years. There were toys in the room. . . . The trainable teacher had been trying to teach Karen and a few others to read, but the special education director they had at the time said, "No, these children can't read." . . . A psychologist had once told us that Karen would be able to read some day, and she wanted to learn. We didn't think that Karen would get anymore out of the trainable class. We begged them to test her. . . . We petitioned the Board. . . . A psychologist from the state said, "She's not ready." I felt like crying. . . . [A year later] we had her tested by a private psychologist. . . . He said that her speech needed improvement but that her vocabulary was almost normal rather than retarded. . . . He thought she should be in the educable class. . . . They finally moved her. . . . She may always be in that class, but at least she's learning something again. (Mother of a Down syndrome child, reported in Darling, 1979, p. 175)

At Children's Hospital, Tony was in a class with active, bright kids. . . . He just sat in the corner and played in the sandbox. . . . Then he went to the School for the Blind, which is geared for the totally blind child. . . . They mostly concentrated on teaching Braille. Finally, Tony . . . had to leave the school. They said [he was] retarded. . . .

After Tony . . . [was] labeled retarded by the School for the Blind, [he] started in the [city] Public School System, but they had no appropriate program either. . . . After three years we started fighting. . . . The Board of Education said, "We've got all kinds of retarded programs. We'll just put [him] in one of those." . . . I visited the programs, and there wasn't one child in a wheelchair. . . . I said, "How [is my child] going to get around? How [is he] going to go on these stairs?" . . . They kept saying "No" to us. . . .

We were lucky at this time because [my husband had changed jobs and] was in the school system and knew a lot of people. And they were guiding us and telling us where to write, each step of the way. We went right to the top. . . . A program was established within two weeks. (Mother of a multiply handicapped child, reported in Darling, 1979, pp. 176–177)

Michael started first grade at the Oakmont School [a facility that served all disabled children within the region]. It was an old, noisy building . . . and it seemed that each year he did the same thing as the year before. . . . There was no separation by age. They just didn't know what to do with the kids. . . .

I talked to everyone, even [our state senator]. . . . He said, "You can't expect things to happen overnight." . . . After awhile . . . parents got together. We . . . decided we wanted our kids in our own school district. . . .

Several parents got together and went to [our school district]. They were building a new elementary school. . . . I didn't know if mainstreaming would be better. I only knew it couldn't be worse. . . . They weren't going to put in an elevator. They wanted to build a tennis court instead. . . . They didn't want to provide transportation. . . . Then, we couldn't get him on and off the bus. . . . They supplied a helper. . . . You eventually get what you need . . . if you're very persistent, but they always leave you with the feeling that they're doing you a favor . . . to provide your son with an education. (Mother of a child with spina bifida, reported in Darling & Darling, 1982, pp. 137–138)

Special-education legislation of the 1970s and 1980s (P.L. 94-142, P.L. 98-199, P.L. 99-457) has mandated that children with disabilities receive a free and appropriate public education in the "least restrictive environment." However, for a number of reasons, including ignorance, fear, and the limited resources of school districts, the promise of the legislation has not become a reality for many children. Because of poor knowledge about their legal rights, many parents have not challenged their children's educational placements. Public awareness has been growing, however, and more and more parents are questioning educators about their children's programs.

One study (Orenstein, 1979) of parents who did challenge the system found that many parents waited months before securing an evaluation. After evaluations were completed, parents were sometimes pressured into accepting inadequate educational plans by school personnel who used "tactics such as blaming the parents for their child's problems, claiming that the child had emotional problems . . . rather than learning problems, using excessive jargon . . . , and offering only minimal levels of special services until parents complain or threaten to use appeals processes."

Parents may challenge their children's educational plans for a variety of reasons. One common complaint involves placement in an inappropriate setting. Parents may wish to have their child placed in an integrated setting rather than a special school or classroom; in other cases, they want more special programming for their children. The former case is illustrated by this experience, related by the mother of a child with spina bifida:

When Ellen entered kindergarten, she was in a special needs class in the morning and mainstreamed in the afternoon. . . . [In the special needs class], she was with children whose needs were much more demanding than Ellen's. . . . Some were retarded. . . . At the end of the year we had a meeting. The first grade was on the second floor [Ellen was in a wheelchair]. . . . They said we should keep her in the special needs class. I was furious. . . . She had done so well in the mainstreaming class. . . . I wanted her in a regular first grade and I suggested moving the class downstairs. . . . They wanted Ellen in the special needs class because it was easier for *them*, not for any other reason. (Darling & Darling, 1982, p. 140)

Another common parental complaint involves the lack of coordination among the various educational settings through which children move during the school day. In the past, when special-education children were completely segregated from regular instruction, coordination was not a problem. With the implementation of newer legislation, however, working relationships have had to be developed between special-education administrators, evaluators, and teachers on the one hand, and regular classroom teachers, principals, and guidance counselors, on the other. As Scanlon, Arick, and Phelps (1981) have shown, regular classroom teachers generally do not attend conferences at which children's Individualized Education Plans are developed. Parents often complain that regular classroom teachers are not prepared for children with disabilities.

Another type of problem involves disagreements about the kinds of services schools are required to provide to disabled children. Parents may believe that related services, such as physical therapy, are needed in order for their children to receive an appropriate education; school systems may disagree. Some children require special health services in order to attend school. Children with spina bifida, for example, may require catheterization one or more times a day. In the past, parents had to come to the school to perform this simple procedure, often at great inconvenience. As a result of one family's persistence, however, the Supreme Court ruled several years ago that clean intermittent catheterization is indeed a necessary related service that must be provided by the school district.

Behavior Problems

Baxter (1986) found, in a study of families with retarded children, that the major stressors associated with the care and management of the child were (1) behavior management problems and (2) the child's continued dependence. The first is discussed here and the second, in the next section.

Baxter found that although concern about the child's physical needs tended to decrease with the age of the child, worry about the child's behavior in public increased over time. Behavior management problems commonly occur in conjunction with such disabilities as mental retardation. The following description of a deaf–blind child illustrates some of the forms that these problems may take:

When he gets off the bus Friday afternoon after a week at the residential school for the blind, he lies on the sidewalk kicking and screaming while his mother runs frantically to and from the house with various foods which might appease his anger. Over the weekend no one in the household is permitted to make program selections on the television because Johnny takes charge of the dial. Most of the night the family lies awake to the sound of ear-piercing screams, and the hours of quiet when they at last lapse into grateful sleep bring the morning rewards of ransacked kitchen shelves and mutilated books. (Klein, 1977, p. 310)

Such nonnormative, disruptive behavior may limit the family's opportunities for social participation. As one mother of a mentally retarded child with cerebral palsy explained:

He's hard to take with us. I always have to get a babysitter or I'll stay home. . . . It's really like having a little baby, only he doesn't outgrow it. . . . And we don't as a rule have people over—because he doesn't go to sleep. (Darling, 1979, p. 171)

DeMyer and Goldberg (1983) have reported that the aspect of family life most affected by an autistic child is family recreation. Baxter (1986) has noted that parents are most willing to take such children to gatherings involving family and friends and least willing to take them to places involving other persons.

Baxter found that certain social situations produced considerable stress:

1. formal social occasions where the child does not conform to norms
2. other persons' homes where coping with the child's behavior is difficult
3. public settings where behavior management is a problem
4. restrictive settings that do not readily allow parents to withdraw from the situation
5. social situations where the child engages in deviant forms of interaction with other people

Parents feel stress when their child's behavior calls attention to the family. Although most try to explain the child's disability to friends or strangers, some simply control their feelings and say nothing or move away from the distressing encounter. Birenbaum (1970) has shown that some parents may try to hide their children's behavior problems by cleaning the house before guests arrive or controlling the home setting in other ways.

Although the extent of a child's behavior problems may be related to the nature of the child's disability, even families with severely disabled children may be able to achieve some degree of normalization if they have adequate social support. Bristol and Schopler (1984) have shown that family adaptation is more closely related to perceived adequacy of informal support than to the severity of the child's disability in the case of autistic children, and families without support may suffer considerable social isolation as a result of their children's behavior. As Bristol (1987) has shown, single parents may be especially vulnerable to such stress, yet we should not assume that social support is lacking in all such cases. Baxter (1986) has shown, too, that small families tend to experience greater stress in care and management than larger families.

Continuing Dependence

As nondisabled children grow older, they become less dependent on their parents. By the end of the preschool years, they are able to feed and dress themselves and take care of their toileting needs. Later they become able to go about the neighborhood without supervision, and eventually they can stay home alone, without the need for babysitters. Demands on parents' time thus decrease. Disabilities may limit the ability of children to achieve such increasing independence, however.

Even families with highly dependent children can achieve normalization if they have access to good support services such as low-cost, specially trained babysitters or respite care. A special camp in Arkansas, for example, cares for school-aged children with disabilities 48 weekends a year in order to provide relief for families:

> Julie Mills, a severely mentally handicapped 10-year old with a speech impairment, attends the camp.
>
> "It allows us to be together the whole weekend, to go shopping at our will or just sit around and watch television," Julie's mother, Sherry Mills, said of time alone with her husband, Carl. "We become a little closer, get to know each other. It's almost like a date."
>
> Susan and Mike Walker send their 7-year-old daughter Rachel to the camp so they can spend time with their 9-year-old daughter Dawn.
>
> Rachel suffers from seizure disorders and mental and physical disabilities, Mrs. Walker said, and caring for her can deprive Dawn of attention. ("Camp Cares for Handicapped Kids," 1986)

On the other hand, when such resources are not available, maintaining a normalized lifestyle can be difficult, as in the case of these parents of deaf–blind children:

Several sets of parents have admitted they have never been on a vacation alone, and very few go out on the weekend because it is nearly impossible to locate a babysitter who will tackle this unusual charge for a reasonable fee. Respite care is a rare and dear luxury. With the deaf–blind youngster functioning as the focal point in these otherwise uneventful weekends, many parents become rivals in finding means to compensate for the child's lack of sensory input. (Klein, 1977, p. 311)

Financial Burden

Childhood disabilities have an economic impact on families in addition to their psychosocial costs. This impact includes both direct costs, such as expenses for childcare, medical care, therapy, and special equipment, and indirect costs, such as lost work time, special residential needs, and interference with career advancement.

Direct Costs

In a nationwide survey of 1,709 families with physically disabled children, Harbaugh (1984) found that the largest single out-of-pocket expense was for babysitting. This finding is not surprising, considering the continued dependence of children with disabilities discussed in the last secion. Yet because of the costs involved, some parents of disabled children may actually use babysitters less than parents of nondisabled children, even though their needs are greater.

Harbaugh reports that, after babysitting, physical and occupational therapy costs were the greatest out-of-pocket expense for the families in his study. These and other medically related services are not always covered by health insurance, and Harbaugh found that the average monthly cost to families for these services (in 1984) was $162—a significant portion of the family budget for many.

Physician visits and hospitalizations are also expensive for these families, especially when they are not covered by private health insurance or public medical assistance. In one study (Butler et al., 1987), only 22% of privately insured disabled children have all their visits to physicians paid by their insurance plans. Another study (Select Committee on Children, Youth, and Families, reported in Morris, 1987) estimated that 10.3% of disabled children and 19.5% of disabled children in poverty have no health insurance. In addition, 40% of all disabled children below the federal poverty level are not covered by Medicaid. Butler and colleagues also note that continuity of insurance coverage is a problem. During 1980, only 67% of poor children were covered continuously by Medicaid. For privately insured families, job changes may mean discontinuity in coverage.

The Select Committee on Children, Youth, and Families of the U.S. Congress (reported in Morris, 1987) found that the annual expenses for hospital and physician services for a child with a disabling chronic condition ranges from $870 to $10,229, depending on the condition's severity. In contrast, the cost of these services for a nondisabled child averages about $270 a year. (For a further discussion of hospital costs, see Darling, 1987).

Medical equipment and supplies are also very expensive. The cost of a standard child-sized wheelchair, for example, is currently approximately $800. Children with severe physical disabilities may also need special equipment for feeding, toileting, and other activities of daily living. Newer computerized equipment, which can greatly improve quality of life, is even more expensive. A computerized system that can synthesize speech, for example, currently costs between $3,500 and $4,000. Most health insurance plans do not yet cover such items.

Although medically related costs will vary by disability, two recent studies found total expenses of this nature to be over $100,000 to raise a child to age eighteen. In a study of families of spina bifida children, the total cost of medical care and equipment from birth to age 18 was $108,000 to $192,000 in 1982 dollars (Lipscomb, Kolimaga, Sperduto, Minnich, & Fontenot, 1983). Similarly, a study of families of children with cerebral palsy (Morris, 1987) found an average cost of $126,631 for disability-related expenses over the same time period.

Other Direct Costs

A child's disability may also require housing or vehicle modifications, such as ramps, lifts, or widened doorways to accommodate a wheelchair. Klein (1977) notes, too, items such as locks for cabinets and bars for windows in the case of deaf–blind children. Additional items are noted by the father of four teenagers with a cerebral palsy–like syndrome:

> Our kids have a phone. It's essential. Other kids can go out and play. We can't afford it but we have it. . . . We also can't afford the swimming pool, but water's the best therapy. . . . Where else can they go and swim almost every day in the summer? The city don't have it, so I have it. (Darling, 1979, p. 180)

Indirect Costs

Other, hidden costs may also be associated with childhood disability. Because these children require access to services and greater commitments of their parents' time than other children, the family's overall economic situation may be adversely affected.

As a mother quoted earlier in the chapter noted, her family moved to a more expensive community than they could afford because a good preschool program was located there. Similarly, another parent has written:

> We were forced to leave the Aurora . . . Public School District for the express purpose of obtaining an appropriate public school education for our son. . . .
>
> The private sector is willing to educate these children—at huge expense. As one professional said to me: "Our attitude even here is, we'll take your house and your second car. Your husband has to get a second job; then we'll help you with your child." Thus, we left Aurora . . . knowing that we would eventually lose our home if we didn't. (Reader's Forum, 1985, p. 7)

● Some parents may reject opportunities for career advancement because services for their children may not be as good in a new location. The amount of parents' time required by a child's special needs may also interfere with career advancement or a parent's having a job at all. Lipscomb and colleagues (1983) found that the average weekly work reduction among parents of children with spina bifida was 5 hours for fathers and 14 hours for mothers. In 1982 dollars, the resulting average annual income loss for these families ranged from $8,000 to $17,000. Morris (1987) notes cases of a mother who forfeited an annual salary of $30,000 to transport her child to speech and physical therapy and a parent who quit work and stayed home for 15 years to care for her disabled child.

Stigma and Its Consequences

As noted in Chapter 8, individuals with disabilities in our society are likely to encounter stigma in their interactions with others. Goffman (1963) has shown, further, that parents and others who associate with the disabled are likely to bear a "courtesy stigma" of their own. As children get older, their disabilities generally become more visible and, thus, more stigmatizing.

Baxter (1986) found that the attribute most likely to attract attention to a disabled child was speech, not appearance or behavior. Parental stress was also related to the quality of their child's speech. In order to prevent stigma-producing encounters, then, families may have to structure their lives to avoid social situations that would require their children to speak or perform roles that would otherwise call attention to their disabilities. Such children, then, may not be taken to see Santa Claus at Christmastime or to visit casual acquaintances. Parents' lifestyles may be limited as a result.

Physical Barriers

A final obstacle to normalization involves physical barriers in the environment. Individuals with disabilities and their families may be prevented from full social participation by stairs, narrow doorways, and hilly terrain. Our society is structured, both socially and physically, to meet the needs of the nondisabled. Although accessibility has been increasing in recent years, families with disabled children are still limited in their housing choices, vacation destinations, and general freedom of movement.

CATALYSTS TO NORMALIZATION

The strength of families is demonstrated by the fact that, given the many obstacles that exist, most are still able to achieve a nearly normal lifestyle; normalization is, in fact, the most common mode of adaptation found among families of children with disabilities in our society. Achievement of a normalized lifestyle may be related less to the degree of a child's disability or parents' coping abilities than to the *opportunity structure* within which the family resides.

Opportunity Structures

All families do not have equal access to opportunities for normalization. These opportunities include:

- access to satisfactory medical care and medically related services
- availability of an appropriate educational program
- supportive relatives and friends
- access to respite care and daycare if needed
- adequacy of financial resources
- presence of accepting neighbors
- quantity and quality of household help
- access to behavior management programs if needed
- availability of appropriate recreational programs
- access to special equipment if needed
- presence of friends and social opportunities for the disabled child
- adequacy of available transportation

Families' opportunity structures can be changed. Such changes may occur when a family moves to a new neighborhood or encounters a helpful professional. Opportunity structures are also changed by new

laws and court decisions and through parental activism and disability-
rights movements. Professionals can play an important role in working
with families to change their access to existing opportunities and to
create opportunities where none exists.

Changes in Support Networks

As we noted in the last chapter, parents commonly become immersed in
support groups consisting of others like themselves when their children
are young and newly diagnosed. Continued immersion in such homogeneous groups can eventually become an obstacle to normalization, or
integration in "normal" society, however. As a result, parents often
decrease their involvement in segregated support networks as their children get older. As one mother explained:

> We went to the Association pretty regularly for two years. But after awhile
> we felt that they did not have that much to offer . . . as far as help to us. . . .
> We just got too busy to go to the meetings. Karen didn't have a lot of
> problems. (Darling, 1979, pp. 161-162)

Parents may also decrease their involvement with other families of
the disabled by encouraging their children's friendships with nondisabled children in the neighborhood or at school. As one mother of a child
with spina bifida explained, her daughter has some friends at "myelo"
clinic but she does not see them elsewhere. "They live too far away," and
the mother will not go out of her way because she wants her daughter to
be "as normal as possible." (Darling, 1979, p. 193)

Although parents may choose to become integrated into "normal"
society, their success will depend on their opportunity structures—"normal" society must accept them. A summary description of the family of
the spina bifida child described above illustrates such a successful adaptation:

> The mother reported that relatives thought the baby was "fantastic" and
> were very supportive during the first few months. Elizabeth attended a
> nursery school with nondisabled children and was then mainstreamed in
> public school. She has always been well accepted by the other children.
> Grandparents and other family members live nearby and continue to be
> highly supportive. They babysit so that the parents can take short vacations
> alone. The parents have decreased their involvement in a parents' associa-
> tion and, at the time they were interviewed, were preoccupied with the
> "normal" concerns of running a business, wanting to buy a house, and
> preparing for a new baby. (Based on Darling, 1979, pp. 191-193)

Placement out of the Home: A Form of Normalization

In writing about families of severely retarded children, Farber (1975) describes a "principle of minimal adaptation." He argues that families disrupt their patterns of living as little as possible to adjust to a problem situation and that parents who have difficulty living with a severely retarded child move through a progression of minimal adaptations:

1. Labeling phase: The bases for existing role arrangements are removed.
2. Normalization phase: This is based on the pretense of maintaining normal roles (most families remain in this phase and do not proceed further).
3. Mobilization phase: Normality claims become difficult to maintain.
4. Revisionist phase: This involves isolation from community involvements and role renegotiation.
5. Polarization phase: Parents attempt to locate the source of their difficulty within the family.
6. Elimination phase: Normality is maintained by excluding the offending person.

Farber notes that parent-oriented families are more likely than child-oriented families to reach the elimination phase, as are families that were coping poorly prior to the birth of the child. Movement through phases is also influenced by social and cultural expectations, not only by internal family dynamics.

Movement from one phase to another may occur more frequently at turning points in family life. If a mother becomes chronically ill, for example, she may not be able to continue caring for a disabled child at home. Similarly, if a family's support network changes (as, for example, in the case of the death of a grandparent who had helped with childcare), the parents will be more likely to move toward the elimination phase, opting for an alternative, such as institutionalization of the disabled child.

Changes in the child can also lead to placement out of the home. As nonambulatory children grow and become heavier, caring for them at home becomes more difficult. Some severely retarded children also become more difficult to handle as they grow and become more mobile. In some cases, parents may come to believe that a child's special needs can be better met in a residential treatment facility than at home. Meyers and colleagues (reported in Blacher, 1984) have noted that the proportion of severely and profoundly mentally retarded children residing in their natural homes drops sharply at school age.

Seltzer and Krauss (1984) note four characteristics associated with residential placement:

1. child characteristics (level of retardation, behavior problems, age, degree of care needed)
2. family characteristics (socioeconomic status, race, marital satisfaction)
3. informal supports (friends and family)
4. formal supports (social and psychological services, respite care, skills training)

MacKeith (1973) suggests three principles that can be presented to families to help them make decisions about residential placement:

1. In our culture, most people live with their families and do better if they do so.
2. People go away from home if thereby they are able to get treatment and education that are better—and sufficiently better to outweigh the disadvantages of being away from home.
3. People go away from home if other people in the family are suffering from their continued presence.

Questions about residential placement are more likely to arise at turning points in the lives of children and their parents—at school-entry age, at the time of leaving school, and when parents become older and unable to care for their child at home.

Residential placement enables some families to achieve normalization when alternatives are not available or acceptable. Through some means, then—social support, access to resources, or removal of the disabled child from the home—most families are able to have a normalized lifestyle. *Normalization is the most common mode of adaptation among families with disabled children during the childhood years.* In the next section we look at other adaptations and present a typology of family adaptations based on a model of differential opportunity structures.

A TYPOLOGY OF ADAPTATIONS

The Crusadership Mode

Although normalization is the most common parental adaptation through most of the childhood years, for some parents normalized routines remain elusive. In particular, parents whose children have unusual disabilities, continuing medical problems, or unresolved behavior problems may have difficulty finding the social supports necessary for normalization. Some of these families adopt a *crusadership* mode of adjustment in an attempt to bring about social change.

Unlike parents who have achieved normalization, these parents may become *more* involved in disability associations and segregated support groups as their children get older. In a study of families of children with birth defects, Goodman (1980) found that parents who acknowledged serious problems in their lives and the lives of their children were more likely to be involved in parent groups. Parents' associations tend to draw their active membership from parents of younger children (who have not yet achieved normalization) and a smaller number of parents of older children with unresolved problems. When normalization cannot be attained, associations and the activities they provide may fill important needs. As the father of four disabled teenagers said: "The [Association] is our kids' only social life. . . . I'm on the Board and I'm referee of the soccer team" (Darling, 1979, p. 162). Such parents sometimes come to play leadership roles in state and national disability groups.

The goal of crusadership is normalization, and families who adopt this mode strive to achieve that goal in a variety of ways. Some become involved in campaigns to increase public awareness of their child's disability. Others testify before congressional committees in an attempt to promote legislation favorable to the disabled. Still others wage legal battles or challenge the school system to establish new programs. Crusaders, then, are advocates who try to change the opportunity structure for their own and other people's children. (For a further discussion of crusadership and parent activism, see Darling, 1988) Some eventually achieve normalization and withdraw from involvement in advocacy groups and roles; a few, however, may continue to advocate on behalf of others in an altruistic mode.

Altruism

Because the ultimate goal of most parents is normalization, altruism is not common. As noted above, parents generally decrease their involvement in organizations and activities that emphasize their stigmatized status in society as their children get older. The departure of families who have achieved normalization from these organizations is unfortunate for the parents of younger children in need of successful role models. Not all such families abandon organizational activity, however.

A few families who have achieved normalization remain active in segregated groups for the sake of others, and individuals from such families are often found in leadership roles in national disability associations. Their motivations vary. Some are truly caring, humanistic people; some have a strong sense of justice; some are applying the principles of their religion; and others simply enjoy the social aspects of participation or the prestige resulting from their leadership roles. Altruists, then, are those who *choose*, for whatever reason, to associate with the disabled even though they have access to opportunities for integration into "normal" society.

Resignation

At the opposite pole from the altruists are the families who, despite their inability to achieve normalization, never become involved in crusadership activity at all. In her study of parent groups, Goodman (1980) found that many parents did not participate as a result of lack of knowledge. Such parents are doubly isolated: They are stigmatized by "normal" society, and yet they never become integrated into alternative support groups. Some may become fatalistic, whereas others may have mental health problems resulting from stress.

Parents who become resigned to their problematic existence may lack access to supportive resources for a number of reasons. Some may live in isolated rural areas where no parent groups exist. Others may not be able to search for support because of poor health, lack of transportation, or family problems apart from the disabled child. In the lower socioeconomic classes, especially, the burdens of daily life—of simple survival—may take precedence over concerns relating to a child's disability. Families who are isolated from the mainstream of society because they do not speak English or in which the parents are themselves disabled may not have access to the lay or professional referral networks that provide information on available resources. Crusadership and altruism are luxuries that presuppose some free time and the absence of competing demands on that time, often making those modes of adaptation most appropriate for middle-class families.

A Model of Modes of Adaptation

By the time their children have entered adolescence, then, most parents have adopted a characteristic mode or style of adaptation to their children's disabilities. These modes are shown in Table 3-1. The reader should keep in mind that these modes are ideal types that are only approximated by real families. Some families move back and forth be-

TABLE 3-1. Modes of Adaptation Among Parents of Children with Disabilities

Mode of adaptation	Type of Integration[a]	
	"Normal" society	Alternative subculture (disability as a "career")
Altruism	+	+
Normalization	+	−
Crusadership	−	+
Resignation	−	−

[a]+, Integration achieved; −, integration withdrawn or not achieved

tween modes as their needs and opportunities change. Ideal types help us to understand family lifestyles, but they should not be used to stereotype families or to predict their responses in any given situation.

All parents, then, have differential levels of access to two opportunity structures: (1) "normal," or mainstream, society and (2) the small subculture of the disabled, consisting of parent support groups, advocacy organizations, special-needs media, and state and national associations. In general, parents who have equal access to both structures will choose a normalization mode rather than the segregated mode of altruism. Parents who do not have equal access to both structures will choose crusadership if their access to normalized structures is severely restricted and resignation if their access to the subculture of the disabled is restricted as well.

These modes of adaptation are similar to those described by Radley and Green (1987) in the case of adjustment to chronic illness. Normalization is paralleled by their "active-denial" mode, which is characterized by fighting the illness and by retaining social activities and minimizing symptoms. Altruism is paralleled by "secondary gain," wherein the illness becomes the context for the pursuit of other rewarding activities. Crusadership is similar to "accommodation," which is characterized by changes in lifestyle ("illness as an occupation"). Finally, resignation mirrors the "resignation" mode, in which the loss of social activity is accompanied by a sense of being overwhelmed by the illness and subject to its vicissitudes. Radley and Green suggest that these modes reflect a psychological process of self-acceptance. In the case of parents of disabled children, access to social resources may be a more important determinant of mode of adaptation than parents' levels of "acceptance."

More research is needed to increase our understanding of how parents become integrated into different opportunity structures. The social processes involved may not be significantly different from those found in studies of social movements or social networks in general. Kazak and

Wilcox (1984) found that networks of families with disabled children tended to be more dense than those of comparison families, suggesting that various members of these families' support networks knew each other. A more "dense" or closely knit network may serve to isolate families from contacts with resources outside of the network. Kazak (1987) suggests that a greater understanding of social networks would be helpful to professionals interacting with these families.

As children with disabilities approach adolescence, the adjustment strategies adopted by their families during the childhood years may become problematic. When children leave school, parents are faced with planning for the future and confronting questions about whether their children will be able to play adult roles. These concerns are discussed in the next section.

APPROACHING ADULTHOOD:
A THREAT TO NORMALIZATION

Adolescence is a stressful time for most families, whether their children are disabled or not. Blumberg, Lewis, and Susman (1984) identify a number of tasks that adolescents must accomplish: (1) establish identity, (2) achieve independence, (3) adjust to sexual maturation, (4) prepare for the future, (5) develop mature relationships with peers, and (6) develop a positive self-image and body-image. In addition, Brotherson, Backus, Summers, and Turnbull (1986) note some tasks that are unique to families with developmentally disabled young adults:

- adjusting to the adult implications of disability
- deciding on an appropriate residence
- initiating vocational involvement
- dealing with special issues of sexuality
- recognizing the need for continuing family responsibility
- dealing with the continued financial implications of dependency
- dealing with a lack of socialization opportunities for the disabled outside of the family
- planning for guardianship

Continuing Dependence

In the typical family, the "launching" stage, when children leave home, creates stresses that have been called the empty-nest syndrome. As the child becomes an adult, all of the parental energies that have been bound up for so long in childrearing are no longer needed for that purpose. Many parents, and especially those who have not developed occupational or other interests outside the home, experience some anomie during this period in their lives. On the other hand, Clemens and Axelson (1985) have noted that in families with *nondisabled* children, the continued presence of adult children in the home can be stressful because it violates social expectations—parents expect the empty-nest syndrome to be only a temporary crisis in their lives. Parents of disabled children may find themselves in a similar situation as their children approach adulthood. The empty-nest syndrome is an experience they would *welcome*. As one father said:

> We'll never reach the stage that other people reach when their children leave home, and that's depressing. . . . I also wonder what will happen to Brian when he no longer looks like a child. (Darling, 1979, p. 184)

Although some disabled children of normal or nearly normal intelligence, whose physical problems are not too severe, *do* achieve independence during later adolescence and adulthood, many are not able to do so. The mentally retarded and those with physical problems that prevent the mastery of self-help skills will continue to be dependent on others to some extent for the rest of their lives.

Most parents of disabled children begin to have concerns about the future from the day they suspect that something is wrong with the child. During the infancy and childhood periods, however, they develop rationalizations that enable them to see the future in positive terms or push it out of their minds. Until their children reach middle adolescence, parents of disabled children almost universally seem to adopt an ideology of "living one day at a time." This ideology is expressed by the mother of a 9-year-old with spina bifida:

> In high school, Ellen's going to be excluded. I always picture Ellen as being left out. So far, it hasn't happened, but as kids get older being alike is so much more important. She'll probably have trouble in school—and what happens when she gets out of school? I don't like to think about it. We just take each year as it comes. (Darling & Darling, 1982, p. 155)

As a child moves through adolescence and approaches adulthood, parents are forced to begin thinking more seriously about the future. Some parents who had hoped that their child would someday be independent, may reassess their situation at this time and come to realize that independence is an unrealistic goal. The parents of a 15-year-old expressed these concerns:

We've been a little down . . . in the past year. . . . He's getting to be an adult.
. . . He's never going to make it on his own. . . . The present is fine. We can
manage it. . . . Our basic concern is the future. . . . We are getting older. We
need babysitters constantly. . . . It's a continuation of care. . . . Joe really
can't be left alone. . . . What if something happens to us? That's our basic
fear. (Darling & Darling, 1982, p. 156)

Parents such as these typically embark on a search for solutions that
is similar in some ways to the searches undertaken by younger parents
whose children have just been diagnosed. They search for such things as
appropriate living and employment arrangements, financial and legal
advice, and social, recreational, and, when deemed appropriate, sexual
opportunities for their children. Suelzle and Keenan (1981) found that
perceptions of unmet service needs were more widespread among parents
of young adults than among parents at any other time in the life cycle. As
noted earlier, they found that needs for family support and services such
as counseling and respite care exhibited a U-shaped function: They were
high among parents of preschoolers and young adults and lower among
parents of school-aged children. As adulthood approaches, then, the
normalization adaptation, so common among families during the childhood years, is likely to be threatened by a new awareness of unmet needs.

Exploring Alternatives for the Future

Living Arrangements

Although physically disabled, many mentally normal adults are able to
live independently with supports such as modified housing, equipment,
or vehicles. These individuals need to be included in planning for their
own futures, and some may become involved, like their parents, in
crusadership to make normalized ways of life more accessible to them.

For the adult who cannot achieve true independence, a number of
alternatives may be available, depending on where they live and their
financial resources. At one extreme is institutionalization; at the other are
various forms of community-living arrangements. Although residential
alternatives have continued to grow during the last decade, studies indicate that most disabled adults still reside in relatively large settings
(Krauss & Giele, 1987). Waiting lists for group homes and other smaller,
community-based programs are often long. In more rural areas, such
facilities may not exist at all. Parents have also expressed concerns about
the high rate of personnel turnover in some group homes and the qualifi-
cations of staff there (Darling & Darling, 1982).

In some cases, parents decide to keep their adult disabled children with them for as long as they live; some expect siblings to accept this responsibility; and others rely on various members of the extended family. Most parents realize that none of these arrangements are necessarily permanent, yet many delay in exploring residential alternatives, continuing the wait-and-see ideology so common among parents of younger children. Many of these parents are ambivalent—knowing that eventually their child will have to enter another living situation but also dreading that time. These remarks by the parents of a moderately retarded adolescent are illustrative:

> He's never going to be self-sufficient, which means as long as we are alive, he'll be with us. I'll never permit institutionalization. Perhaps eventually he'll be in a group home situation . . . maybe an adult day program. . . . His brother and sister are being trained to want to take care of him. I don't want them to have him live with them but I want them to keep close ties. . . . We haven't really explored things for the future. . . . We live for today. (Darling & Darling, 1982, p. 158)

Employment Opportunities

Normalization for adults in most segments of society includes independent employment. Yet individuals with disabilities may be limited, either by their disabilities or by employer attitudes, in their quest for jobs. Parents' concerns about their children's ability to achieve independence generally include the world of work, as evidenced in these comments by the mother of a young adult with spina bifida:

> Right now we're not sure what he'll be able to do and what's available for him to do. . . . I've thought for years, "What will Paul do?" His father and I won't always be around to take care of him. Paul's got to have a reason to get up in the morning. . . .
> Eighteen seemed like a long time away when he was four years old. . . . Now he doesn't have any inkling as to the value of a dollar. . . . I'm concerned about what he will do. . . . Sometimes, I get so angry at Paul. . . . He's waiting for me to come up with an answer. (Darling & Darling, 1982, p. 162)

In some cases, parents must readjust their goals for their children in accordance with their children's disabilities. The mother of a child with Down syndrome said:

> There was a Down's woman who was a dishwasher at work. My first reaction was, "My daughter will not wash dishes for somebody else." Later, I

thought, "Well, maybe she'd like washing dishes." I just want her to do whatever she wants to do. (Darling, 1979, p. 184)

Some disabled individuals may not be able to achieve competitive employment at all but may be able to work in sheltered or supported employment situations. Still others may not be capable of any kind of work. Being able to work for a living is a basic expectation deeply rooted in the American way of life. The capitalist ethic suggests that those who do not work are in some way morally inferior to those who are employed. Consequently, the realization that a severely disabled child might not ever be able to do any productive work is a difficult one for parents.

Social Opportunities

Parents' concerns about social acceptance for their children include a variety of interactional areas: friendship, dating, marriage, recreational opportunities, and opportunities for sexual activity. Getting information may also be difficult. As one mother said:

> I made a feeble attempt to discuss Bruce's sexual development with the pediatrician, but he seemed more embarrassed than I and suggested that I not borrow trouble. . . . Few medical and other professional people seemed interested in the impact which sexuality has on the entire family of a retarded person. (Meyer, 1978, p. 108)

Questions of normalization arise when disabled adolescents attempt to establish relationships with their nondisabled peers:

> Like most teenagers, I became very self-conscious about my appearance and physical state. In childhood, my family and others had accepted my physical limitations with little or nothing said; in my teens, these same limitations started cutting me off from the world. I think the first boy–girl parties that my age group started having were probably the beginning of the social and emotional difficulties that have been greater than my physical ones. (Kiser, 1974, p. 54)

> My cousin and Judy's steady egged me to ask her for a date. I told them I didn't think it was right for me to ask a non-handicapped girl to go on a date because I was in a wheelchair. (Chinn, 1976, p. 75)

Adolescents' attempts to achieve normalization may include rejection of the disabled peer group:

When I graduated from special school, I said, "Thank God, no more handicapped people." And I slipped into college. The first year I didn't have any
friends. My parents said, "Why don't you invite the old high school
friends?" I said, "No, I'm not going to be associated with handicapped
people anymore. I'm finished with that." (Richardson, 1972, p. 530)

In other cases, the disabled peer group becomes the locus of the
adolescent's social life:

His best friend has spina bifida too. He lives [nearby], and they talk all the
time. He doesn't really have any other friends that he sees. . . . He goes to a
spina bifida meeting once a month at City Children's Hospital. . . . He has a
girlfriend in the spina bifida group. They write and talk on the phone
between meetings. (Darling & Darling, 1982, p. 166)

Legal/Financial Needs

When parents realize that their disabled children may outlive them, they
usually become concerned about providing for their children's future
legal and financial security. Finding an estate-planning specialist who
can help them plan for the future is not always easy.

Beyer (1986) notes that if parents leave their assets directly to their
disabled child, the child may not be eligible for government benefits,
such as Supplemental Security Income or Medicaid. He recommends
instead that parents establish a trust for the child, naming a sibling or
other person as the trustee. In all cases, parents should seek out a good
lawyer, preferably one experienced in planning for families with a disabled member.

A recent alternative to family or public guardianship of the disabled
individual is corporate guardianship (Appolloni, 1987). These programs
have been developing in various areas throughout the United States and
have a number of advantages, including standards relating to quality of
life and the possibility of a lifetime commitment.

FAMILY CAREERS IN PROCESS:
AN OVERVIEW OF EMERGENT PATTERNS

Several consistent patterns or styles of adaptation emerge from a review of
the lifestyles over time, or careers, of many families with disabled children.
The major determinant of the career path that any given family will follow
is the social opportunity structure. When supportive resources and services
are available to parents, they are most likely to choose a lifestyle based on

normalization. When the opportunity structure is limited, on the other hand, they may engage in various forms of seekership or crusadership in an attempt to achieve normalization. The modes of adaptation that families adopt commonly change in a patterned sequence over the course of a child's life cycle. These career changes are shown in Figure 3-1.

Immediately after a diagnosis has been issued, parents are generally in a state of anomie; that is, they feel both meaninglessness and powerlessness in relation to their situation. Anomie is also felt by parents who suspect that something is wrong with their child and whose suspicions are not confirmed by a physician or other professional. Most parents feel meaninglessness because they have little knowledge about disabilities in general or their child's disability in particular.

Parents feel powerlessness even after they have satisfied their need for meaning. Once they have obtained a diagnosis, most parents ask: "What can I do about it?" Most parents have a strong need to do all that they can to help their children. However, most parents of disabled infants have little knowledge of treatment programs or educational or supportive services. All too often the professionals who issue diagnoses are themselves unaware of available programs.

Human beings constantly strive to make sense of their experiences. When events seem random and we feel out of control, most of us try to rationalize our experiences and reestablish order in our lives. Consequently, when parents feel anomic, they are likely to engage in behaviors that will restore their sense of meaning and purpose. During their children's infancy, then, most of these parents become engaged in a process of *seekership*—they read books, they consult experts, they write letters, and they make telephone calls—in an attempt to find answers to their questions and alleviate the anomie that they feel.

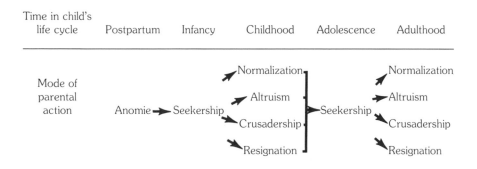

FIGURE 3-1. Career paths of parents of disabled children.

Most parents find the answers they are seeking. As a result, most parental quests end in *normalization*. By the time their children have reached school age, most parents have obtained an accurate diagnosis, found an acceptable pediatrician, and enrolled their child in an appropriate educational or training program. Many parents have also found support through talking to other parents of similarly disabled children. Most parents, then, are able to achieve a nearly normal style of life during the childhood years.

Although the majority of parents choose normalization when it is available to them, a few remain active in parent groups or other advocacy organizations in an attempt to help other parents achieve normalization. Such parents forgo the comforts of a normalized routine and adopt an *altruistic* mode of adaptation.

Because of a limited opportunity structure, some families are unable to achieve normalization. Sometimes their children have more severe or unusual disabilities or they live far away from treatment facilities. When parents do not have access to good medical care, appropriate educational programs, or other services, they may adopt a mode of prolonged seekership, or *crusadership*, and attempt to change the opportunity structure. These parents may join national organizations, go to court to demand that their children's needs be met, or use other means to create necessary services.

Finally, some parents who do not have access to services for their children may also not have access to the means for bringing about change. These parents who are doubly isolated adopt a mode of *resignation*. They struggle alone with difficulties created by the disabled child and often with other problems as well. Resignation is probably a more common outcome among the poor than among parents in the higher social classes.

When the disabled child reaches adolescence, normalization is likely to be threatened. During the childhood years, most parents adopt an ideology of "living one day at a time." Once a child approaches adulthood, however, problems raised by the child's continuing dependence must be faced. Regardless of the adaptation they adopted during the childhood years, then, all parents must eventually make decisions about their child's future. At this time, seekership commonly resumes, as parents search for living arrangements, employment opportunities, or other services that their children will need when they are no longer willing or able to care for them.

Finally, for some parents, the normalization equilibrium will be reestablished after they have located a satisfactory residential placement for their adult child. Other parents may choose to continue in an altruistic mode and remain active in organizations for the disabled even after they have found a place for their own child. Finally, some parents may not be able to locate a satisfactory placement at all and may keep their adult child with them while they adopt a crusadership or resignation mode.

Ideally *all* families should achieve normalization. Social change in the form of more and better services for the disabled could bring normalization to the crusaders and to those who are resigned to their fate. Altruism would, consequently, be eliminated as well for lack of need. Professionals should explore ways to help families expand their opportunity structures, with the goal of making normalization available to all who seek it.

REFERENCES

Appolloni, T. (1987, November/December). Guardianship: New options for parents. *The Exceptional Parent*, pp. 24-28.

Baxter, C. (1986). *Intellectual disability: Parental perceptions and stigma as stress*. Unpublished doctoral dissertation, Monash University, Clayton, Victoria, Australia.

Beyer, H. A. (1986, December). Estate planning: Providing for your child's future. *The Exceptional Parent*, pp. 12-18.

Birenbaum, A. (1970). On managing a courtesy stigma. *Journal of Health and Social Behavior, 11*, 196-206.

Birenbaum, A. (1971). The mentally retarded child in the home and the family cycle. *Journal of Health and Social Behavior, 12*, 55-65.

Blacher, J. (1984). A dynamic perspective on the impact of a severely handicapped child on the family. In J. Blacher (Ed.), *Severely handicapped young children and their families: Research in review* (pp. 3-50). Orlando, FL: Academic.

Blumberg, B. D., Lewis, M. J., & Susman, E. J. (1984). Adolescence: A time of transition. In M. G. Eisenberg, L. C. Sutkin, & M. A. Jansen (Eds.), *Chronic illness and disability through the life span: Effects on self and family* (pp. 133-149). New York: Springer.

Bristol, M. M. (1987). Methodological caveats in the assessment of single-parent families of handicapped children. *Journal of the Division for Early Childhood, 11*, 135-143.

Bristol, M. M., & Schopler, E. (1984). A developmental perspective on stress and coping in families of autistic children. In J. Blacher (Ed.), *Severely handicapped young children and their families* (pp. 91-141). Orlando, FL: Academic.

Brotherson, M. J., Backus, L. H., Summers, J. A., & Turnbull, A. P. (1986). Transition to adulthood. In J. A. Summers (Ed.), *The right to grow up: An introduction to adults with developmental disabilities*. Baltimore: Paul Brookes.

Butler, J. A., Rosenbaum, S., & Palfrey, J. S. (1987). Ensuring access to health care for children with disabilities. *The New England Journal of Medicine, 317*(3), 162-165.

Camp cares for handicapped kids. (1986, April 18). *Johnstown (PA) Tribune-Democrat*, p. 5C.

Chinn, H., Jr. (1976). *Each step of the way*. Johnstown, PA: Mafex Associates.

Clemens, A. W., & Axelson, L. J. (1985). The not-so-empty nest: The return of the fledgling adult. *Family Relations, 34*, 259-264.

Darling, R. B. (1979). *Families against society: A study of reactions to children with birth defects*. Beverly Hills: Sage.

Darling, R. B. (1987). The economic and psycho-social consequences of disability: Family-society relationships. In M. Ferrari & M. B. Sussman (Eds.), *Childhood disability and family systems* (pp. 45–61). New York: Haworth.

Darling, R. B. (1988). Parental entrepreneurship: A consumerist response to professional dominance. *Journal of Social Issues, 44,* 141–158.

Darling, R. B., & Darling, J. (1982). *Children who are different: Meeting the challenges of birth defects in society.* St. Louis: Mosby.

DeMyer, M. & Goldberg, P. (1983). Family needs of the autistic adolescent. In E. Schopler & G. Mesibov (Eds.), *Autism in adolescents and adults* (pp. 228–237). New York: Plenum.

Farber, B. (1975). Family adaptations to severely mentally retarded children. In M. J. Begab & S. A. Richardson (Eds.), *The mentally retarded and society: A social science perspective* (pp. 247–266). Baltimore: University Park Press.

Goffman, E. (1963). *Stigma: Notes on the management of spoiled identity.* Englewood Cliffs, NJ: Prentice-Hall.

Goodman, C. I. (1980). *A study of alternative therapeutic relationships: Parent groups and their members.* Unpublished doctoral dissertation, Case Western Reserve University, Cleveland, OH.

Harbaugh, G. R. (1984). *Costs and "out of pocket" costs of rearing the handicapped child.* Unpublished manuscript.

Kazak, A. E. (1987). Professional helper and families with disabled children: A social network perspective. *Marriage and Family Review, 11,* 177–191.

Kazak, A., & Wilcox, B. (1984). The structure and function of social support networks in families with handicapped children. *American Journal of Community Psychology, 12,* 645–661.

Kiser, B. (1974). *New light of hope.* New Canaan, CT: Keats Publishing.

Klein, C. (1977). Coping patterns of parents of deaf–blind children. *American Annals of the Deaf, 122,* 310–312.

Krauss, M. W., & Giele, J. Z. (1987). Services to families during three stages of a handicapped person's life. In M. Ferrari & M. B. Sussman (Eds.), *Childhood disability and family systems* (pp. 213–229). New York: Haworth.

Lipscomb, J., Kolimaga, J. T., Sperduto, P. W., Minnich, J. K., & Fontenot, K. J. (1983). *Cost-benefit and cost-effectiveness analyses of screening for neural tube defects in North Carolina.* Unpublished manuscript, Duke University, Institute for Policy Sciences, Durham, NC.

MacKeith, R. (1973). The feelings and behaviour of parents of handicapped children. *Developmental Medicine and Child Neurology, 15,* 524–527.

Max, L. (1985). Parents' views of provisions, services and research. In N. N. Singh & K. M. Wilton (Eds.), *Mental retardation in New Zealand* (pp. 250–262). Christchurch. New Zealand: Whitoculls.

Meyer, J. Y. (1978). One of the family. In S. L. Brown & M. S. Moersch (Eds.), *Parents on the team* (pp. 103–111). Ann Arbor: University of Michigan Press.

Mori, A. A. (1983). *Families of children with special needs: Early intervention.* Rockville, MD: Aspen Systems.

Morris, M. M. (1987, July). Health care: Who pays the bills? *The Exceptional Parent,* pp. 38–42.

Orenstein, A. (1979). *Organizational issues in implementing special educational legislation.* Paper presented at the annual meeting of the Society for the Study of Social Problems, Boston, MA.

Radley, A., & Green, R. (1987). Illness as adjustment: A methodology and conceptual framework. *Sociology of Health and Illness, 9,* 179–207.

Reader's forum. (1985, October). *The Exceptional Parent*, p. 7.

Richardson, S. A. (1972). People with cerebral palsy talk for themselves. *Developmental Medicine and Child Neurology, 14*, 524–535.

Scanlon, C. A., Arick, J., & Phelps, N. (1981). Participation in the development of the IEP: Parents' perspective. *Exceptional Children, 47*, 373–374.

Seltzer, M. M., & Krauss, M. W. (1984). Placement alternatives for mentally retarded children and their families. In J. Blacher (Eds.), *Severely handicapped young children and their families: Research in review* (pp. 143–175). Orlando, FL: Academic.

Suelzle, M., & Keenan, V. (1981). Changes in family support networks over the life cycle of mentally retarded persons. *American Journal of Mental Deficiency, 86*, 267–274.

Voysey, M. (1975). *A constant burden: The reconstitution of family life*. London: Routledge & Kegan Paul.

4

Effects on the Family as a System

Given our present state of knowledge, it is risky and misleading to draw firm conclusions about the stresses experienced by families with a disabled child. It is also difficult to ascertain whether these families are better or worse off than comparable families in which there is no special-needs child or adolescent. The research in this area is beset by many methodological problems (Crnic, Friedrich, & Greenberg, 1983), which has resulted in mixed and contradictory results. Nevertheless, some hold that the trauma and unrelenting stress of coping with a disabled youngster is difficult at best, if not immobilizing. This view is reflected in such commentary as the following:

> Some parents overprotect and do not stimulate the child to use the abilities he has. Others are so depressed that they cannot do much for the child. In still others, the sadness is interwoven with a kind of impotent rage toward the world. Many parents are angry at the retarded child, though they try to cover this up, hating to admit feelings of anger toward a helpless child. Most try to do their best in spite of their personal sense of loss and sadness, but some become cool and distant and withdraw from the retardate the sustained warmth and stimulation that he requires even more than other children. Some parents try to quash their own sadness and embark on brisk programs, pushing the children relentlessly toward speech training, toilet training, nursery school, exercises, and a host of other "stimulating" activities. If they push too hard, they overwhelm a vulnerable child and tend to make him withdraw even further. (Bernstein, 1978, pp. 58–59)

More recently Hobbs, Perrin, and Ireys (1986) write:

> Families with a chronically ill child confront challenges and bear burdens unknown to other families. The shock of the initial diagnosis and the urgent

and compelling need for knowledge; the exhausting nature of constant care
unpredictably punctuated by crises; the many and persistent financial concerns; the continued witnessing of a child's pain; tensions with one's spouse
that can be aggravated by the fatiguing chronicity of care; the worries about
the well-being of other children; and the multitude of questions involving
the fair distribution within the family of time, money, and concern—these
are challenges that parents of chronically ill children must face. (p. 80)

After their comprehensive review, Crnic and colleagues (1983) conclude that even though there are inconsistent and contradictory findings,
in general, the available literature suggests that families of retarded
children are at risk for numerous difficulties in comparison to families
with nonretarded children.

Some of what we presently know about families is derived from
empirical data, but much of it is anecdotal. Parents, often writing in the
most poignant terms, describe how it "feels" to parent a disabled child
(see the magazine *The Exceptional Parent*, Helen Featherstone's *A Difference in the Family* [1980], and Turnbull and Turnbull's *Parents Speak
Out* [1985]). No one would challenge these personal accounts in terms of
their veracity and poignancy, yet from a research perspective one needs
to question how representative these views are of the broader population of families with disabled children. With some exceptions, most
parent testimonials have been written by highly educated and articulate
persons.

Much of the research has been from the mother's perspective (which
is reflected in much of the research reported in this chapter), and it is not
unusual for mothers to be asked about the adjustment of other family
members. Even here it is worth noting that although a mother's view of
another family member's functioning has value, this type of information
should not take the place of nor necessarily be interpreted as accurate
information about other family members.

Much of the early literature was concerned with families with mentally retarded children, especially severely mentally retarded children
(Farber, 1959, 1960; Ross, 1964). This left a major gap in our understanding of families with other kinds of handicapped children. Although there
continue to be a disproportionate number of studies published on families of mentally retarded children, the situation is changing, as publications begin to deal more frequently with other disabilities: impaired
hearing (Israelite, 1985), epilepsy (Lechtenberg, 1984), chronic illness
(Travis, 1976; Turk & Kerns, 1985), spina bifida (Tew, Lawrence, Payne,
& Rawnsley, 1977), and autism (Schopler & Mesibov, 1984). These devel-
opments are important, yet their segregated nature implies that families

with children with different handicaps are more dissimilar than alike. We examine this assumption more closely later in this chapter.

The point to be made here is that separate lines of inquiry are developing and imply that some disabling conditions exert a greater stressful influence on the family than others. The truth is probably that we know little about the differential impact of dissimilar conditions on children and youth and their families; but the research, with its segregated literature, may be misleading in that it implies conclusions that are untrue. We have also not sufficiently explored the effects of mild–moderate versus severe disability on the family, although a few authors have made attempts to examine this area (Fewell & Gelb, 1983; Lyon & Preis, 1983). This topic is also explored in this chapter.

As noted above, mothers' experiences have been explored with far greater frequency than those of other family members, and many of the studies cited in this chapter used mothers as subjects. That is beginning to change also, as more attention is being paid to siblings (Grossman, 1972, Seligman, 1983; Wasserman, 1983), fathers (Lamb, 1983), and even grandparents and other extended family (Sonnek, 1986).

Our understanding of families with a disabled child has changed from a singular focus on the mother to one that explores family dynamics and, now, even broader ecological factors (see Chapter 1). This expansion in perspective makes it imperative that we study the multitude of influences on families and not resort to simplistic explanations of family functioning. For example, the research by Kazak and colleagues (Kazak & Marvin, 1984, Kazak & Wilcox 1984) on social support networks and their buffering effect on family stress is but one example of the promising lines of research presently being explored.

In addition to the factors already enumerated, the changing nature of the family has made it even more difficult to study the effects of childhood disability on the family (Hobbs et al., 1986). In response to the changes in family structure, Vadasy (1986) has written recently on single mothers of disabled children. Another area that needs more research attention is family adaptation over time (longitudinal studies). And finally, the implementation of innovative research models needs to be considered more seriously. For example, Goode (1984), in examining in depth the public presentation of a family with a deaf–blind child, utilized a naturalistic/observational model to study this phenomenon.

Against this backdrop, then, which suggests that research on families with disabled children is riddled with more questions and problems than answers, we attempt to examine the factors that have been reported to affect family adjustment.

STAGES OF MOURNING

Chapter 2 discusses in depth the effects of first knowledge of disability on the family; this section reviews the stages parents are thought to experience and explores a few concepts related to early knowledge.

Stage theory, as it has been applied to parents of disabled children, has been the subject of some controversy (Blacher, 1984; Olshansky, 1962; Searle, 1978). The stages noted below have been used in reference to families with disabled children in response to Solnit and Stark's (1961) observation that the birth of a disabled infant is often experienced by the parents as the death of the expected normal, healthy child.

Duncan (1977) adapted Kübler-Ross's (1969) stages, which characterize reactions to impending death. The stages must be viewed flexibly, due to the complexity of families and the unpredictable impact an event may have. Knowledge of these stages can help professionals understand family responses to crises in context and avoid regarding them as inappropriate, chaotic, or pathologic. Also, being aware of these stages enables the professional to intervene in a timely and appropriate fashion.

Kübler-Ross' (1969) stages are:

1. Denial
2. Bargaining
3. Anger
4. Depression
5. Acceptance

Shock and *denial* are a parent's initial response. Denial operates on an unconscious level to ward off excessive anxiety. Denial serves a useful, buffering purpose early on but can cause difficulties if it persists. If, over time and in the face of clear evidence, parents continue to deny the existence of their child's handicap, one needs to be cautious that:

• they do not push their child beyond his/her capabilities;
• they do not fail to enroll their child in early intervention programs;
• they do not make endless and pointless visits to professionals to get an acceptable diagnosis.

The *bargaining* phase is characterized by a type of magical thinking or fantasizing. The underlying theme is that if the parent works extra hard the child will improve. A child's improved condition will be the reward for working hard, being useful to others, and contributing to a worthy cause. During bargaining, parents may join local groups in activities that benefit a particular cause. Another manifestation of the bargaining phase is that parents may turn to religion or look for a miracle.

As parents realize that their child will not improve significantly, *anger* develops. There may be anger at God ("Why me?") or at one's spouse for having produced a handicapped child. Anger is frequently projected onto professionals for not healing the child (doctors) or for not helping the child make significant learning gains (teachers). Anger can also spring from an unsympathetic community, insensitive professionals, inadequate services, fatigue due to long hospital stays, and the like. Also, excessive guilt can turn anger inward, with a parent blaming himself/ herself for the handicap. Anger turned inward often results in depression.

Expressing anger is often cathartic and cleansing; but when parents realize that their angry energy does not change their child's condition and when they accept the chronic nature of the handicap and its implications for the family, a sense of *depression* sets in. For many parents depression is temporary or episodic, although Olshansky (1962) speaks about the "chronic sorrow" parents experience. Depression may coincide with a particular stage in the family life cycle. Developmental transitions imply change and invite comparisons with other children and families. These periods are time bound, and the seriousness of the depression depends on the family's interpretation of an event and on their coping strategies. Also, it is very important to be able to distinguish between clinical depression and milder and normal forms of dysphoria.

Acceptance is achieved when parents demonstrate some of the following characteristics:

1. They are able to discuss their child's shortcomings with relative ease.
2. They evidence a balance between encouraging independence and showing love.
3. They are able to collaborate with professionals to make realistic short- and long-term plans.
4. They can pursue personal interests unrelated to their child.
5. They can discipline the child appropriately without undue guilt.
6. They can abandon overprotective or unduly harsh behavioral patterns toward their child.

In applying these stages to families, one needs to be mindful that families are not homogeneous and that these stages may not apply precisely to some families. For some, these stages are cyclical, recurring when new developmental milestones are achieved or a crisis occurs (e.g., a child's condition worsens). Other factors that affect the manifestation of these stages include the possible impact of one's culture, whether all family members experience the same stage at the same time, how long a particular stage lasts, and what accounts for differences in duration. The literature on this topic, as Blacher (1984) notes, is "surprisingly extensive" (p. 55) and reflects an interest in the initial and continuing experiences of parents. In addition to the precautions about drawing conclusions from the existing research noted early in this chapter, another difficulty has been with the measurement and validation of these stages.

Various studies (see, e.g., Darling, 1979; Kennedy, 1970) have indicated that when families experience stages of adaptation at all, they may complete the entire process within a short period of time. On the other hand, Olshansky (1962) suggests that chronic sorrow is a *normal* reaction to parenting a disabled child and a more meaningful concept than the oversimplistic notion of acceptance/rejection. In this view, a parent who continues to experience sadness about a child's disability can still be competent and caring. Too often, professionals have been quick to label parents as unaccepting or poorly adjusted when they are, in fact, reacting normally to their continuing burden.

CHRONIC BURDEN OF CARE

The chronicity of care that families with a disabled child anticipate is a major feature that distinguishes them from families confronting other crises. As noted in Chapter 3, for some families, the care is necessary 24 hours a day, 7 days a week, and for many years. The stresses can be relentless, draining the family physically and psychologically. Add to this the financial worries that may exist, and the family has the potential for being at risk. The degree to which the family is in trouble may depend on how it conceptualizes or reframes its life circumstance, how supportive family members are of one another, and the availability of social support outside the family.

The burden of care is not only chronic; it can be experienced as a dark cloud that will continue to engulf the family for years to come. Family members can see little relief when they look to the future. Instead of independence, growth, and differentiation, a family may see only despair, dependence, and social isolation. And Seligman and Meyerson (1982) observe that: "The mental health needs of exceptional parents may be cumulative. That is, living with a handicapped child over many years can take its toll psychologically, physically and financially" (p. 103).

In facing the future, family members must decide how they plan to negotiate their special life circumstance. As we note in Chapter 1, flexibility and adaptability are important to successful family living. Without

•becoming intrusive, family members must be able to assume roles not ordinarily assigned by society. For example, siblings may need to help with caretaking more than they otherwise would and fathers may need to assist instrumentally more often and also be more psychologically supportive of the mother. Mothers, so that they do not become enmeshed, have to learn to facilitate, without undue guilt, as much growth and independence as their child is capable of achieving. All in all, over the family's lifespan, members need to adapt, negotiate, and communicate. This is sound advice for all families, but it has special relevance to families in which there is a chronic stressor.

In addition to seeking help within the family, the family system needs to be permeable enough to allow for outside help, such as respite care, when such help is available. For example, Wikler (1981) reports that respite care leads to a decrease in negative maternal attitudes toward the disabled child and increased positive family interaction. Upshur (1982, 1983) reinforces the importance of respite care services and advocates a spectrum of types of respite care to meet different family needs. Receptiveness to outside intervention and help is important in enabling the family to cope with a chronic and potentially stressful situation. And it is within this context that professional psychologists, counselors, social workers, and physicians need to help families adapt to their situation. They may also have to help families *create* such resources where they do not exist.

STIGMA

Mark Twain once wrote:

> There is something that he [man] loves more than he loves peace—the approval of his neighbors and the public. And perhaps there is something which he dreads more than he dreads pain—the disapproval of his neighbors and the public. (in Neider, 1963, p. 344)

In American society today the physically and mentally disabled are often judged on the same basis as "normals," resulting in a degradation or *stigmatization* of the disabled. To the extent that individuals deviate from the societal norm of physical and mental perfection, they are likely to be shunned, ridiculed, avoided, and/or ostracized.

The conditions of stigmatization vary for different disabilities. Goffman (1963) suggests that some disabilities are "discredited," whereas others are "discreditable." A "discreditable" condition is one that is not readily apparent to a layperson. A child with a disfigurement hidden by clothing or a disease such as cystic fibrosis might be able to "pass" as normal in many situations and thus avoid stigma. On the other hand, a child with a more visible defect, such as Down syndrome or severe spina bifida, would be discredited immediately, although the degree of discreditation may vary for different conditions.

Individuals with discreditable defects and their families will sometimes engage in what Goffman calls "impression management" to appear normal. Voysey (1972) mentions the mother of an autistic child who was able to conceal the severity of her child's condition from even the closest family members by cleaning him and the house before visits. Other techniques are noted in Chapter 2.

• Even if the parent is not intentionally trying to "pass," encounters with strangers may be stressful because people generally assume that a child is normal. The parent must then decide whether to "play along" with the assumption of normality.

In the case of "discredited" conditions, which are immediately obvious to strangers, the problems of "impression management" are different. "Passing" as normal is not possible in these cases. Davis (1961) has suggested that when those with visible disabilities come into contact with "normals," a kind of mutual pretense takes place: Both the stigmatized and the normal act as though the disability does not exist. Davis calls this mode of interaction "fictional acceptance" because the normal person does not *really* accept the disabled person as a moral equal.

Typically, interaction between the stigmatized and the normal never moves beyond a superficial level. People are hesitant to become close to the family of a stigmatized person because they, in turn, might be stigmatized. Goffman (1963) suggests that close associates of the stigmatized come to bear a "courtesy stigma" and may suffer similar reactions of avoidance, rejection, or ridicule. For this reason stigmatized individuals and their families may choose their friends from what Goffman (1963) calls their *own*—others who already share a similar stigma.

The notion of social stigma does not apply exclusively to persons with disabilities; it also applies to minority-group members. Although persons with disabilities share certain commonalities with members of other minority groups, Wright (1983) notes that important differences exist. For example, the status implications for disabled persons differ from those of other minority groups in that their affliction is not likely to be shared by other family members or perhaps even by others in the immediate environment. In contrast, members of other minority groups are often surrounded by other persons with whom they share common attributes, such as skin color.

This sense of difference experienced by disabled children is also, by association, felt by others in the family, namely the parents, siblings, and grandparents. In a social or interactional context these "exceptional" families feel devalued, which can result in a sense of shame and stigma.

Studies have rather consistently shown that disabled persons are viewed negatively by the general public (Resnick, 1984). Research has also demonstrated that certain disabling conditions are more acceptable than others and, furthermore, that professionals hold attitudes that are negative (Darling, 1979; Resnick, 1984). Indeed, Resnick (1984), based on his literature review, reports on the negative attitudes held by teachers, counselors, social workers, and physicians. Darling and Darling (1982) note that negative attitudes toward disabled persons are reinforced by training in medical schools and other professional training programs, which may account in part for the negative attitudes professionals hold. (This phenomenon is discussed further in Chapter 9.)

Goffman (1963) states that the predominant social attitude toward those who are different is one of stigma and that stigmatized persons are regarded as morally inferior to those who are "normal." As Newman (1983) has pointed out; "In early societies, illness and disability were seen as the work of evil demons and supernatural forces—disease and disability [were seen] as the scourge of God, as punishment for sin (p. 9)." As suggested above, children are stigmatized, but parents suffer from a "courtesy stigma" because of their association with a handicapped person.

Gliedman and Roth (1980) believe that the destiny of disabled children is to suffer from a greater likelihood of unemployment, underemployment, and lower wages than able-bodied peers. They may also be the victims of limited upward mobility, poverty, marital separation and divorce, frequent hospitalizations, low educational attainment, and social isolation. These outcomes, Gliedman and Roth contend, are not due to one's limitations alone but, more importantly, are a consequence of individual and societal response to disability.

Wikler (1981) believes that families must develop competence in managing uncomfortable social situations. She goes on to say that they

> face hostile stares, judgmental comments, murmurs of pity, and intrusive requests for personal information whenever they accompany their child to the grocery store, on the bus, or to the park. (p. 282)

Wikler notes further that families with a mentally retarded child are subject to an increase in the number of stressful encounters as the discrepancy between the child's size and mental functioning increases. However, professionals can help families cope with awkward social situations.

It could be that the rather positive portrayals of disabled persons in films and television has positively affected attitudes. Nevertheless, our present state of knowledge regarding public and professional sentiment about disabled persons informs us that attitudes are indeed negative. Thus social ostracism may be added to the other burdens families must endure.

One study found that adolescents who suffered from cystic fibrosis had major difficulties with their self-image compared to similarly aged victims of asthma or cancer (Offer, Ostrov, & Howard, 1984). Cystic fibrosis is a lethal genetic disease in which chronic respiratory and digestive problems delay growth and sexual development, resulting in a more noticeable difference in physical appearance. In speculating on their findings, Offer and colleagues (1984) remark that "in illnesses in which the social stigma is easily noticed by others (i.e. cystic fibrosis), the self-image system is impaired. The greater the stigma, one might assume, the greater the impairment" (p. 72). In her review of the research on families of adolescent victims of cystic fibrosis, McCracken (1984) reports that families often experience poor communication; a general lack of time and energy for personal, marital, and family activities; marital discord; depression; and repressed hostility. Thus the child's difficulties due to the characteristics of the disease and the associated social stigma affect the entire family.

Such sobering information about attitudes toward disabled persons must be factored into our conception of the family with a disabled child. At minimum, we, as professionals, must carefully examine our own attitudes toward disability and toward families with special-needs children lest they interfere with our performance in subtle ways. Personal examination of our own attitudes is important, and an appropriate place to begin exploring them would be in professional training programs.

MARITAL ADJUSTMENT, DIVORCE, AND SINGLE PARENTHOOD

Hobbs and colleagues (1986) state that divorce adds to the stress of illness and that many disabled persons live in households with only one parent. (There is a growing population of single parents in society in general.) Vadasy (1986) notes also that single parents of disabled children will experience greater stresses in their family system than parents in intact families. Yet most assumptions about the single parents of disabled children are intuitive, because empirical data is scarce.

One study reported that single mothers of handicapped children felt that there were too many time demands, which hindered their personal growth (Holroyd, 1974). These mothers also felt that they had many problems, that the family was not well integrated, and that they had significant financial problems. Beckman (1983) discovered that single mothers reported more stress than control mothers, and Wikler (1981) reports that mothers rated their greatest needs as being respite care, then financial assistance, and then personal and social support. She also found that these mothers were less likely to be employed, more likely to be on welfare, and prone to feel that they would not remarry.

Vadasy (1986) notes that the role functions assumed by family members of intact families are shared, thereby decreasing the burden on any one family member. Perhaps the most support a single parent can expect from the family is from his/her own parents. Other potential problems for single parents include economic, physical, and emotional needs. Vadasy pleads for researchers and those responsible for social policy to address seriously the needs of this underserved population.

The information regarding marital problems and divorce in families with handicapped children is sparse and contradictory (Crnic et al., 1983). Gabel, McDowell, and Cerreto (1983) report that marital difficulty is one of the more frequently reported adjustment problems. Their re-search review shows that marital problems include more frequent con-flict, feelings of marital dissatisfaction, sexual difficulties, temporary separations, and divorce. Farber (1959) found marital conflict to be com-mon, especially in families containing a retarded boy aged 9 years or older. Conversely, some families report no more frequent problems than comparison families with no handicapped child (Bernard, 1974; Dorner, 1975; Martin, 1975; Waisbren, 1980); and some marriages have been reported to improve after the diagnosis of a child's disability.

Although the data regarding marital dissatisfaction and divorce are contradictory, we do know that some marriages are under stress but are able to cope, while others simply fail. Our task should probably be to understand why some families disintegrate while others thrive. Crnic and colleagues (1983) believe that future investigations should help differen-tiate the child and family characteristics, as well as other ecological factors, that distinguish families that cope well from those that do not. Zucman (1982) speculates about the emergence of certain family dynam •ics. For example, while attending to the needs of a disabled infant or child, the mother unwittingly moves away from her husband; feeling abandoned, the husband may turn to others for solace or at least distance himself from the family as a means of self-protection. Siblings often respond to a parent's excessive attention to a disabled brother or sister by feeling abandoned, angry, and resentful; perhaps the same dynamic oper-ates with husbands.

Harris (1983) makes the important observation that a family's focus on the disabled child as the source of family problems may in fact be a red herring that distracts parents from more fundamental issues about their relationship. She makes the cogent point that professionals need to discriminate family problems caused by a child's disability from those that would have arisen under any circumstances. Problematic marital relationships can be made considerably worse by the birth of a special-needs child. Schipper (1959) found that in those families who had serious personal and/or financial problems *prior* to the birth of their Down syndrome child, the child sometimes became "the straw that broke the camel's back." It is probably a myth that such a child—or any child, for that matter—can bring a troubled marriage together.

After a thorough review of the literature on families of severely handicapped children, Lyon and Preis (1983) conclude that these families must contend with a number of stressors, but in general the research reveals mixed conclusions regarding the impact such a child has on the family. These authors also make note of the major methodological problems inherent in much of the research and conclude that, in the absence of clear evidence that these families are coping badly, professionals should focus on such practical matters as concrete information, respite services, financial help, and other supportive services to help with logistical problems. Lyon and Preis (1983) conclude that: "Rather than to continue to view these families as functioning pathologically we might better and more productively focus upon those practical matters that are of great concern to the families themselves" (p. 221).

From the above overview, what can we conclude about marital harmony among families with a disabled child? One conclusion may be that marital dysfunction may have occurred even without the presence of a disabled child; in some families the child may aggravate latent problems. Another conclusion is that families can cope successfully with the help of family and community supports. And finally, one consequence of marital discord is divorce and single parenthood, an area that deserves much more attention than it has thus far received.

FAMILIES WITH CHILDREN
WITH DIFFERENT HANDICAPS

Although research on families with children with differing disabling conditions is increasing, the available research is too meager to allow any definitive conclusions. Even so, based on the characteristics of a child's condition, one may speculate on the effects certain child attributes have on the family.

The unpredictability of the behavior of autistic children and the social–interpersonal ramifications experienced by families cause considerable stress (Bristol, 1984; Schopler & Mesibov, 1984). Even as we learn more about the biological bases of this developmental disability, parents of autistic and schizophrenic children are still often considered responsible for their child's illness and thereby suffer the social stigma that accompanies this disorder. Bristol (1984) states that for families with an autistic child, the following constitute high-risk factors: ambiguity of diagnosis, severity and duration of the illness, and lack of congruity with community norms. Cantwell and Baker (1984) cite research indicating that families are affected by the multiple failures of their autistic children, that mothers appear the most severely affected, that spousal affectional bonds tend to be weakened, that siblings are affected, and that family difficulties do not diminish as the child grows older.

A recent study by Tartar (1987) shows that 27% (or 13 out of 47 subjects) of parents of head trauma victims had a DSM-III diagnosable psychiatric disturbance that became manifest after the offspring's accident. The disturbance was primarily associated with high levels of anxiety and depression. Notably, it was the behavioral, not the physical, aspect of the offspring's disability that was most closely associated with parental disturbance.

The unpredictability of epileptic children's seizures may result in family members' constant vigilance for seizure activity (Lechtenberg, 1984). Public attitudes toward persons with epilepsy resemble those toward persons with mental illness, thereby creating a major stressor for the family. Travis (1976) notes that families with a hemophilic child need to be constantly vigilant of their child's bleeding episodes and that families with children with heart disease need to be cautious about bringing home infections. All of these characteristics of the child's disability cause stress in the family and may precipitate a major family crises when there are other existing family problems. As Tartar (1987) points out, the contribution of the parents' characteristics together with the demand characteristics of the child's disability "underscores again the complex dynamic and reciprocal relationship between parent and offspring with the characteristics of one affecting the reactions of the other" (p. 83).

As with most handicapping conditions, the effects of a deaf child on the family are mixed (Luterman, 1984). However, hearing-impaired children are often also impaired in their communication, which can be a source of considerable frustration for family members. Levine (1960) reports that deaf children are often socially less mature than their hearing peers and that they are more than twice as likely to have emotional problems. Also, hearing-impaired youngsters are often educated in segregated environments; this enables them to develop communication skills, grow personally, and acquire academic knowledge, but it also isolates them from the larger "normal" community and prevents them from establishing stronger ties with family members.

Fewell and Gelb (1983) report that the *degree* of visual loss in blind children has important implications for both the child and the family's reaction to the child. Just as children with impaired vision try to "pass" as normally sighted, parents, too, are caught in the dilemma of not wanting to identify their children's differences. Although children who are blind may struggle with their mobility, and there is some evidence of their delayed development and aberrant social behavior, the fact that a blind child can think, communicate, and carry on with the chores of daily living makes blindness less devastating to the child and the family than other disabilities (Fewell & Vadasy, 1986).

For physically disabled children, it is their mobility that is most affected, which, in turn, affects their ability to perform self-care functions. Physical impairments can take a variety of forms, such as a loss of limbs or a paralysis due to accident or disease. The nature and characteristics of the physical impairment may determine the type of adjustment the child and the family must make. For example, quadriplegia holds numerous implications for how family members choose to assist with frequent caretaking duties. Muscular dystrophy, a degenerative disease, means that the child and family need to adjust to an increasing level of dependency as the disease progresses. Numerous other physical disorders, many of which are rare and leave the family with few others to identify with, may cause adjustment problems.

A new medical procedure that allows child and adolescent victims of end-stage renal disease to perform dialysis at home has been reported by LePontois, Moel, and Cohn (1987). Four or five exchanges are required daily for these children, yet home treatment permits them to reduce hospital visits and allows them to be ambulatory, active, and more in touch with family and peers. Although responsibility for the dialysis procedure shifts somewhat from the parents to the patient during adolescence, the family is often "burned out" by years of home care and parents can lose hope in the possibility of a satisfying future for themselves. Conflicting messages from professionals (for example, be careful to maintain sterile techniques to prevent serious illness but don't become so anxious that separation and individuation are prevented) result in feelings of hopelessness, helplessness, and depression in family members.

Mullins (1979) reports that the physical needs of children with cancer have effects on the entire family: "The medications, hospitalizations, repeated transportation for treatment, and extended care at home will be a drain on family finances and physical resources" (p. 266). If the cancer is terminal, the family needs to prepare for the child's imminent death. This can be a crisis of major proportions and requires considerable family adjustment before and after the child's death.

Cystic fibrosis, one of the most common chronic diseases of childhood, requires the family to comply with a prescribed home regimen. The home care of the child is difficult and chronic, and failure to carry out treatment can contribute to the progression of the disease and eventual death (Dushenko, 1981). In regard to compliance with home treatment for children with cystic fibrosis, Patterson (1985) reports that age is a factor in that children are more reluctant to adhere to prescriptions as they grow older. Also, the family's commitment to home treatment may wane in the face of the reality that their child is moving into the terminal stages of the disease. Patterson notes further that communication in these families often declines in a situation that is difficult and requires the continued expression of hope and mutual support. McCracken (1984) reports that families with children with cystic fibrosis have multiple problems, and Offer and colleagues (1984) hypothesize that an adolescent's problems are exacerbated by short stature and an appearance indicating a lower maturational level. Social stigma, as noted earlier, adds to the disability.

It is impossible to conclude with any certainty how the *type* of a child's disability will affect the family. Factors other than severity of handicap may play an important role in determining family adaptation (Crnic et al., 1983). For example, several researchers have found that the quantity and quality of community resources and family support have an impact on the family's ability to cope (Darling, 1979; Korn, Chess, & Fernandez, 1978; Wortis & Margolies, 1955). More recently, researchers have sought to determine more specifically which aspects of social support are most helpful to families, and how (Dyson & Fewell, 1986; Kazak & Marvin, 1984; Kazak & Wilcox, 1984).

Based on her research, Beckman (1983) found that mothers of disabled children experienced significantly more stress if their offspring had a greater number of or unusual caregiving demands, were less socially responsive, had more difficult temperaments, and displayed more repetitive behavioral patterns. Beckman's research is important in that it represents a departure from other studies by examining specific child characteristics rather than medical labels. Certainly, within any one disability category we would find a wide range of behaviors and other child attributes. Furthermore, Beckman's results are supported by those of Tartar (1987), who found that it was the behavioral, not the physical, aspects of their child's disability that was most distressing to parents.

In the face of inconclusive research data, we feel that it is incumbent upon us to educate professionals regarding the numerous variables that may affect family adjustment and to persuade them to keep these in mind when evaluating a family's level of functioning. However, as further research avenues are explored, it seems to us that Beckman's (1983) approach deserves attention. The effects that specific attributes of disabled children (or the demand characteristics of the disability) may have on the family is a more productive line of inquiry than lumping all children with a particular label into one diagnostic category and assuming that they are all alike. It is also certain that child characteristics must be viewed within the context of the family's structural and interactional patterns. However, it appears from current research that a disabled child's aberrant behavior is the most likely cause of family stress.

THE SEVERITY OF DISABILITY

Perhaps a more productive avenue for research than type of disability is the impact severity of disability has on family functioning. Severity has implications for caregivers in terms of dependency, increased attention for the disabled child (perhaps at the expense of other family members), frequent contact with medical personnel and other service providers, and the prospect of lifelong care.

The placement of children into categories of mild, moderate, and severe disabilities is somewhat arbitrary. Diagnostic ambiguity is particularly evident between the mild and moderate categories. However, Fewell and Gelb (1983) briefly differentiate these categories:

1. Mild: This category includes children whose disabilities require special services but who have substantial areas of normal functioning.
2. Moderate: This category includes children who are markedly deficient in at least one area while functioning normally in others.
3. Severe: This category includes children with handicaps that pervade most, if not all, areas of functioning.

According to Fewell and Gelb (1983), children in the less severe categories are more difficult to assess educationally and in terms of emotional adjustment, making treatment alternatives less obvious. Furthermore, the ambiguity about diagnosis may cause families to go to many sources in search of a favorable diagnosis (called "shopping"), thus delaying initiation of a treatment plan and thrusting the family into a state of stress. The more "normal-like" a child appears, the more likely parents may be "stuck" in the denial stage and engage in more "shopping." Parents who deny their child's disability seem to experience more tension between professionals (especially school personnel) and themselves. For children with mild or moderate disabilities, treatment may need to be modified as the child develops and other problems appear, decrease, or increase. More moderate disabilities may become worse over time or improve.

Children who are mildly or moderately disabled (especially those who fall into the "mild" category) are often considered "marginal" in that they do not clearly fit into either the disabled or the normal category. A person who is marginal can claim partial membership in two worlds but is not completely acceptable to either (Stonequist, 1937). Fewell and Gelb (1983) argue that intermediately handicapped people will have more adjustment problems than more severely handicapped individuals. Marginality implies ambiguity not only in terms of diagnosis but also in terms of the parents' concerns about the child's future, social acceptance, and level of functioning. But it seems that social adjustment may have the most severe impact on the child and family. In this regard, Watson and Midlarsky (1979) speculate that a mother's overprotective behavior toward her retarded child is not caused by guilt; it is the consequence of her perception that normal individuals have negative attitudes toward retarded people. Fewell and Gelb (1983) make the cogent point that the family's difficulty with the social destiny of their stigmatized child is inevitable and normal, not a sign of pathologic functioning.

Fewell and Gelb (1983) speculate further that a child with a less severe disability creates stress for the family due to the "uncertainty of not knowing in a given situation whether the child will be accepted or rejected" (p. 178). Certainly, in school situations and in one's immediate community, concerns about acceptance and belonging are paramount, especially during adolescence. A child who is not disabled but who has a physical disfigurement, such as a cleft palate or facial scars, certainly will face ridicule and experience shame from peers. As suggested earlier, a family that has a child who is devalued due to a disability also experiences a sense of stigma and lower status:

> The effect of the moderate disability on functioning is, according to our definition, limited. The moderately handicapped are not of themselves socially deviant. They are penalized, however, by virtue of the "handicapped" label. They are identified with the severely handicapped, although they could as easily be identified with the nondisabled. Their social isolation is no less palpable for being undeserved, and it strongly affects their parents. (Fewell & Gelb, 1983, p. 179)

A study of mothers of thalidomide-deformed babies found that social factors were a major concern in the parents' reactions (Roskies, 1972). Moreover, as time went on the importance of social factors to the mothers increased.

The concept of "spread" has relevance to children with milder disabilities and, by association, their families. If a person has an undesirable characteristic and is viewed as less adequate only in that regard, the judgment would be a realistic one. But realistic appraisal of others is more the exception than the rule. For example, physique (being obese or slender) evokes a wide variety of impressions and feelings about people. Specific characteristics may be legitimately inferred from physique (an obese person may have physical restrictions), but the person *as a whole* is sometimes evaluated (for example, the obese person is also viewed as depressed, socially isolated, low in self-esteem, and lacking sexual relationships). Global devaluations are problems of some significance in that persons with atypical characteristics are considered to be less worthy, less valuable, and less desirable.

Dembo, Leviton, & Wright (1956) introduced the term *spread*, which refers to the power of single characteristics to evoke broader inferences about a person. Early research indicated that a handicapped person's characteristics, traits, and behaviors are inferred beyond their disability (Musseen & Barker, 1944; Ray, 1946, both cited in Wright, 1983). Because of spread, the degree of disability is often perceived as more severe than it actually is. An illustration of spread is when a sighted person speaks unusually loudly to a person who is blind, as if blindness implies a hearing impairment as well.

The phenomenon of spread is evident in the way parents of disabled children are sometimes viewed. As a consequence of disability in the family, some parents are as subject to spread as are their afflicted sons and daughters. Because of a disabled child, parents may be viewed as deeply troubled and burdened—or as extraordinarily brave and courageous. The numerous factors that contribute to family adjustment, as well as the complex nature of their interactions, are typically disregarded. By association, then, certain feelings and other characteristics may be attributed to family members of mildly disabled children. The all-too-ready judgment, on the basis of disability in the family, that a person's life is a tragedy from which there is no reprieve may be a fairly common perception.

In their article on parenting moderately handicapped persons, Fewell and Gelb (1983) discuss family adjustment to children who have vision and hearing problems, physical impairments, and learning disabilities. They conclude their review of these conditions by stating that:

> In most cases, the presence of a child with a moderate impairment creates the following concerns: the dilemma of being educated with the nondisabled or the handicapped; the stress of heavy involvement in physiotherapy; the stress of acknowledging the existence of the handicap or simply covering it up. (p. 192)

Lyon and Preis (1983) report that children with severe disabilities constitute an extremely low-incidence population and are really a heterogeneous population with different characteristics, needs, and abilities. Although severely disabled children are heterogeneous, there are a number of problems and difficulties that characterize these children and their families' responses to them.

Intellectual deficits are one characteristic of this population. These children may be substantially cognitively delayed and may not even acquire the most rudimentary conceptual abilities. In addition, they may remain extremely limited in the acquisition and use of language.

Another problem common among severely disabled children is the presence of physical disabilities. A chief culprit here is cerebral palsy, which, along with other physical impairments, can affect such basic movements as walking, using one's hands, speaking, and eating. The presence of major physical handicaps is exceedingly restrictive to the impaired child and places a great burden on the family.

A third characteristic, according to Lyon and Preis (1983), is sensory impairment. Many severely disabled children suffer from various degrees of visual and/or auditory deficits. It is not uncommon for children with sensory impairments to have varying degrees of retardation and physical handicaps as well.

A major consequence of severe impairment is that these children also manifest great difficulty in developing appropriate social skills. Social skill deficits may be associated with mental retardation or childhood autism. These children characteristically demonstrate bizarre behavior through unintelligible or repetitive speech, self-stimulation, and even self-destructive behavior. These behaviors are difficult to treat and often necessitate extensive effort and commitment by the family to remedy or even tolerate them (Lyon & Preis, 1983). We already know from the research of Beckman (1983) and Tartar (1987) that a disabled child's behavior can be a major stressor in the family.

It would seem from this brief review of children with severe disabilities that the consequences for the family would be insurmountable. For some families this is surely so, but the evidence regarding negative impact is unclear. Much of the fault for this equivocation lies in the fact that research in this area is not abundant and that the work that has been reported is poor from an empirical point of view. Nevertheless, the literature does provide some preliminary evidence about how these children may contribute to stress for the family.

Several researchers conclude that severely disabled children have a negative effect on siblings. Gath (1974) reports that older sisters have a higher incidence of psychiatric disturbance, while Grossman (1972) observes that siblings may experience a variety of negative emotional reactions, such as fear, death wishes, and anxiety. Lyon and Preis (1983) note that one consistent finding has been that older female siblings may experience difficulty due to the excessive caretaking burdens placed on them. On the other hand, Caldwell and Guze (1960) and Kibert (1986) found no evidence of negative impact on siblings. (A more detailed discussion of siblings appears in Chapter 5.)

In terms of the family, Farber's (1959, 1960) pioneering studies show that overall family integration of families who keep their severely mentally retarded child at home is affected negatively. Gath (1974) found families of severely handicapped children to evidence more negative emotions, while other researchers have reported role tension, increased divisiveness within the family, negative emotionality, and increased financial burdens (Caldwell & Guze, 1960; Dunlap & Hollinsworth, 1977; Farber, 1960; Hormuth, 1953). In a recent study designed to compare families of severely mentally retarded, educable mentally retarded, and trainable mentally retarded children, Blacher, Nihira, and Meyers (1987) found that parents of severely retarded children reported the greatest amount of negative impact on family adjustment. Family adjustment was defined as the "extent to which the retarded child affects the atmosphere in the home, relationships among family members, agreement as to discipline of the child" (p. 315). The excessive caretaking responsibilities of the families apparently influenced family adjustment. However, on the measures of marital adjustment ("extent to which the retarded child has influenced the parents' marriage" [p. 315]), no differences were found among the three groups. Blacher and colleagues' results reinforce those found by others, who explain that the demanding care of a severely disabled child is more likely to disrupt family routines and social lives than marital harmony. A further finding was that there are no differences among the three groups on the coping scores, reflecting the equal ability to deal with day-to-day events. Humphrey and Jacobson (1979) argue that the negative effects have been overstated and the positive effects ignored. This is similar to the conclusion reached by Lyon and Preis (1983), based on their literature review.

Lyon and Preis (1983) also note that frequently reported problems by families of severely handicapped children include financial difficulties and the burden on the practical day-to-day operations and logistics of the family. They concur with Jacobson and Humphrey (1979) that these families have been pathologized too often in the past and that with adequate services (and these families need many) families with severely handicapped youth do manage to cope. When families experience severe stress, they argue, it is usually due to the failure of the service delivery system, not necessarily a consequence of the disabled child. Indeed, of the many services needed by families with a severely impaired child, perhaps one of the most critical, and in some communities least available, is respite care (Lyon & Preis, 1983; Upshur, 1982, 1983).

In contrast to the aforementioned authors, Blacher (1984) concludes from her review that:

> The impact of a severely impaired child on the family appears to be profound, pervasive, and persistent. It is reasonable to assume that parents feel the effects of such a child throughout infancy, early childhood, during the school years, and beyond into adult life. (p. 41)

And Crnic and colleagues (1983) comment that the "research in this area suggests that parents of retarded children are at the least a group at high risk for emotional and personality difficulties" (p. 128).

Although Blacher (1984) and Crnic and colleagues (1983) tend to view the effect of a severely disabled child more negatively than others, they do note that extrafamilial and intrafamilial support buffer the hardships. The availability and quality of social support is generally viewed as a critical factor in a family's ability to cope—a fact that should not be lost to those in a position to affect public policy.

It seems that a characteristic that differentiates families with a severely or multiply handicapped child from those with a moderately disabled child is the burdensome, unrelenting chronicity of care. The burden of multiple needs can also place stress on the family system. For families with a mildly or moderately disabled child, it appears that the ambiguity of the affliction, the marginality of the child and the impact this has on social acceptance, constitutes a major obstacle. The evidence to date supports the conclusion that marital harmony is comparable across levels of severity. And finally, the aberrant behavior of the child appears to cause stress in the family no matter how mild or severe the disability is.

In the end, perhaps, when one considers whether it is best to posit type of disability or severity of disability as more debilitating to the family, the most useful construct may come from Hill's (1949) model of stress. Recall from Chapter 1 that a key to a family's experience of stress is the c factor, which refers to how the family interprets a particular event. This is similar to Ellis's (1962) conception of neurotic behavior in individuals, which holds that it is not the event itself, but the meaning attributed to the event, that determines how one will respond. In addition, as Chapter 2 indicates, family responses are shaped by social interaction. These views of human behavior suggest that a key intervention with distressed families would be to help them reorganize their thinking, which in turn would affect their outlook and thus their behavior. Perhaps a combination of constructive thinking about their situation and adequate family and community support would constitute a meaningful strategy for professionals to consider in helping families.

One conclusion from this review is that it is too simplistic to base one's evaluation of family functioning on whether a child has a particular type of disability or whether the child is moderately or severely disabled. Phenomenological thinkers have argued that the most meaningful reality is that which the person, or in this case, the family, perceives. It is only by "walking in the shoes" of another that we can truly understand someone else's pain.

OTHER FACTORS THAT AFFECT THE FAMILY

Stress, its causes and consequences, has probably been studied more than any other construct with regard to families with exceptional children (Beckman, 1983; Friedrich, 1979; Friedrich & Friedrich, 1981; Houser, 1987; Wikler, 1981). Some of the research indicates that stress caused by a child's handicap is a major factor in the lives of family members. Other studies report the reverse to be true. Houser (1987), for example, reports that fathers of mentally retarded adolescents were no more stressed than a control group of fathers of nonretarded adolescents. This positive outcome conflicts with other studies on fathers (Andrew, 1968; Cummings, 1976; Holt, 1958). Dyson and Fewell (1986) found that parents of severely handicapped young children were significantly more stressed than a control group. Beckman (1983) indicates that single mothers reported more stress than mothers in intact homes but also found that two child characteristics, age and sex, were not related to the amount of stress experienced by mothers, a finding that contradicts that of other studies (Bristol, 1984; Farber, 1959). These studies reflect the mixed and contradictory results found in the literature.

In understanding stress in context it is important to acknowledge that stress is a common human condition and is caused by intrapsychic, familial and extrafamilial factors. Furthermore, based on the available evidence on families with a disabled child compared to those with nondisabled children, we cannot say that these families experience more or less stress than the general population. Furthermore, it is misleading to assume, even in studies that demonstrate stress in families with disabled children, that stress is necessarily dysfunctional. Low levels of stress over relatively short periods of time may be perfectly adaptive. High levels of stress over long periods of time, however, need to be taken seriously:

> Considerable evidence suggests that high stress levels, if chronically sustained, may contribute significantly to a lowering of one's energy levels,

ineffective cognitive processes, performance failures, ruptures in interpersonal relationships, flattened affect, a weakened immune system, and degenerative diseases of various kinds. (Matheny, Aycock, Pugh, Curlette, & Cannela, 1986, p. 500)

Perhaps the research question that needs to be asked is whether stress levels of family members are high or low and whether they are sustained over long periods of time, rather than simply assessing whether stress presently exists or not. Clearly, the exploration of this phenomenon has captured the interest of researchers, but different questions regarding stress and families need to be formulated before meaningful conclusions can be reached.

The interest in stress research has sparked a corresponding interest in coping behaviors. Coping which can take several forms, has as a major component social support. Indeed, social support, both within and outside of the family, is generally viewed as buffering the effects of stress. In assessing families, then, a useful approach would be to evaluate the demand characteristics of the child's disability, determine the coping resources within the family, and ascertain the social supports available to help reduce negative effects. In this regard Matheny and colleagues (1986) provide an in-depth discussion of coping resources (e.g., social support, beliefs/values, and self-esteem) and coping behaviors (e.g., assertive responses, tension reduction, cognitive restructuring). The interested reader may wish to consult Matheny and colleagues' article for further information.

Zucman (1982) believes that professionals should be wary of families that are socially isolated. She asserts that social isolation has a tendency to increase as the child grows older but feels that a major contributor is the "insufficient help received from the social and professional environment" (p. 29). Linked to the family's withdrawal is the denial of the child's disability and concomitant unrealistic view of the child's future. Presumably, when families defend against the reality of their child's disability, they remove themselves from needed services and withdraw from relationships with other families. Their withdrawal would indicate, however, that there is some unconscious recognition of the child's problems. Whatever the cause, a family's withdrawal from social interaction is a serious concern.

Although the evidence is inconclusive, there is some indication that children with physical disabilities are at risk for abuse or neglect (White, Benedict, Wulff, & Kelley, 1987). One problem with the research in this area is its failure to determine more precisely whether child or family characteristics—or perhaps a combination of the two—are linked to abuse and neglect. However, from their review White and colleagues (1987) report that the most consistently reported demographic factor associated with child abuse or neglect is low socioeconomic status (SES). (Child abuse among high SES families tends to be underreported, however). Stress is also caused by poor economic conditions, as well as by too much change too quickly, poor general coping and parenting skills, and social isolation. A major child characteristic causing stress, is low birth weight or prematurity. Premature infants are ill more often, cry more, and are more irritable; they may thus overwhelm their parents.

And finally, increased family stress may be caused by major personality problems in one or both of the parents. In her study of 48 parents of traumatic head injury children, Tartar (1987) found that 73% of the study sample met criteria for at least one type of preexisting psychiatric disorder, which stands in marked contrast to a baseline prevalence rate of 38%. Tartar posits the intriguing hypothesis that prospective head trauma victims live in more stressful environments due to the presence of psychiatric illness in a parent. She concludes that suffering a severe head trauma is not a random event but is more likely to occur when there is a psychiatric disorder in at least one parent. Tartar's study and White and colleagues' (1987) review of child neglect and abuse reinforce the notion that family dysfunction can have its roots in a number of child or parent characteristics.

Although much of the literature in this field has stressed the negative impact of a disabled child on the family, other studies have noted *benefits* created by the presence of such a child in the home. These include: (1) increased family cohesion, (2) increased involvement, and (3) personal growth (Darling, 1986).

The following parent comments suggest that for some, childhood disability seems to strengthen rather than weaken the family:

> All of us have gained a certain awareness and a certain compassion. . . . Coming across a problem that can't be solved is a maturing thing.

> I think my children will be better human beings. . . . They will be more understanding . . . more prepared for difficulties in life . . . more loving.

> Elizabeth has enriched our life. I wouldn't change it for the world. . . . Elizabeth has taught me love and patience and how to give of myself. (Darling, 1979, pp. 165, 172, 187)

The vast literature on the negative impact of disabled children on families must be balanced by a greater recognition of family strengths. More research is needed on the positive effects that arise from the misfortune of childhood disability.

REFERENCES

Andrew, G. (1968). Determinants of Negro family decisions in management of retardation. *Journal of Marriage and the Family, 30*, 612–617.

Beckman, P. J. (1983). Influence of selected child characteristics on stress in families of handicapped infants. *American Journal of Mental Deficiency, 88*, 150–156.

Beit-Jones, M. S., & Kapust, L. R. (1986). Temporal lobe epilepsy: Social and psychological considerations. *Social Work in Health Care, 11*, 17–33.

Bernard, A. W. (1974). A comparative study of marital integration and sibling role tension differences between families who have a severely mentally retarded child and families of non-handicapped (Doctoral dissertation, University of Cincinnati). *Dissertation Abstracts International, 35A*(5), 2800–2801.

Bernstein, N. R. (1978). Mental retardation. In A. M. Nicholi (Ed.), *The Harvard guide to modern psychiatry* (pp. 551–556). Cambridge, MA: Harvard University Press.

Birenbaum, A. (1979). The social construction of disability. *Journal of Sociology and Social Welfare, 4*, 89–101.

Blacher, J. (1984). Sequential stages of parental adjustment to the birth of a child with handicaps: Fact or artifact? *Mental Retardation, 22*, 55–68.

Blacher, J., Nihira, K., and Meyers, C. E. (1987). Characteristics of home environments of families with mentally retarded children: Comparison across levels of retardation. *American Journal of Mental Deficiency. 91*, 313–320.

Bristol, M. M. (1984). Family resources and successful adaptation to autistic children. In E. Shopler & G. B. Mesibov (Eds.), *The effects of autism on the family* (pp. 289–310). New York: Plenum.

Caldwell, B., & Guze, S. (1960). A study of the adjustment of parents and siblings of institutionalized and non-institutionalized retarded children. *American Journal of Mental Deficiency, 64*, 839–844.

Cantwell, D. P., & Baker, L. (1984). Research concerning families of children with autism. In E. Shopler & G. B. Mesibov (Eds.) *The effects of autism on the family* (pp. 41–63). New York: Plenum.

Crnic, K. A., Friedrich, W. N., & Greenberg, M. T. (1983). Adaptation of families with mentally retarded children: A model of stress, coping, and family ecology. *American Journal of Mental Deficiency, 88*, 125–138.

Cummings, S. T. (1976). The impact of the child's deficiency on the father: A study of fathers of mentally retarded and of chronically ill children. *American Journal of Orthopsychiatry, 46*, 246–255.

Darling, R. (1979). *Families against society: A study of reactions to children with birth defects.* Beverly Hills: Sage.

Darling, R. B. (1987). The economic and psychosocial consequences of disability: In M. Farrari & M. B. Sussman (Eds.). *Childhood disability and family systems* (pp. 45–64). New York: Haworth.

Darling, R. B., & Darling, J. (1982). *Children who are different: Meeting the challenges of birth defects in society.* St. Louis: Mosby.

Davis, F. (1961). Deviance disavowal: The management of strained interaction by the visibly handicapped. *Social Problems, 9*, 120–132.

Dembo, T., Leviton, G. L., & Wright, B. A. (1956). Adjustment to misfortune: A problem of social-psychological rehabilitation. *Artificial Limbs, 3*, 4–62.

Dorner, S. (1975). The relationship of physical handicap to stress in families with an adolescent with spina bifida. *Developmental Medicine and Child Neurology, 17*, 765–776.

Duncan, D. (May, 1977). *The impact of a handicapped child upon the family.* Paper presented at the Pennsylvania Training Model Training Sessions, Harrisburg, PA.

Dunlap, W. R., & Hollinsworth, J. S. (1977). How does a handicapped child affect the family? Implications for practitioners. *Family Coordinator, 26,* 286-293.

Dushenko, T. (1981). Cystic fibrosis: Medical overview and critique of the psychological literature. *Social Science in Medicine, 15B,* 43-56.

Dyson, L., & Fewell, R. R. (1986). *Sources of stress and adaptation of parents of young handicapped children.* Unpublished manuscript, University of Washington, Seattle.

Ellis, A. (1962). *Reason and emotion in psychotherapy.* New York: Lyle Stuart.

Farber, B. (1959). Effects of a severely mentally retarded child on family integration. *Monographs of the Society for Research in Child Development, 24* (2, Serial No. 71).

Farber, B. (1960). Perceptions of crisis and related variables in the impact of a retarded child on the mother. *Journal of Health and Social Behavior, 1,* 108-118.

Featherstone, H. (1980). *A difference in the family.* New York: Basic Books.

Fewell, R. R., & Gelb, S. A. (1983). Parenting moderately handicapped persons. In M. Seligman (Ed.), *The family with a handicapped child* (pp. 175-202). New York: Grune & Stratton.

Fewell, R. R., & Vadasy, P. F. (1986). *Families of handicapped children.* Austin, TX: Pro-Ed.

Friedrich, W. N. (1979). Predictors of the coping behaviors of mothers of handicapped children. *Journal of Consulting and Clinical Psychology, 47,* 1140-1141.

Friedrich, W. N., & Friedrich, W. L. (1981). Psychosocial assets of parents of handicapped and nonhandicapped children. *American Journal of Mental Deficiency, 5,* 551-553.

Gabel, H., McDowell, J., & Cerreto, M. C. (1983). Family adaptation to the handicapped infant. In S. G. Garwood & R. R. Fewell (Eds.), *Educating handicapped infants* (pp. 455-493). Rockville, MD: Aspen.

Gath, A. (1974). Sibling reactions to mental handicap: A comparison of the brothers and sisters of mongol children. *Journal of Child Psychology and Psychiatry, 15,* 187-198.

Gliedman, J., & Roth, W. (1980). *The unexpected minority: Handicapped children in America.* New York: Harcourt Brace Jovanovich.

Goffman, E. (1963). *Stigma: Notes on the management of spoiled identity.* Englewood Cliffs, NJ: Prentice-Hall.

Goode, D. A. (1984). Presentation practices of a family with a deaf-blind child. *Family relations, 33,* 173-185.

Graham, P., & Rutter, M. (1983). Organic brain dysfunction and child psychiatric disorder. *British Medical Journal, 3,* 695-700.

Grossman, F. K. (1972). *Brothers and sisters of retarded children: An exploratory study.* Syracuse, NJ: Syracuse University Press.

Harris, S. L. (1983). *Families of the developmentally disabled.* New York: Pergamon.

Hill, R. (1949). *Families under stress.* New York: Harper & Row.

Hobbs, N., Perrin, A., & Ireys, S. (1986). *Chronically ill children and their families.* San Francisco: Jossey-Bass.

Holroyd, J. (1974). The questionnaire on resources and stress: An instrument to measure family response to a handicapped member. *Journal of Community Psychology, 2,* 92-94.

Holt, K. S. (1958). *The impact of mentally retarded children upon their families.* Unpublished doctoral dissertation, University of Sheffield, England.

Hormuth, R. P. (1953). Home problems and family care of the mongoloid child. *Quarterly Review of Pediatrics, 8,* 274-280.

Houser, R. A. (1987). *A comparison of stress and coping by fathers of mentally retarded and non-retarded adolescents.* Unpublished doctoral dissertation, University of Pittsburgh.

Humphrey, R. A., & Jacobson, R. B. (1979). Families in crisis: Research and theory in child mental retardation. *Social Casework, 60,* 597-601.

Israelite, N. K. ((1985). Sibling reaction to a hearing impaired child in the family. *Journal of Rehabilitation of the Deaf, 18,* 1–5.

Kazak, A. E., & Marvin, R. S. (1984). Differences, difficulties, and adaptation: Stress and social networks in families with a handicapped child. *Family Relations, 33,* 67–77.

Kazak, A. E., & Wilcox, B. L. (1984). The structure and function of social support networks in families with handicapped children. *American Journal of Community Psychology, 12,* 645–661.

Kennedy, J. F. (1970). Maternal reactions to the birth of a defective baby. *Social Casework, 51,* 410–416.

Kibert, R. P. (1986). *A descriptive study of the perceptions of normal college age siblings in families with a mentally retarded child.* Unpublished doctoral dissertation, University of Pittsburgh.

Korn, S. J., Chess, S., & Fernandez, P. (1978). The impact of children's physical handicaps on marital quality and family interaction. In R. M. Lerner & G. B. Spanier (Eds.), *Child influence on marital and family interaction.* New York: Academic.

Kübler-Ross, E. (1969). *On death and dying.* New York: Macmillan.

Lamb, M. E. (1983). Fathers of exceptional children. In M. Seligman (Ed.), *The family with a handicapped child* (pp. 125–146). New York: Grune & Stratton.

Lechtenberg, R. (1984). *Epilepsy and the family.* Cambridge, MA: Harvard University Press.

LePontois, J., Moel, D. I., & Cohn, R. A. (1987). Family adjustment to pediatric ambulatory dialysis. *American Journal of Orthopsychiatry, 57,* 78–83.

Levine, E. S. (1960). *Psychology of deafness.* New York: Columbia University Press.

Luterman, D. (1984). *Counseling the communicatively disordered and their families.* Boston: Little, Brown.

Lyon, S., & Preis, A. (1983). Working with families of severely handicapped persons. In M. Seligman (Ed.), *The family with a handicapped child* (pp. 203–232). New York: Grune & Stratton.

Martin, P. (1975). Marital breakdown in families of patients with spina bifida cystica. *Developmental Medicine and Child Neurology, 17,* 757–764.

Matheny, K. B., Aycock, D. W., Pugh, J. L., Curlette, & Canela, K. S. (1986). Stress coping: A qualitative and quantitative synthesis with implications for treatment. *The Counseling Psychologist, 14,* 499–549.

McCracken, M. J. (1984). Cystic fibrosis in adolescence. In R. W. Blum (Ed.), *Chronic illness and disabilities in childhood and adolescence* (pp. 397–411). Orlando, FL: Grune & Stratton.

Mullins, J. (1979). *A teacher's guide to management of physically handicapped students.* Springfield, IL: Thomas.

Neider, C. (Ed.). (1963). *The complete essays of Mark Twain.* New York: Doubleday.

Newman, J. (1983). Handicapped persons and their families: Philosophical, historical, and legislative perspectives. In M. Seligman (Ed.), *The family with a handicapped child* (pp. 4–25). New York: Grune & Stratton.

Offer, D., Ostrov, E., & Howard, K. I. (1984). Body image, self perception, and chronic illness in adolescence. In R. W. Blum (Ed.), *Chronic illness and disabilities in childhood and adolescence* (pp. 59–73). Orlando, FL: Grune & Stratton.

Olshansky, S. (1962). Chronic sorrow: A response to having a mentally defective child. *Social Casework, 43,* 190–193.

Patterson, J. M. (1985). Critical factors affecting family compliance with home treatment for children with cystic fibrosis. *Family Relations, 34,* 79–89.

Resnick, M. D. (1984). The social construction of disability. In R. W. Blum (Ed.), *Chronic illness and disabilities in childhood and adolescence* (pp. 29–46). Orlando, FL: Grune & Stratton.

Roskies, E. (1972). *Abnormality and normality: The mothering of thalidomide children.* Ithaca, NY: Cornell University Press.

Ross, A. O. (1964). *The exceptional child in the family.* New York: Grune & Stratton.

Schipper, M. T. (1959). The child with mongolism in the home. *Pediatrics, 24,* 132-144.

Schopler, E., & Mesibov, G. B. (1984). *The effects of autism on the family.* New York: Plenum.

Searle, S. J. (1978). Stages of parents reaction. *The Exceptional Parent, 8,* 27-29.

Seligman, M. (1983). Sources of psychological disturbance among siblings of handicapped children. *Personnel and Guidance Journal, 61,* 529-531.

Seligman, M., & Meyerson, R. (1982). Group approaches for parents of handicapped children. In M. Seligman (Ed.), *Group psychotherapy and counseling with special populations* (pp. 96-116). Baltimore, MD: University Park Press.

Solnit, A. J., & Stark, M. H. (1961). Mourning and the birth of a defective child. *Psychoanalytical Studies of the Child, 16,* 523-537.

Sonnek, I. M. (1986). Grandparents and the extended family of handicapped children. In R. R. Fewell, & P. F. Vadasy (Eds.), *Families of handicapped children* (pp. 99-120). Austin, TX: Pro-Ed.

Stonequist, E. V. (1937). *The marginal man: A study in personality and culture conflict.* New York: Scribner's.

Tartar, S. B. (1987). *Traumatic head injury: Parental stress, coping style and emotional adjustment.* Unpublished doctoral dissertation, University of Pittsburgh.

Tew, B. J., Lawrence, K. M., Payne, H., & Rawnsley, K. (1977). Marital stability following the birth of a child with spina bifida. *British Journal of Psychiatry, 131,* 79-82.

Travis, C. (1976). *Chronic illness in children: Its impact on child and family.* Stanford, CA: Stanford University Press.

Turk, D. C., & Kerns, R. D. (1985). *Health, illness, and families.* New York: Wiley.

Turnbull, H. R., & Turnbull, A. P. (1985). *Parents speak out: Then and now.* Columbus, OH: Merrill.

Upshur, C. C. (1982). Respite care for mentally retarded and other disabled populations: Program models and family needs. *Mental Retardation, 20,* 2-6.

Upshur, C. C. (1983). Developing respite care: A support service for families with disabled members. *Family relations, 32,* 13-20.

Vadasy, P. F. (1986). Single mothers: A social phenomenon and population in need. In R. R. Fewell & P., F. Vadasy (Eds.), *Families of handicapped children* (pp. 221-249). Austin, TX: Pro-Ed.

Voysey, M. (1972). Impression management by parents with disabled children. *Journal of Health and Social Behavior, 13,* 80-89.

Waisbren, S. E. (1980). Parents' reactions after the birth of a developmentally disabled child. *American Journal of Mental Deficiency, 84,* 345-351.

Wasserman, R. (1983). Identifying the counseling needs of the siblings of mentally retarded children. *Personnel and Guidance Journal, 61,* 622-627.

Watson, R. L., & Midlarsky, E. (1979). Reaction with mothers with mentally retarded children: A social perspective. *Psychological Reports, 45,* 309-310.

White, R., Benedict, M. I., Wulff, L., & Kelley, M. (1987). Physical disabilities as risk factors for child maltreatment: A selected review. *American Journal of Orthopsychiatry, 57,* 93-101.

Wikler, L. (1981). Chronic stresses of families of mentally retarded children. *Family Relations, 30,* 281-288.

Wortis, H. Z., & Margolies, J. A. (1955). Parents of children of cerebral palsy. *Medical Social Work, 4,* 110-120.

Wright, B. A. (1983). *Physical disability—A psychosocial approach.* (2nd ed.). New York: Harper & Row.

Zucman, E. (1982). *Childhood disability in the family.* New York: World Rehabilitation Fund.

5

Effects on Siblings

Until recently, professionals have either neglected or consigned to secondary importance the effect a disabled child in the family context has on siblings. Children who share in the anticipation and excitement of a new brother or sister also share in the grief and pain that accompanies the birth of a chronically disabled infant. Until recently, the literature on family adaptation has focused on the parents, with a particular emphasis on mothers. Recent observations on siblings, however, suggest that some of these children may be at risk psychologically (DeLuca & Solerno, 1984; Seligman, 1983; Trevino, 1979).

The study of the effects of a disabled brother or sister on nondisabled siblings is emerging as a significant area of research and concern. We need considerably more research before we fully understand disabled and nondisabled brothers and sisters, their respective roles in the family, and the reciprocal effects they have on each other. Even so, it would be useful to review what we presently know about this population so that we can understand and serve siblings in an effective manner.

The following chapter, then, is an examination of the factors that influence a sibling's adjustment. The discussion is based on existing research and commentary, augmented by the personal accounts of siblings and their parents.

THE SIBLING BOND

Sibling relationships are usually the longest and most enduring of family relationships. The permanence of this relationship makes it possible for two individuals to exert considerable influence over the other through longitudinal interactions. As Powell and Ogle (1985) note: "Siblings provide a continuing relationship from which there is no annulment" (p. 12).

Like any intense, long-term relationship, sibling relationships are cyclical. Bank and Kahn (1982) observe that siblings follow a life cycle of their own. They provide a constant source of companionship for one another during the early childhood years. During these early years, there is considerable contact between them, but it is also common for children to extend themselves to others outside the immediate family, drawing on the social skills they have developed together. During adolescence, siblings manifest ambivalence about their mutual relationship, yet they still rely on one another as confidants and advisors. In adulthood, siblings may interact less often due to marriage and/or geographic distance. Even so, during this period siblings may provide long-distance support and encouragement as they face the vicissitudes of adult life. In addition, as aunts and uncles they provide unique support networks to one another's children. And finally, in old age, when their own children move on to increased independence and spouses pass away, siblings continue to provide a social network for one another; it is not unusual for sibling relationships to become reestablished or intensified once again in a manner similar to the first stages of their lives together.

The many changes in contemporary family life add to the importance of studying the sibling bond. Bank and Kahn (1982) suggest that the following realities of family life may result in increased sibling contact and emotional interdependence:

1. Because fewer children are born, family size is decreasing. Also, children tend to be closer in age, resulting in more intense contact between siblings.

2. Siblings provide a longitudinal source of support to one another as longevity increases.

3. Siblings may rely on each other more because of frequent moves by the family and the difficulties in developing friendships.

4. Siblings are confronted with family disintegration and new configurations as divorce and remarriage rates remain high. Such changes in family structure surely affect sibling relationships, although the nature of these changes is not well understood.

5. Parental stress affects the availability of parents to their children. Such periods of parental emotional absence influence sibling relationships.

Children are growing up in a mobile and complex world in which opportunities for contact, constancy, and permanence have decreased*:

> Children are biologically propelled by these biological needs . . . to turn for satisfaction to any accessible person. In a worried, mobile, small family, high-stress, fast-paced, parent-absent America, that person can be a brother or sister. (Bank & Kahn, 1982, p. 15)

*Excerpts from Bank and Kahn (1982) are copyright by Basic Books, Inc. Reprinted by permission.

In the past we have not sufficiently acknowledged the intense, long-term, and complex nature of sibling relationships. Now that we have begun to focus on this subsystem of the family, we are beginning to comprehend the immense value in understanding sibling relationships and in fostering their positive growth. It may well be that in families in which a disabled child resides we need to be particularly sensitive to the siblings' experience. Even the limited knowledge available suggests that although siblings are unaffected by or even benefit from this experience, other siblings simply do not fare well.

THE NEED FOR INFORMATION

Due in part to parents' reluctance to communicate about their disabled children, siblings often have a limited understanding of their afflicted brother or sister's condition. In her review of studies on siblings, Wasserman (1983) notes that there is a startling lack of information about the disability, its manifestations, and its consequences. Limited or poor information confuses siblings in regard to several factors:

1. being held responsible for a particular condition;
2. whether it is transmittable;
3. if and how one should communicate to family and friends about the disability;
4. what implications the disabled child has for the siblings' future;
5. how one should respond to discomforting feelings such as anger, hurt, and guilt;
6. how to relate effectively to one's disabled brother/sister and to others in one's environment.

In *Living with a Brother or Sister with Special Needs: A Book for Sibs*, Meyer, Vadasy, and Fewell (1985) have published a helpful resource. Their sensitive and down-to-earth work addresses the many feelings and questions siblings have about their special circumstances. Such areas are addressed as typical sibling concerns regarding the future; educational and social services for children and their families; and feelings that siblings often experience. In addition, the authors provide short, readable, and accurate explanations of the etiologies, manifestations, and prognoses of a number of disabling conditions.

As suggested above, parents often are unable or unwilling to share information with their nondisabled children or they may provide inaccurate information. For example, one of our colleagues had been told as a youngster that her sister suffered from asthma when, in fact, she had cerebral palsy. Asthma may have been more acceptable than cerebral palsy in a family in which social appearances were paramount.

In regard to the provision of information, Murphy, Paeschel, Duffy, and Brady (1976) observed in their discussion groups with siblings of Down syndrome children that the type of information requested appears to be related to age. Children aged 6 to 9 years asked questions about motor development and speech, discussed what their brothers and sisters could and could not do, and were interested in the medical and biological information presented to them. Concerns about the future became evident among the 10- to 12-year-old children, while the older adolescents showed concern about their own chances of bearing a handicapped child. The observations by Murphy and colleagues hint at a potentially rich and useful area of future study: Is there something to be gained from homogeneously aged sibling support groups whose focus corresponds with their developmental level?

Siblings tend to have two views about the cause of a brother's or sister's disability. One view comes from the information they have gotten from their parents and from professionals. The other view is their "private" version which is often not verbalized. The private view may reflect confusion or a cause–effect relationship fueled by fear, guilt, and magical thinking in an effort to make sense of an overwhelming and perplexing situation. For example, a sibling might attribute a disability to a benign fall or accident or because he/she had a cold or sore throat that had been passed on to a disabled brother or sister. As Sourkes (1987) suggests, it is important to obtain the sibling's private version of the cause of the disability. Information can be provided and misconceptions can be replaced by fact after the child's view is obtained. Important information such as the cause of the disability may need to be repeated more than once, especially with young children. Parents and professionals must be alert to the reemergence of guilt feelings associated with a child's "private" reasoning as it pertains to causality.

Siblings have sought to be more open about their circumstances, their feelings, and their need to be better informed. They have found that they are not alone and, indeed, have discovered that disability in the family—and the family's reaction to it—is shared by others. Along with the welcome discovery that others share this life situation, siblings are speaking out so that parents and professionals will understand their special plight. And finally, siblings—aided by the newly established Sibling Information Network*—are encouraging a wider dissemination

*Sibling Information Network, School of Education, Box U-64, Room 227, University of Connecticut, Storrs, CT 06268. The network also publishes a newsletter where, in addition to providing information, siblings share their feelings regarding their life with a handi-

of basic information about handicapping conditions and the siblings' experience so that siblings, parents, and professionals can be better informed. It is only with accurate and fairly complete knowledge that professionals can move toward stated treatment goals. And armed with this knowledge, siblings will be in a better position to perceive their situation unambiguously and with less fear. Service providers need to understand that siblings will respond with less anxiety when they are presented with accurate information in a compassionate and understanding manner.

CARETAKING RESPONSIBILITY

Another important issue is the responsibility children feel for their disabled sibling. Excessive caretaking can result in anger, resentment, guilt, and quite possibly subsequent psychological disturbance, especially if the nondisabled sibling receives limited parental attention.

A disabled child in the family absorbs a great deal of time, energy, and emotional resources. Before they are ready, children may be pressed into parental roles they are ill prepared to assume. As Myers notes, such youngsters may move too rapidly through the developmental stages so necessary for normal growth:

> From the time Roger began going to physicians and consultants, it seemed to me that I carried a five-hundred-pound lead weight around in the front of my brain. Never out of my mind was the idea that my brother was retarded, needed special attention, needed special care, and that I had to provide some of it.
>
> My role in those days was someone who was always around to help care for Roger. That was my mother's phrase. My father called me his "good right arm." Roger himself called me "Dad" before he corrected himself and called me "Bobby."
>
> I never felt I dressed like a kid, never felt comfortable with the clothes I wore, never felt I knew how to act as a boy or a teenager. I was a little man. (Myers, 1978, p. 36)

The tremendous burden visited upon children as they assume responsibility for a disabled sibling is vividly expressed by Hayden (1974):

---

capped brother/sister. Similarly, the Committee of the National Alliance for the Mentally Ill publishes a newsletter, *The Sibling Bond*. This newsletter reviews relevant publications, provides information, and publishes sibling essays. Their address is National Sibling Network, 5112 15th Avenue South, Minneapolis, MN 55417.

The responsibility I felt for Mindy was tremendous. One year, when my "babysitting" duties involved periodic checking on my sister, Mindy wandered away between checks. After a thorough but fruitless search of the neighborhood, my mother hysterically told me that if anything happened to Mindy, I would be to blame. I felt terrified and guilty. I was seven. (p. 27)

Kirkman's (1985) study of adult siblings shows that resentment and anger over caretaking can be a multidetermined response. In her Australian study she found that a few of her 151 sibling subjects reacted negatively to their parents because of the parents' failure to provide adequate attention to their handicapped brother/sister. This is what one sibling said: "I feel angered at both my parents for lack of understanding and effort to truly help him. They have neglected their responsibility to their son and have lost my respect in this regard" (p. 3).

It is often difficult for adults to accept their circumstances when they compare their lot to that of others who appear to be more successful or less troubled. Children find their lives with a disabled sibling even less comprehensible when they compare their family to families with "normal" children:

The whole situation is profoundly unfair. It is unfair that the family must live with schizophrenia, autism, blindness, or retardation while others do not. It is unfair that some children must function as adjunct parents even before they go to school, while others successfully avoid responsibilities of all sorts well into their second decade. The brothers and sisters of the handicapped child learn to cope with this unfairness, and with their own response to it, the sorrow and the anger. (Featherstone, 1980, p. 162)

Siblings may experience "survivor's guilt" for their healthy lives, which are in sharp contrast to those of ill or retarded siblings (Bank & Kahn, 1982). They may experience considerable guilt over the advantages they have and the only recourse to expiate such guilt lies in taking care of the ill sibling. The danger occurs when the well sibling remains "in the service" of the disabled one through much of his/her life because of guilt and forced obligation.

Family size seems to be related to the extent to which a sibling experiences caretaking responsibility. This observation is borne out by Grossman's (1972) research, namely, that the college students she interviewed from two-child families found life with a retarded sibling more stressful than those with a number of normal siblings. It could be that in larger families, where more siblings are available to help, there is more shared responsibility. More recently, however, Simeonsson and Bailey (1986) list as a negative adjustment factor that of residing in a large family. An important consideration may be whether larger families have sufficient resources; if not, there may be chronic family tension.

Research also reveals that the gender of nondisabled brothers and sisters plays a significant part in caretaking (Farber, 1959). Female siblings are more subject to caretaking behavior than males and may thus be more prone to psychological maladjustment. However, this early observation of the relationship of gender and maladjustment has been questioned by recent information that males sometimes fare more poorly than females and that sibling age, age spacing, and sex may interact in complex ways (Simeonsson & Bailey, 1986). In regard to age, children who are younger than their disabled siblings may experience "role tension" when the older disabled child becomes the youngest child socially (Farber, 1960). In such instances, the nondisabled siblings may be expected to care for and subordinate their needs to their disabled brother or sister. Nevertheless, females probably do assume more caretaking roles than males, but perhaps this does not necessarily lead to maladjustment.

Indeed, McHale and Gamble (1987) speculate that problems should not be attributable to caregiving per se; how disabled children *behave* when they are being cared for by their siblings may create tensions. Therefore, these authors would discourage a realignment of family roles and responsibilities and instead teach children behavior-management skills. McHale and Gamble also report from their research that children were more depressed, anxious, and had lower self-esteem when they were dissatisfied about how their parents treated them relative to the other children in the family. These findings held for siblings of both disabled and nondisabled brothers and sisters. Parental "fairness" seems to be an important concern for siblings.

Grossman (1972) found that socioeconomic status is related to the amount of responsibility a nondisabled sibling might assume for a disabled brother and sister. The more financially able a family, the better prepared they are to secure necessary help from sources outside the family.* Families that are less secure financially must rely on resources within the family. Financial problems produce additional stress and can detract from general stability when excessive and unreasonable demands are placed on family members. In families stressed primarily because of limited financial resources, a disabled child may even be blamed as the source of the financial woes. In such instances service providers must be alert to the potential for abuse of the disabled child.

According to Travis (1976), the burdening of siblings with the care of chronically physically ill children seems to be common. Travis reports

*It is worth noting here that, due to family values, there may be considerable resistance to securing outside help, irrespective of the family's financial situation.

that siblings who have been excessively burdened may leave home during their adolescence. She observes that signs of mounting resentment among siblings can be seen in hasty or unkind physical care. However, in close-knit families, the care of a disabled child may be viewed as a shared responsibility.

Travis points out that some chronically ill children enslave their physically normal siblings—"Hand me this, pick up that." Chronically ill children have been observed to be verbally abusive toward their nondisabled siblings, presumably because of envy and confusion. In an informal study by Holt (1958), nondisabled children were reported to have suffered repeatedly from unexpected physical attacks by their disabled siblings. Disabled or ill children may resent their sibs for having escaped the condition they must confront daily. Although rarely mentioned in the literature, the disabled child's anger can be devastating for the other children (Sourkes, 1987). Poor sibling relationships may require counseling or at minimum an attempt by parents to encourage open communication between their children.

Responsibility for the physical well-being of a chronically ill child can be taken to great lengths. In instances in which the sick child must be guarded from infection—for example, in chronic heart disease—Travis (1976) reports that mothers warn their healthy children to avoid crowds for fear of bringing home infections. Such responsibility for the welfare of one's ill brother/sister places an inordinate burden on nondisabled siblings, with possible implications for their subsequent adjustment. Siblings in a hemophilic family, for example, may bear an enormous amount of responsibility in helping to prevent their brother's/sister's "bleeds."

Siblings may be burdened by excessively high aspirations to compensate for parental disappointments and frustrations. The responsibility for high achievement may fall on the shoulders of nondisabled siblings, some of whom may intellectually or psychologically be unable to attain in a manner compatible with parental expectations.

Michaelis (1980) observes that a disabled child's schooling may fall to normal siblings:

> Although using the services of the siblings to help implement the education programs for the handicapped child may at first seem like an obvious solution, it may be the beginning of more problems for the school, the family, the siblings, and even the handicapped child. It is important that siblings are not expected to be their "brother's keeper" to the extent that their own social and academic learning is hampered by the responsibility. (p. 102)

All parents reflect on the future of their children—their education, marriage, career. Parents of disabled children worry even more about the future as they fret about many of the same issues parents of nondisabled children do; in addition, they are concerned about such issues as the extent to which their child will be able to achieve independence, how they will be able to care for their disabled offspring in their later years, and who will care for the child once one or both parents are dead.

In instances where a sibling needs lifelong care or supervision, nondisabled brothers and sisters understandably look anxiously to the future. They wonder whether the responsibility their parents at present assume will later fall to them. They wonder whether they can cope with the decisions that need to be made in future years, in addition to worrying about whether they can physically or psychologically manage to care for their disabled sibling. A further, related concern of some significance is the doubt a sibling may have about whether his/her future or present spouse will accept or be able to cope with the disabled brother/sister.

A child's sense of obligation for a disabled brother/sister should thus be a major concern for the professional. Exploring the extent to which a sibling feels or expects to assume responsibility for a disabled family member is very important. How a sibling envisions the way he/she will manage life's future demands depends in part on whether there are vestiges of resentment and anger toward the parents and the disabled sibling from earlier interactions. Professionals ought to help siblings consider how much obligation should be assumed if there are other able family members. For some a central issue will be whether they can, without guilt, abandon the powerful burden of responsibility their parents have placed on them out of their own anxieties about the future care of their disabled child.

IDENTITY CONCERNS

Featherstone (1980) points out that in the wake of a disability, young children may be concerned about "catching" it. She notes that anxiety about this is exacerbated when siblings learn that the disability was caused by a disease like rubella or meningitis. In a videotape in which parents talked about the effects cancer had on the family, one of the concerns voiced was that well children feared that they, too, would be stricken with the disease (Western Psychiatric Institute and Clinic, 1980). Sourkes (1987) notes that the fear of taking ill with cancer runs high among siblings. Siblings need reassurance that there is little likelihood of getting the same disease nor is the illness contagious. Siblings should be encouraged to pursue their own activities and relationships that can help counteract the sense of identification implied in sibling relationships.

Young nondisabled siblings may have anxieties that they will become blind or deaf in the future (Marion, 1981). Siblings may believe that if a disability can happen to a brother or sister, then it can happen to them. Believing this, a child may choose to "leave" the family, which is facilitated by the parents' preoccupation with the disabled sibling (Bank & Kahn, 1982).

Children have been known to develop somatic complaints in their attempts to gain attention from their parents (Luterman, 1979; Marion, 1981; Sourkes, 1987). Luterman observes that in siblings of hearing—impaired children it is not uncommon for them to develop a pseudosensory deficit as an attention-getting behavior. Furthermore, Lechtenberg (1984) notes that siblings of epileptic children have an inordinate fear that they will develop the disorder—a fear disproportionate to the possibility that they will acquire epilepsy or another seizure disorder.

Similarly, Michaelis (1980) notes that as a consequence of a strong sibling identification, the nondisabled child may feel overly responsible to the disabled sibling in order to justify psychologically the fact that he/she is not the disabled one. Moreover, siblings may feel responsible for the disability, particularly when a newborn is deeply resented and the child has fleeting thoughts about a brother or sister's demise. The notion of overidentifying with a disabled brother or sister may be attributable in part to age, age spacing, and gender similarities between the disabled and nondisabled siblings (Breslau, 1982).

As noted below, the development of an identity separate from that of a disabled sibling is of considerable importance:

> The issue of being similar to or different from the retarded sibling permeated many of the meetings and seemed to be a source of enormous concern for all of the group members. In fact the experience with this group suggests that the main task of siblings of defective children is to avoid identifying with them. (Grossman, 1972, p. 34)

Siblings who are not informed about the nature and consequences of their brother's/sister's disability may be confused regarding their own identity (Wasserman, 1983). If adolescents are ignorant of the nature of the disability, identity issues are sure to arise, since this period of development is marked by considerable struggle over self-worth and self-identity. Feigon (1981) consistently observed in her sibling support groups a strong identification with the disabled sibling that resulted in feelings that one is or will become handicapped. And Bank and Kahn (1982) speculate that relatively undifferentiated siblings may share symptoms with their disabled brother/sister, whereas siblings who have successfully separated tend to act more independently.

The type of disablement of chronically ill children may bear a relationship to identity problems. Tew and Lawrence (1974) conclude from their study that siblings of slightly handicapped children are most disturbed, followed by siblings of severely and moderately disabled children. It may be that identity confusion and one's ability to differentiate oneself from a brother/sister is a consequence of the perceived similarity of the other. In other words, the less "abnormal" the sibling, the more likely issues of identity may surface. However, Lobato (1983) and Kirkman (1985) point out that the research appears to support the position that there is no simple linear relationship between severity of disability and sibling adjustment. The same conclusion holds when one considers the type of impairment (Lobato, 1983). For siblings of the seriously emotionally disturbed, Bank and Kahn (1982) comment that:

> Every well sibling that we have interviewed has, at one time or another, feared the possibility of becoming like a seriously disturbed brother or sister. Some siblings do not dwell on this fear, while others allow themselves to be haunted and dominated by the possibility that they could wind up in serious trouble or in a mental hospital. (p. 253)

With young children particularly, professionals should help parents understand the concerns of nondisabled siblings. Parents are often unaware of the needs of their nondisabled children. In a recent study Wallinga, Paquio, and Skeen (1987) found that parents thought their healthy children were coping considerably better than the children thought they were. The parents' participation in the study enabled them to realize for the first time how much they had neglected their healthy children.

Professionals can help siblings express their identity concerns and their worries about contamination. Support groups of similarly aged youngsters are useful mechanisms for eliciting feelings and concerns. Siblings may feel different or odd about their experiences and feelings but are comforted in a group context.

CAREERS

Basic life goals of nondisabled siblings may be affected when a disabled child is present in the family. A child's career descision may be shaped by having interacted with and cared for a less able brother or sister. Children are cognizant of others' reactions to their disabled sibling, adding to their sensitivity to interpersonal dynamics. The continuous act of caring for a disabled youngster, especially in a loving family, may become internalized to the extent that it influences career decisions in the direction of the helping professions.

As Farber (1959) and Cleveland and Miller (1977) found in their studies, normal siblings internalize helping norms and turn their career endeavors toward the improvement of humanity or at least toward life goals that require dedication and sacrifice. The following comments by a sister of a mentally retarded, cerebral palsied, and epileptic child reflect the thinking behind the decision to prepare for a service career:

> Having Robin as a member of our family caused me to undergo a great deal of introspection which led me to insights into certain aspects of my character that needed to be changed. My contact with him, coupled with some sound advice from my parents, also unquestionably influenced my decision to pursue a career in special education. I had originally intended to enter the field of chemistry, and indeed I completed a bachelor's degree in that area. However, something about my choice bothered me. I enjoyed the lab work and the excitement of scientific discovery, but something was missing. It wasn't until my father, during the course of one of our "What are you going to do with your life?" discussions, pinpointed the problem when he quoted the following statement made by the philosopher Kierkegaard: "The door to happiness opens outward." What this meant to me was that one could find true happiness through serving others. The choice of a career then became obvious to me. What better way was there to serve others than to enter the field of special education where I could help people like my brother lead more fulfilling lives? (Helsel, 1978, p. 112)

Although Illes (1979) did not investigate career objectives per se of siblings of cancer victims, she did report that her subjects exhibited compassion, tolerance, and empathy—characteristics valued in the helping professions. Indeed, Skrtic, Summers, Brotherson, and Turnbull (1984) speculate that a sibling's identification with a disabled brother/sister and a desire to understand his/her problems provide the impetus to choose a career in education or in the human services.

Without adequate research data, the theoretical leap from the development of compassion, tolerance, and empathy to the selection of a particular career goal may be too great. In fact, siblings who have developed such attitudes and who believe they have already made a significant contribution to a stressful life circumstance may seek out fulfillment in careers outside the helping professions. In a videotape* of a group of

---

*The Other Children: Brothers and Sisters of the Developmentally Disabled. Available from Siblings for Significant Change, 105 East 22nd Street, New York, NY 10010.

siblings expressing their personal views of life with a disabled brother/ sister, a sister of an autistic brother spoke about her wish to pursue a career unrelated to the helping professions. She felt that she had contributed considerably to the welfare and development of her brother and now felt that she wanted something "for herself" in a non-human-service-oriented profession. Moreover, Israelite (1985), in a small-scale study of siblings of hearing-impaired children, found that subjects indicated their desire to pursue careers that are unrelated to the human service professions.

In his family of ten siblings, including an autistic brother, Laureys (1984) reports that a brother is an art therapist, a sister is in special education, a brother is in a woodworking business, a sister is a graphic artist, a brother is studying business, a sister is studying language and drama, a sister is studying journalism and literature, a brother is a high school star wrestler who has not yet chosen a career, and he himself is a lobbyist in government.

There is thus insufficient data for firm conclusions about the relationship between being a sibling of a disabled brother/sister and choosing a particular career path. There is only enough information for some armchair speculation about the impact of a disabled child on a sibling's career choice.

ANGER AND GUILT

Anger is an emotion common to human beings. Some handle the expression of anger better than others, while some deny that they experience anger at all. Siblings of disabled children may experience anger more often and perhaps more intensely than siblings of nondisabled brothers and sisters. Whether siblings harbor or openly express their feelings of anger and resentment depends on a number of factors:

1. the extent to which a sibling is held responsible for a disabled brother or sister
2. the extent to which a disabled sibling takes advantage of (manipulates) a brother or sister
3. the extent to which the disabled child restricts his/her sibling's social life or is considered a source of embarrassment
4. the extent to which a disabled child requires excessive time and attention from the parents and takes time away from the other children
5. the extent to which the family's financial resources are drained by the disabled child's needs
6. the number and gender of siblings in the family

7. the overall accommodation parents have made to their special circumstances

Anger may arise in relation to numerous conditions in a family with a disabled child:

> Children feel angry: at parents, at the disabled child, at the wider world, at God or fate, perhaps at all four. Some blame their mother and father for the disability itself (just as they blame them for any new baby). A handicap creates unusual needs; many children envy their brother or sister this special attention. And older children may rage secretly about the sometimes colossal sums of money spent on diagnosis and therapy-resources that might otherwise finance family comforts and college tuition. (Featherstone, 1980, p. 143)

Reactions from acquaintances or strangers to a disabled brother or sister may lead to open expressions of hostility, as illustrated in the following comments from a college student:

> I heard some guy talking in the back about Mark and how stupid he was, and you could make him do anything and he is so gullible, and all this kind of stuff. I walked back to the kid and slugged him in the face. . . . I always felt that I had to protect him from someone, from teasing, from fights, and any other kids trying to put things over on kids who are at a disadvantage to them. If you love somebody you cannot help but get emotionally involved in that. (Klein, 1972, pp. 12, 13)

Siblings may be placed in a difficult bind. Parental demands that a child care for and protect the disabled sibling clash with those of the child's playmates, who may encourage shunning; and then one's own ambivalent feelings (anger, guilt, love, protectiveness) toward the disabled sibling and resentment toward the parents for demanding that one love and take care of a brother or sister result in a tension-filled situation.

> Wherever I went, Mindy went too. . . . I was often excluded from neighborhood games because of my sidekick. And then there was the unwritten family rule that I must leave with Mindy whenever my playmates made fun of her. They often did mock her, of course, and we would leave—except for one time which to this day gives my conscience no rest, when I joined in. I lost many playmates by having to side with Mindy. I felt neglected by my family and shunned by my peers. I was a very lonely little girl. (Hayden, 1974, p. 27)

Feeling ignored and unappreciated for one's achievements leaves lifelong scars on normal siblings. Hayden (1974) continues:

Mindy's achievements always met with animated enthusiasm from our parents. In contrast it seemed, mother and daddy's response to my accomplishments was on the pat-on-the-back level. I was expected to perform well in every circumstance. I wanted my parents to be enthusiastic about my accomplishments, too. I didn't want to have to beg for praise. I didn't want to be taken for granted. I wanted to be noticed. (p. 27)

Angry feelings surface when siblings perceive that their mother must carry the burden of care for a disabled child without their father's help. Work, recreation, or community involvement can keep fathers from contributing. In such instances, it is useful for professionals to distinguish between fathers who are legitimately occupied from those who are "too busy" because they wish to deny or avoid their anxiety-provoking family situation. Nondisabled siblings probably sense their father's motivations, which can add to their anger toward him (see Chapter 6 for more on fathers).

A friend of one of us (M. S.), in her late 60s, mentioned recently that she still harbors angry and resentful feelings about her youth due to the attention her diabetic sister received from her parents. The friend expressed surprise that her feelings, while distant in time, continued to evoke a strongly negative intensity.

Very young children, too young to understand verbal explanation, may interpret preoccupation with a disabled family member as rejection, and school-aged siblings feel resentment, anger, and guilt due to the elevated anxiety within the family (Sourkes, 1987). Siblings feel angry toward the parents and competitive (and guilty) toward the disabled child. According to Sourkes, siblings suffer as much as, and sometimes more, than child cancer victims with regard to having their emotional needs met within the family. Other issues related to sibling anger are reflected in the following passage:

A painful issue is the siblings' anger at the parents for not having been able to protect the patient from the illness. Parents may be perceived as having played a role in the occurrence of the illness. Young siblings may come to this conclusion through a magical juxtaposition of events. Older siblings may wonder why the parents didn't check the patient's symptoms earlier, echoing the parents' own self-questioning. The siblings are shaken by having a life-threatening illness strike so close, and insecure in the parents' ability to protect them. (Sourkes, 1987, p. 173)

Professionals need to help siblings understand the source of their anger and to understand the universality of angry feelings. For siblings of emotionally disturbed children, Bank and Kahn (1982) note that:

Aggressiveness is one natural way through which siblings communicate. But when one sibling is defective, or is seen as defective and needs special treatment by parents, the well child must learn to inhibit, to refrain from aggressive taunts and actions. To establish himself as "well", he must give up and suppress these vital angry parts of himself, or submerge or hide them, lest he further injure his vulnerable sibling. Further, the well sibling learns not to rock the parents' boat, not to roil already troubled waters. Inhibition of anger also means that other forms of spontaneity—such as kidding, humor, and "messing around"—get squelched. The relationship between disturbed and rigidly avoidant siblings is serious and drab and lacks playfulness. (pp. 259–60)

Professionals should help parents facilitate the expression of anger experienced by nondisabled children, and they should be sensitive to parents who discourage the open expression of feelings. It is also important to take note when parents are made anxious by their child's feelings. Again, sibling support groups are an excellent resource for the expression and acceptance of angry feelings. A group of peers who share a particular life circumstance has powerful healing powers.

COMMUNICATION AND ISOLATION

Featherstone (1980) observes that the presence of a disabled child in the family inhibits communication. She believes that the lack of communication within a family over a child's disabling condition contributes to the loneliness normal siblings experience. Siblings may sense that certain topics are taboo and that "ugly" feelings are to remain hidden; they are thereby forced into a peculiar kind of loneliness—a sense of detachment from those one typically feels closest to. Trevino (1979) believes that family secrets or implicit rules forbidding the discussion of a problem force siblings to pretend that circumstances are other than they are. For some parents, discussing their disabled child with their nondisabled one is as threatening as a discussion of sex.

Siblings may not ask questions of their parents because of their wish to protect them. Children fear that the parents may lack the capacity to tolerate the illness and that their questions may precipitate family tensions. Such a pattern of diminished communication spreads to other aspects of family life, producing a generalized web of silence.

The existence of a child with a disability is a total family problem, and siblings need to be involved in the total family communication process. Often decisions that bear on the disabling condition are made without prior discussion with or explanation to siblings who may be affected by them. We therefore encourage open communication within the family to help reduce unpleasant side effects.

Some parents "teach" their children that aggression toward a disabled sibling is bad, disloyal, and rebellious. As a result, angry feelings are kept hidden or discharged in the parents' absence.

> Rather than invigorating the relationship with the give-and-take of insults and punches, easily dished out and quickly forgotten, the well sibling must be wary of hostile impulses toward a sick brother or sister, or risk being charged with kicking the crippled or hurting the handicapped. The well sibling, being presumed to have many riches and advantages is expected to show restraint, charity, kindness, and loyalty. Being a true-blue Boy Scout is, of course, impossible; and well siblings may vent their dammed-up anger in sneaky and violent ways. (Bank & Kahn, 1982, pp. 260–61).

Powell and Ogle (1985) also believe that communicating to children about their afflicted brother or sister is difficult, yet not impossible. They offer the following communication guidelines to help the parent–child relationship:

1. Display active (not passive) listening.
2. Take the time.
3. Secure needed knowledge.
4. Be sincere and honest.
5. Respond in a comprehensive fashion.
6. Adopt an open attitude.
7. Provide balanced information.
8. Be aware of nonverbal communication.
9. Follow up earlier communication.

Communicating the nature of a child's disability to a nondisabled son/daughter is difficult yet essential. Children sense underlying feelings, regardless of the actual words used; therefore open and honest communication is important within the family. Pearlman and Scott (1981) believe that what is communicated to children should be based on a child's age and ability to comprehend and assimilate. They believe that parents should be aware of certain key words in their communication with children. For example, the words *better* and *worse* invite comparisons, whereas *different* and *cannot* convey that limitations are not due to anything anyone did or did not do. These authors urge parents to begin a dialogue with their children as soon as possible; McHale and Gamble (1987) believe that siblings tend to keep their worries and problems to themselves, which makes it difficult for parents or others to know about their private concerns.

Professionals should encourage parents to open channels of communication between them and their children. Some of the internalized feelings that siblings experience can be quite intense and frightening.

In regard to schoolwork, Michaelis (1980) notes that siblings may resent that the disabled child is "playing" when they themselves must work so hard. Explaining the educational methods used with the disabled child and the skills that are being taught will help make it possible for the sibling to be supportive rather than critical and resentful. Also, young siblings may not understand that their brother/sister has certain cognitive limitations and as a result spends less time studying and in other learning activities.

Wentworth (1974) reports that nondisabled siblings want their parents to be honest with them above all else. Wentworth believes that nondisabled siblings need to know what caused the disability, how severe the disability is, and what the prognosis is. He urges parents to answer inquiries as truthfully as possible according to the siblings' age and level of comprehension.

Peer reactions may further isolate siblings from their social group. Children who feel rejected by their peers and are largely ignored by their parents are youngsters at risk. Add the caretaking responsibility siblings may assume and the making of emotional disturbance may be set in motion. And finally, Featherstone (1980) comments on the frustration and isolation nondisabled siblings feel when they are unable to communicate with a disabled brother/sister:

> The difficulty of "knowing" an autistic or profoundly retarded child, or the child with a severe communication disorder, can frustrate siblings as much as parents. They yearn for a relationship of equals, for someone with whom they can play and tell secrets, someone who shares their child-view of an adult world. Even when the normal siblings perform some of these functions, they sometimes imagine the special relationship they might have with this brother if he were more accessible. The abled-bodied member of a two-child family may feel very much alone. (p. 159)

FOR BETTER OR WORSE

Trevino (1979) is unequivocal in her view that nondisabled siblings are children at risk. She believes that the research, as sparse and inadequate as it is, is suggestive of several factors that contribute to emotional disturbance, such as the number of nondisabled siblings, siblings' age and gender, parental reaction to the disabled child, and the like.

Researchers and clinicians view the potential for psychological harm differently. Poznanski (1969), San Martino and Newman (1974), and

Trevino (1979) appear to be the most pessimistic about the effects of a disabled child on nondisabled sibling adjustment. Poznanski reports that psychiatrists treat more siblings of disabled children than disabled children themselves. Trevino believes that nondisabled children with a combination of certain characteristics and circumstances are children at risk who require psychological intervention. For San Martino and Newman, guilt provides the foundation for subsequent difficulties siblings are likely to experience. From their interviews of 239 families, Breslau, Weitzman, and Messenger (1981) found conflicting results regarding sibling adjustment. They did, however, discern a marked trend toward aggressive behavior and confused thinking by nondisabled siblings.

Both Featherstone (1980), from personal experience and in recounting the experiences of others, and Grossman (1972) and Kibert (1986), from their research on brothers and sisters in college, take a more cautious view of the effects of a disabled sibling on normal children. They believe that a disabled child in the family may have differential outcomes: little impact, negative impact, or positive outcome on subsequent adjustment and coping. Farber's (1959, 1960) research tends to support the same conclusion, which is further reinforced by Klein (1972) and Schreiber and Feeley (1965). Grakliker, Fishler, and Koch (1962) did not find any adverse effects reported by the siblings interviewed in their study, nor did McHale, Sloan, and Simeonsson (1986) in their study of siblings of autistic and mentally retarded brothers and sisters. This study is particularly noteworthy because they had 90 carefully selected subjects and included a matched control group. Although statistical differences between groups were not significant, children with disabled siblings had more variable experiences, with some children reporting very positive and some describing very negative relationships with their disabled brothers and sisters. McHale and colleagues note that children who reported difficult relationships worried about the disabled child's future (perhaps sensing some implication for themselves), perceived parental favoritism toward the disabled child, and experienced rejecting feelings toward their brother/sister. The more positive children viewed their parents and peers as reacting positively to the disabled child; they also had a better understanding of the disability.

In another well-conducted study, siblings of chronically ill children were reported to be as well adjusted as control subjects (Tritt & Esses, 1988). However, the siblings of the ill children were perceived by their *parents* as having more behavioral problems (withdrawal and shyness).

Bank and Kahn (1982) observe that adjustment can be affected by the age and developmental stage of the nondisabled sibling. Furthermore, the chronicity of the condition determines whether the sibling must cope with a time-limited or more chronic situation, and the rate of onset, especially with a mentally ill sibling, can be a source of confusion. The stigmatizing aspects of a disabled sibling's condition should also be considered. In a public situation, a well-behaved Down syndrome young-ster will be less noticed than a drooling, bent figure in a wheelchair.

From an empirical point of view, the question of whether siblings are unaffected, helped, or harmed by the presence of a disabled brother/sister remains open to speculation. Available data have not yet deter-mined the prevalence of emotional problems among siblings residing with a disabled brother/sister compared with that in "normal" families. The factors that interact and subsequently lead to psychological difficul-ties are many and combine in complex ways.

While some contributors to the professional literature are uncom-promisingly pessimistic about the impact of a disabled child on family members, others are very optimistic, especially parents and siblings who have written about their experiences. In reviewing much of the research and commentary about siblings, one may be left with the impression that largely negative effects are to be expected. This is simply not true.

For example, Illes (1979) reports that siblings of cancer victims are compassionate, tolerant, empathic to parents, and appreciative of their own health. Such positive sentiments underscore both the capacity of children to function under stress and the important contributions they make to their families. McHale and Gamble (1987) believe that a sibling's experiences may give rise to more mature, other-oriented, and humanitar-ian interests in the long-term (p. 154). Glendinning's (1983) British study, in which she interviewed in depth 17 parents (mostly mothers) of severely handicapped children, revealed that siblings were seen to face life optimistically. Drotar (quoted in Wallinga et al., 1987) argues that a child's chronic disability brings family members together. A common adversity tends to mobilize positive efforts on behalf of a child, which in turn tends to benefit the family. Furthermore, Simeonsson and Bailey (1986) note that siblings who have been actively involved in the manage-ment of their disabled family member tend to be well adjusted. It is difficult to integrate this observation with the studies that caution against excessive caretaking. It is possible that shared family caretaking and responsibility, along with expression of affection to all children in the family, promote a healthy, loving environment.

In their research Grossman (1972) and Kibert (1986) report that a number of college students who reported on their relationship with their retarded brother/sister appeared to have benefited from this experience. "The ones who benefitted appeared to us to be more tolerant, more compassionate, more knowing about prejudice" (Grossman, 1972, p. 84). In support of Grossman's findings, Miller (1974) found that a number of nondisabled siblings who had experienced involvement in the growth and development of a retarded sibling exhibited a sense of pride that they had been a part of it. Diane, a nondisabled sibling, said the following in her interview with Klein (1972):

> I always felt there was something very different about our family. Of course, you know, Cathy being that difference. Because of her difference there was a degree of specialness or closeness about us that, I do not know, it was sort of a bond that made us all very, very close. We all pitched in and helped each other out. (p. 14)

Another sister, this one of a mentally retarded, cerebral palsied, and epileptic boy, reflects:

> I do not mean to imply that life with Robin has been all goodness and light. I have seen the strain that the responsibility of his constant care has placed upon my parents. I worry about the increasing frequency of his seizures and about what would happen to him should my parents become unable to care for him. Robin, himself, like all brothers I suppose, can be truly aggravating. It makes me angry to see him try to weasel his way out of doing things that I know he is capable of doing. Just the other day, I was scolding him for not clearing his place at the table. I guess my sisterly bossing was too much for him. He pointed at me and angrily made the sign for handcuffs—his way of indicating that I should be put in jail.
>
> All in all, I feel that Robin has brought much good into the lives of my family. He has taught us a great deal about acceptance, patience, individual worth, but most of all about love. (Helsel, 1978, p. 112, 113)

And after a lengthy discussion of brothers and sisters of disabled youngsters and their adaptation to this special circumstance, Featherstone (1980) remarks:

> I have focused, up until now, on the difficulties that the abled-bodied child faces. These problems are real enough, and assume major importance in the lives of some children. Nonetheless, the sheer length of my discussion creates a misleading gloomy impression. It may suggest that for the brothers and sisters of the disabled the developmental path is strewn with frightful hazards, that all but the most skillful parents can expect to see their "normal" children bruised irreparably by the experience of family living. The truth is quite otherwise. (p. 163)

From this review of the literature one realizes that our knowledge of siblings is still in its infancy. However, we advise professionals to heed the admonition that sibling adjustment is dependent on numerous intertwined variables and that a simple etiological explanation is impossible.

The impact of a disabled child may be "for better or for worse" and may depend on various mediating variables.

REFERENCES

Bank, S. P., & Kahn, M. D. (1982). *The sibling bond.* New York: Basic Books.
Breslau, N. (1982). Siblings of disabled children: Birth order and age-spacing effects. *Journal of Abnormal Child Psychology, 10,* 85–96.
Breslau, N., Weitzman, M., & Messenger, K. (1981). Psychologic functioning of siblings of disabled children. *Pediatrics, 67,* 344–353.
Chinn, P. C., Winn, J., & Walters, R. H. (1978). *Two-way talking with parents of special children.* St. Louis: Mosby.
Cleveland, D. W., & Miller, N. (1977). Attitudes and life commitments of older siblings of mentally retarded adults. *Mental Retardation, 15,* 38–41.
DeLuca, K. D., & Solerno, S. C. (1984). *Helping professionals connect with families with handicapped children.* Springfield, IL: Thomas.
Farber, B. (1959). Effect of severely retarded child on family integration. *Monographs of the Society for Research in Child Development, 24* (Whole No. 71).
Farber, B. (1960). Family organization and crisis: Maintenance of integration in families with a severely mentally retarded child. *Monographs of the Society for Research in Child Development, 25* (Whole No. 75).
Featherstone, H. (1980). *A difference in the family.* New York: Basic Books.
Feigon, J. (1981). A sibling group program. *Sibling Information Network Letter, 1,* 2–3.
Gath, A. (1974). Sibling reactions to mental handicap: A comparison of the brothers and sisters of mongol children. *Journal of Child Psychology and Psychiatry, 15,* 187–198.
Glendinning, C. (1983). *Unshared care.* London: Routledge & Kegan Paul.
Grakliker, B. V., Fishler, K., & Koch, R. (1962). Teenage reactions to a mentally retarded sibling. *American Journal of Mental Deficiency, 66,* 838–843.
Grossman, F. K. (1972). *Brothers and sisters of retarded children.* Syracuse, NY: Syracuse University Press.
Hayden, V. (1974). The other children. *The Exceptional Parent, 4,* 26–29.
Helsel, E. (1978). The Helsels' story of Robin. In A. P. Turnbull & H. R. Turnbull (Eds.), *Parents speak out* (pp. 81–98). Columbus, OH: Merrill.
Holt, K. S. (1958). The home care of severely retarded children. *Pediatrics, 22,* 746–755.
Illes, J. (1979). Children with cancer: Healthy siblings' perceptions during the illness experience. *Cancer Nursing, 2*(5), 371–377.
Israelite, N. (1985). Sibling reaction to a hearing impaired child in the family. *Journal of Rehabilitation of the Deaf, 18*(3), 1–5.
Kibert, R. P. (1986). *A descriptive study of the perceptions of normal college age siblings in families with a mentally retarded child.* Unpublished doctoral dissertation, University of Pittsburgh.
Kirkman, M. (1985). The perceived impact of a sibling with a disability on family relationships: A survey of adult siblings in Victoria, Australia. *Sibling Information Network Newsletter, 4,* 2–5.
Klein, S. D. (1972). Brother to sister: Sister to brother. *The Exceptional Parent, 2,* 10–15.
Laureys, K. (1984). Growing up with Brian. *Sibling Information Network Newsletter, 3,* 5–6.
Lechtenberg, R. (1984). *Epilepsy and the family.* Cambridge, MA: Harvard University Press.
Lobato, D. (1983). Siblings of handicapped children: A review. *Journal of Autism and Developmental Disorders, 13,* 347–364.

Luterman, D. (1979). *Counseling parents of hearing-impaired children*. Boston: Little, Brown.

Marion, R. L. (1981). *Educators, parents, and exceptional children*. Rockville, MD: Aspen.

McHale, S. M., Sloan, J., & Simeonsson, R. J. (1986). Sibling relationships with autistic, mentally retarded, and non-handicapped brothers and sisters. *Journal of Autism and Developmental Disorders, 16*, 399–414.

McHale, S. M., & Gamble, W. C. (1987). Sibling relationships and adjustment of children with disabled brothers and sisters. *Journal of Children in Contemporary Society, 19*, 131–158.

Meyer, D., Vadasy, P., & Fewell, R. R. (1985). *Living with a brother or sister with special needs*. Seattle: University of Washington Press.

Michaelis, C. T. (1980). *Home and school partnerships in exceptional children*. Rockville, MD: Aspen.

Miller, S. (1974). *An exploratory study of sibling relationships in families with retarded children*. Unpublished doctoral dissertation, Columbia University, New York.

Murphy, A., Paeschel, S., Duffy, T., & Brady, E. (1976). Meeting with brothers and sisters of Down's syndrome children. *Children Today, 5*, 20–23.

Myers, R. (1978). *Like normal people*. New York: McGraw-Hill.

Pearlman, L., & Scott, K. A. (1981). *Raising the handicapped child*. Englewood Cliffs, NJ: Prentice-Hall.

Powell, T., & Ogle, P. (1985). *Brothers and sisters: A special part of exceptional families*. Baltimore: Brookes.

Poznanski, E. (1969). Psychiatric difficulties in siblings of handicapped children. *Pediatrics, 8*, 232–234.

San Martino, M., & Newman, M. B. (1974). Siblings of retarded children: A population at risk. *Child Psychiatry and Human Development, 4*, 168–177.

Schreiber, M., & Feeley, M. (1965). A guided group experience. *Children, 12*, 221, 225.

Seligman, M. (1983). *The family with a handicapped child*. Orlando, FL: Grune & Stratton.

Simeonsson, R. J., & Bailey, D. B. (1986) Siblings of handicapped children. In J. J. Gallagher & W. Vietze, *Families of handicapped persons* (pp. 67–77). Baltimore: Brooks.

Skrtic, T., Summers, J., Brotherson, M. J., & Turnbull, A. (1984). Severely handicapped children and their brothers and sisters. In J. Blacker (Ed.), *Severely handicapped young children and their families*. Orlando, FL: Academic.

Sourkes, B. M. (1987). Siblings of the child with a life-threatening illness. *Journal of Children in Contemporary Society, 19*, 159–184.

Tew, B., & Lawrence, K. (1975). Mothers, brothers and sisters of patients with spina bifida. *Developmental Medical Child Neurology, 15* (Suppl. 29), 69–76.

Travis, G. (1976). *Chronic illness in children: Its impact on child and family*. Stanford, CA: Stanford University Press.

Trevino, F. (1979). Siblings of handicapped children: Identifying those at risk. *Social Casework, 60*, 488–493.

Tritt, S. G., & Esses, L. M. (1988). Psychosocial adaptation of siblings of children with chronic medical illness. *American Journal of Orthopsychiatry, 58*, 211–220.

Wallinga, C., Paquio, L., & Skeen, P. (1987). When a brother or sister is ill. *Psychology Today, 42*, 43.

Wasserman, R. (1983). Identifying the counseling needs of the siblings of mentally retarded children. *Personnel and Guidance Journal, 61*, 622–627.

Wentworth, E. H. (1974). *Listen to your heart: A message to parents of handicapped children*. Boston: Houghton Mifflin.

Western Psychiatric Institute and Clinic. (1980). *An intruder in the family: Families cope with cancer* [videotape]. Pittsburgh: University of Pittsburgh.

6

Effects on Fathers and Grandparents

In the investigation of families with a disabled member, the focus of attention generally is on the affected person. A present-day case in point is in the area of geriatrics, where victims of Alzheimer disease are the central focus. While research continues on those afflicted with this disease, there is a fledgling but growing body of literature on family members who care for and must cope with Alzheimer patients. Similarly, parents of disabled children, who fall on the other end of the lifespan spectrum from the ill elderly and their families, have been studied with increased frequency since the late 1950s. The fact that a disabled child resides within a reactive larger system, affects it, and in turn is affected by it is increasingly acknowledged by researchers.

After the affected child, mothers have been the most studied family member. In part, this is probably due to their greater accessibility, but it also, and perhaps more importantly, reflects the fact that mothers give birth and are considered natural caregivers and nurturers. Also, in the past mothers typically stayed at home to raise the children while fathers worked outside the home. Within the context of a family systems perspective, which stresses that all family members are affected by a crisis, fathers, siblings, and grandparents are, in more recent years, being considered important influences. The present chapter, then, examines the least studied family members, fathers and grandparents. The study of siblings, which now has a modest research base, is considered in the previous chapter.

FATHERS

Lamb (1983) notes that only after the publication of an early study on infant attachment and a later paper reconceptualizing the "maternal deprivation" literature did there emerge a realization that, in emphasiz-

134

ing mothers, researchers had lost sight of the broader context in which children are raised. Prior to that the role of the father in child development and family functioning had been undervalued. This diminution of the father's influence can be attributed, in part, to Freud's (1936) theories emphasizing the mother as the primary influence in the development of children. Bowlby (1951) contributed to this belief by suggesting that the father's role in child development was secondary to that of the mother. Thus, until the 1970s, the mother's role in the family overshadowed that of the father.

The last decade has witnessed a marked reversal in this trend. As noted by Hornby (1988), this evolution is illustrated in the widely read childcare books by Benjamin Spock. In the 1946 edition Spock stressed the support that fathers should provide mothers. In the 1957 edition he suggested that fathers become involved in childcare, though as secondary to mothers. In his 1985 edition he suggested that the father's responsibility in child development should be equal to the mother's. Hornby notes that further evidence for the elevation of the importance of fathers has been the increase in publications on fathers in the last several years.

Hornby (1988) and Pruett (1987) speculate further about the reasons for the escalated interest in fathers. Accompanying the increase in the number of mothers who work has been a corresponding focus on alternative caretakers for children. A likely resource for alternative care is fathers. The shortening of the work week has meant that fathers have more time to spend with their families. Furthermore, changes in child custody laws have led to an increased number of single-parent fathers and fathers with joint custody. The growth of feminism has relaxed traditional sex roles, making less rigid the identification of women with motherhood and men with breadwinning. Also, the adoption of family systems models has meant that all members of the family are considered important. And finally, as the following section illustrates, the dearth of information on fathers and fathering has propelled researchers to investigate this family role from a number of perspectives.

Fathers' Effects

In the past children were viewed as malleable organisms waiting to be shaped by outside socialization processes. As noted by Lamb (1983), we are now more aware that each child has individual characteristics that not only affect the way the child is influenced by external forces but also contribute to the child's shaping of the socializers themselves. Therefore, socialization is viewed as a bidirectional process, with influences flowing in two directions.

According to Lamb (1983) and Meyer, Vadasy, Fewell, and Schell (1985), nurturing emotions are not unique to mothers; fathers also seem to know instinctively how to interact with their infants and how to care for them. Furthermore, fathers are interested in their infants and want to be actively involved with them. In fact, during infancy the father's sensitivity to his infant's distress is just as acute as the mother's.

Other studies reviewed by Lamb and by Meyer and colleagues reveal some differences between mothers' and fathers' behaviors with their infants that begin to emerge shortly after the infant's birth. Mothers tend to engage more in caretaking, while fathers tend to play more with their infants. Fathers are more vigorous with their infants; they are more likely to pick up, toss, and generally be rougher than mothers, who are more likely to play such games as peek-a-boo or hide-and-seek. However, fathers, like mothers, adapt their play to their children's developmental level, suggesting that both fathers and mothers are equally sensitive to their children's developmental changes. These general observations would suggest that fathers are competent nurturers and caretakers.

Fathers and Disabled Children

Change causes stress and the birth of *any* child is stress inducing for the parents. The birth of a child means that both parents must readjust their marital roles in order to assume new responsibilities. Feelings of elation and joy may give way to fatigue and doubt as the parents worry about their competence as parents, and they may experience ambivalence over their loss of freedom. Therefore, there are normal stresses preceding, during, and after the birth period. Add to this tension the birth of a child with a disability and a full-scale crisis may be set in motion.

Our understanding of fathers of disabled children is based on little more than a handful of studies. According to Hornby (1988), the first published study of fathers of disabled children was by Eisenberg in 1957. Eisenberg's study, which was based on the clinical impressions of the author, found that 85 out of 100 fathers showed evidence of serious personality disorders, such as an obsessive, detached, and humorless personal style. It is worth noting that this article appeared during the period when it was common to blame the parents for their children's birth defects and their reaction to these defects.

In his review of more recent studies, Lamb (1983) notes that fathers and mothers initially respond differently to the news that they have produced a child with a disability. Fathers tend to respond less emotionally and focus on possible long-term concerns, whereas mothers respond more emotionally and are concerned about their ability to cope with the burdens of childcare.

Generally speaking, fathers are more concerned than mothers about the adoption of socially acceptable behavior by their children, especially their sons, and they are more anxious about the social status and occupational success of their offspring. As a result, fathers are more concerned than mothers about the long-term prospects of their disabled children, and they are probably more affected by the visibility of the disability.

Because of the high expectations fathers have of their sons, they may be especially disappointed when they have disabled sons. The behavioral consequences of this disappointment, according to Lamb (1983), are manifested in extremes of intense involvement and total withdrawal, whereas fathers seem to have limited, routine involvement with their disabled daughters. Houser's (1987) recent study, however, does not support the contention that fathers are more distressed by a disabled boy than a disabled girl, suggesting that more research is needed in this area.

In a frequently cited study, Cummings (1976) found that fathers of mentally retarded children are more depressed and experience lower self-esteem and confidence in their roles as fathers than fathers of nondisabled children. They also reported less enjoyment of their children than the fathers of the control group. However, a more recent study notes that fathers reported fewer symptoms of distress, higher self-esteem, and more internal locus of control than mothers (Goldberg, Marcovitch, MacGregor, & Lojkasek, 1986). The results of this study run counter to Cummings's investigation and suggest that fathers may adjust more favorably now than in the past. This may be due to more enlightened attitudes and the availability of greater support systems. On the other hand, as the researchers speculate, their findings might support the idea that men tend to deny and suppress uncomfortable emotions.

Fathers' reactions to their disabled children may have implications for the responses of other family members. For example, Peck and Stephens (1960) found a strong relationship between the degree of paternal acceptance of the disabled child and the amount of acceptance and rejection generally observed in the home. This suggests that the father's reaction might set the tone for the entire family. Lamb (1983) speculates that this may reflect the fact that fathers obtain less satisfaction from disabled than from nondisabled children. Furthermore, it supports the notion that the father's involvement is discretionary, that is, that fathers can increase or decrease their involvement, whereas mothers are expected to show the same commitment to all children. Not only is the development of the disabled child likely to be affected when the father chooses to withdraw, but the entire family suffers. Indeed, Houser (1987) found that the fathers who experience high levels of stress tend to cope by employing an escape-avoidance strategy.

Family systems theory would suggest that as the father pulls away, other family members are affected and will react to the father's behavior. As the father withdraws, the burden of care, for example, falls to other family members, particularly the mother. Feelings of anger and resentment will fester as tension in the family mounts. The father's avoidance of the family as its members struggle to cope with the added pressures of attending to a disabled child will set into motion a negative and dysfunctional dynamic.

Meyer and colleagues (1985) note that the father's emotional difficulties may be masked by his need to be stoic and in control of his emotions. Men may find it difficult to express sadness or grief, because to express these feelings is often perceived as a sign of weakness. When the infant's mother is experiencing shock or depression, the father may suppress his own feelings because they are not "manly" and/or because he wishes to support his wife by being "strong."

A father's stoic behavior can be viewed by professionals as a more manageable reaction. The male physicians quoted below seem to feel more comfortable communicating distressing information to fathers than to mothers:

> Usually I prefer to tell the father. The mother is in an emotional state after having just given birth.
>
> Usually I tell the father, and, based on his knowledge of his wife, we decide on a course of action. . . . I do this for psychological reasons. My feeling is that you can deal more easily with the father. It's emotionally easier.
>
> If I had a choice, I'd probably prefer talking with the father first and let him help me make the decision about talking to the mother.
>
> I call the father and ask him what he wants me to do. I wait until I can reach the father before I talk to the mother.
>
> I try to talk to the obstetrician to find out if it's the mother's first baby or if she's anxious or apprehensive. . . . I always tell the father right away. (Darling, 1979, p. 206)

In his fathers' discussion groups, Smith (1981) found that the group members distrusted male displays of emotion and that the fathers learned as children that "real men" are always in control of their emotions and that "big boys don't cry." Smith believes that these masculine behaviors place considerable stress on the father and make it harder for him to express and be attuned to his own feelings.

For the men in the fathers' discussion groups, these facets of the stereotypic masculine role were quite restrictive and presented obstacles to the men's coming to terms with their children's handicaps and with their own feelings as parents of exceptional children. In particular, these men displayed stereotypical instrumental traits such as a reluctance to show one's emotions, a need for independence and self-reliance, and a need to "fix" problematic situations. (Smith, 1981, p. 12)

Smith points out that as fathers of disabled children these men experienced a variety of intense emotions that they could not easily express or confront. For example, many felt anger at the physicians who initially informed them of their child's disability, believing that these doctors were unnecessarily abrupt and unsympathetic. Furthermore, the fathers found themselves dependent on the expertise of professionals. This dependence was difficult for the fathers, because it made them feel less in control and less competent as parents. Males grow up to be "fixers" who actively confront problems. Passivity in the face of a crisis is threatening to men who have learned that they must be "strong", avoid showing weakness (mainly by suppressing emotions), and be able to resolve difficult situations competently. Perhaps the most poignant frustration is that fathers simply cannot "fix" their child's disability.

For most of the fathers, their involvement in the discussion groups represented the first time they had acknowledged to anyone—to their wives or even to themselves, that they had such strong feelings resulting from the birth of their disabled child.

Josh Greenfeld (1978) describes the powerful and contradictory feelings he experiences as he reflects on life with his autistic son Noah*:

I thought continually that soon I will have to kill Noah. The monster that has long been lurking in him increasingly shows its face. And just as the day may come when I can no longer bear to take care of him, I could not bear to see him mistreated—or maltreated—in a state hospital like Camarillo or Letchworth Village.

He will become a hopeless grotesque with less than endearing manners. He keeps putting his fingers to his lips and then spit-touching the nearest object or person. He pinches, he scratches, he pulls hair. This morning he suddenly pulled Foumi's [Greenfeld's wife] hair after she had chastised him for his finger-spitting. I heard her crying and rushed to free her from his grasp.

Killing him would be a kindness. His brain has stopped working; he has not been functioning anyway. I dread it but I see myself killing my son not as a myth but as a fact. My dreams now are dreams of prison. Isolation. A

winding down of my life in solitude. It seems absurd, I know. But could I
ever bear to see Noah suffer, killed softly and cruelly, day after day? No.

There is a man from Santa Barbara who killed his brain-damaged son a
few years ago. He put a gun to the boy's head and squeezed the trigger, then
called the police. He's in prison now. But he'll get out eventually. (pp. 282–
283)

Noah is quick to scream, to clutch, to demand, to be unreasonable. He is a
tyranny I will never quite learn to live with. He is an obsession I will never
learn to live without. (pp. 94–95)

Smith believes that support/discussion groups for fathers are an
important emotional resource that will benefit fathers and indirectly will
have a positive effect on the entire family. Indeed, as Meyer and colleagues (1985) emphasize, the support that the father can provide to his
wife and other family members is another reason it is important that
fathers learn to cope with their child's disability.

We know, then, that some fathers of disabled children may reject the
child and withdraw; they may experience a lowered sense of competence
and self-esteem; and they may experience considerable frustration as they
confront the masculine injunctions they have learned to exercise in the
face of powerful emotions. The issue then becomes how a father might
learn to be more accepting of his child and his unenviable circumstances
as a parent, as well as how he can come to terms with emotions that are
not easily expressed. Lamb (1983) believes that intervention efforts should
be directed toward fathers more systematically than they have until now.
Certainly the discussion group model proposed by Smith (1981) seems to
be the type of intervention that can help ameliorate some of the problems
noted above. But perhaps the most promising venture is the one that has
been developed at the University of Washington.

Starting in 1978, fathers of young disabled children in Seattle, Washington, were exposed to a group format that provided information and
social support (Vadasy, Fewell, Greenberg, Desmond, & Meyer, 1986).
The basic structure was that fathers met twice monthly for 2 hours. They
brought their disabled children with them to sessions organized by two
male facilitators, one a professional and one the father of a disabled child.
The meetings included activities in which fathers and children participated together, such as songs, dances, and games. Time was set aside for
fathers to meet without their children so that they could discuss their
concerns. And finally, at some meetings, guests were invited to speak on
topics selected by the fathers. Mothers were often invited to attend the
presentations, and special family meetings were scheduled at holidays
and occasionally at other times. This format allowed fathers to acquire

information, experience emotional support from other fathers, discuss feelings and more practical concerns, and develop strong attachments to their young disabled children.

The fathers' workshop manual, developed by the investigators at the University of Washington, describes in detail how to initiate a fathers' group, how to select and train leaders, and how to plan for the various components of the meetings (Meyer et al., 1985). Since 1980, participating families have been the subjects of research on the program's impact on parents' stress levels and coping abilities. An early report showed that mothers and fathers who had been participating in the program had lower stress and depression levels and higher satisfaction levels regarding their social supports than parents newly entering the program (Vadasy, Fewell, Meyer, & Greenberg, 1985). In a later evaluation of 45 sets of parents, it was found that both mothers and fathers reported significantly decreased depression (Vadasy et al., 1986). Fathers reported a decrease in stress and grief and an increase in pessimism about the future.

The fathers' information needs decreased over time, and mothers reported increased satisfaction with social supports, increased family cohesion, and decreased stress and rigidity in family control over time (Vadasy et al., 1986). The outcomes for the study were very positive and support the value of fathers' groups not only for the father but for the entire family. The unanticipated finding regarding the fathers' increased pessimism, according to the investigators, may be due to the fathers' ultimate acceptance of the children's limitations. It may also reflect the fact that knowledge is a double-edged sword.

In summary, some modest research efforts suggest that fathers may have a variety of adverse reactions to the birth of a disabled child. Fathers who are coping poorly tend to find it difficult to be supportive of their wives. When fathers experience stress and withdraw from their families, other family members (especially the mothers) must take up the slack, resulting in family tensions. Furthermore, there is some evidence that fathers may cope better with a disabled daughter than son. A promising resource for fathers seems to be a support group format that can help them attach more positively to their young disabled children, gain information, and discuss their common problems in a supportive context. Further research is needed, too, on the positive effects a disabled child may have on fathers.

GRANDPARENTS

A systemic view has to incorporate the complexity of intergenerational relationships affecting contemporary family life. Yet much of the literature on families has focused on the nuclear family, with little mention of grandparents. To conceptualize the family apart from its ancestral past is to ignore an integral aspect of its present life. Some argue that the influences from previous generations are of considerable importance for understanding the nuclear family's dynamics (Bowen, 1978). Others note that the grandparent–grandchild relationship has the potential for affecting the development of children in a way that is different from other relationships (Baranowski, 1982).

The traditional view of grandparents as the domineering, controlling family matriarch or patriarch has given way to a more positive view. As noted by Wilcoxon (1987), grandparents now view their roles as being less associated with power and control and more related to warmth, indulgence, and pleasure without responsibility. Contemporary roles, then, seem to be multidimensional and supportive. Kornhaber and Woodward (reported in Wilcoxon, 1987) identify the following grandparent roles:

- historian—a link with the cultural and familial past
- role model—an example of older adulthood
- mentor—a wise adult experienced in life transitions
- wizard—a master of storytelling to foster imagination and creativity
- nurturer/great parent—an ultimate support in family crises and transitions

Becoming a grandparent confers a special status on a person. Grandparents witness the emergence of a new generation, giving them the satisfaction of seeing their grandchildren take on new and fulfilling roles—a source of considerable pride.

In some ways grandchildren provide a new lease on life for their grandparents. The birth of a grandchild can both signal renewal of present life and offer intimations of immortality. As Gabel and Kotsch (1981) note:

> The sense of surviving through the grandchild may help soothe the increasing infirmities of advancing age and the approaching reality of death. Grandchildren also offer renewal, because grandparents can relive the joys of their own early parenthood as they watch their children in this early phase of life. Furthermore, playing with and occasionally caring for young grandchildren supplies grandparents with a revived feeling of importance and purpose in life. To the delight of many grandparents, this new lease on life is purchased at a relatively low cost. They can often enjoy their grandchildren without the burdens of the ongoing caretaking responsibilities and the stress of parenthood. (p. 30, 31)

People are becoming grandparents earlier in their lives and will continue in this role for longer periods than in previous generations (Meyer & Vadasy, 1986). The grandparent role is often assumed when one is in one's 40s or 50s, younger than grandparents in the past. Also, increased life expectancy means that some people will assume grandparent roles for almost half their lives. Zinsmeister (1985) estimates that in the near future, grandparents will comprise increasingly larger percentages of our population.

Approximately three-fourths of the elderly live within 30 minutes of at least one child, making regular contact between nuclear and extended family a reality (Stehower, 1968). Almost half of U.S. grandparents see a grandchild every day (Harris and Associates, 1975). And recent state laws protecting grandparents' rights to continue their relationships with their grandchildren after divorce demonstrate how seriously grandparents regard their roles and how important this relationship is to them (Vadasy, Fewell, & Meyer, in press).

In summary, then, we know that there will be more persons becoming grandparents as this century comes to a close. Earlier views that grandparents are interested in control and tend to meddle in their children's lives have been replaced by the perception of grandparents as supporters and helpers to their adult children and nurturers to their grandchildren. Furthermore, and perhaps most important, grandparents are affected by what happens in the nuclear family and, in turn, affect those family members.

Given these characteristics of grandparents, what might be expected when one is confronted with a grandchild with a disability? The next section will attempt to answer this question.

Grandparents and Childhood Disability

As one grandmother put it:

> There is a very special magic between grandparents and grandchildren. There is a joy, a delight, an unencumbered relationship. The responsibility of parenthood is over. Grandparents have an opportunity to sample the mysteries and watch with awe the unfolding of a new personality. This new unique human being is a stranger, but is hauntingly familiar. He is the link between our past and the future. But what happens when this link, this delight, this claim to immortality is born less than perfect? What is the relationship then between grandparent and grandchild? (McPhee, 1982, p. 13)

The remainder of this chapter will attempt to address the questions posed by McPhee. Indeed, when a disabled child is born grandparents must face the disappointment of a less-than-perfect baby and ponder the relationship between this child and themselves. They must also reflect on their relationship with their own children and how they will interact with this newly constituted family of which they are a part.

A major concern of the parents is how their own parents (and in-laws) will accept the disabled baby. Writing about her experience with her mother-in-law, Pieper (1976) chronicles their reactions to each other after the birth of her son. Pieper's mother-in-law was reluctant to visit her in the hospital and later accused Pieper of burdening her husband for life. Attempting to cope with such an assault, Pieper chose to try to understand the special mother–son relationship rather than, in her own pain, strike out at her mother-in-law.

> She is my husband's mother! Just as I could gaze on that son of mine— looking for all the world like a plucked chicken, even to the black sutures near his butt—and feel a fierce protectiveness, so she could feel nothing less for the son she had loved for so much longer.—I was supposed to present their son with a fine, healthy, and above all "normal" child.—Instead, I had given birth to a "defective baby." In so doing I had threatened her son's well-being—or her image of it. I had threatened his financial future, his emotional make-up, his position in the community and his independence. Her harsh words to me in the hospital were a way of expressing the same protectiveness toward her son that I was now feeling towards mine. (Pieper, 1976, p. 7)

A relationship that floundered had, with the insight and wisdom of the mother, been restored. Pieper understood a mother's protective feelings toward her son. She further understood that her mother-in-law grew up when deviancy was tolerated even less than it is today. In addition, the philosophy of the "bad seed" might have flourished, in that at some level the grandmother might have felt that she herself had passed on the defective gene that resulted in the birth of the disabled child. This can be threatening and anxiety provoking to a relative. As expressed by McPhee (1982): "That diagnosis set both sides of the family busy rattling skeletons trying to prove that each was pure and not responsible for the present suffering" (p. 14).

Generally speaking, an event that usually reassures grandparents that the future will be carried on by the baby instead introduces uncertainty about what the future holds for the family. The birth of a grandchild with a disability evokes different emotions from those produced by the birth of a healthy grandchild (Meyer & Vadasy, 1986). Grandparents experience a dual hurt, not only for their grandchild but also for their own child, whom they may see as burdened for life. The grandparents' wish for their child's happiness is shattered as they see their offspring preparing to cope with a family crisis that will not go away and cannot be easily remedied.

According to Meyer and Vadasy (1986), grandparents, perhaps to avoid the pain of reality, often deny a grandchild's problem ("there's nothing wrong with her"), trivialize it ("she will grow out of it"), or fantasize about unrealistic cures. Grandparents who deny the existence of the disability and those who reject the child can prove difficult burdens to the parents, who are attempting to cope with the crisis. They must attend to their own pain while at the same time they are compelled to cope with their parents' and in-laws' reactions.

Although we know little about how grandparents react to the birth of a grandchild with a disability, it is likely that they experience a mourning period for the loss of the idealized grandchild they had expected. Just as the parents experience the "death" of the expected normal, healthy child, so, too, may the grandparents feel a great loss and mourn the death of what they had wished for. They may go through the same stages as the parents: denial, grief, anger, and eventually acceptance. Reporting on the reactions of grandparents who attended the grandparents' workshops at the University of Washington, Vadasy and colleagues (in press) report that their initial reactions were most often sadness (67%), shock (38%), and anger (33%). Forty-three percent reported that they continued to feel sad long after they first learned of their grandchild's disability, but 57% expressed eventual acceptance of the problem.

Grandparents may be mourning at the same time as the parents. In the crisis-laden initial period of discovery, both parents and grandparents may be experiencing great loss and grief; they may therefore be unable to be supportive of one another. According to Gable and Kotsch (1981), grandparents may be in a state of "diminished capacity" for providing help to the child's parents. Whatever the initial reactions, professionals need to be cognizant of what different family members are experiencing so that they can take these reactions into account in counseling.

Grandparents may feel anger when a child with a disability enters the family. A common pattern is the paternal grandmother's expression of resentment toward her daughter-in-law, as noted in the relationship described above by Pieper. The hurling back and forth of accusations between family members heightens the sense of crisis. Not only does the mother already feel guilty about the birth, but she is also made to feel even more guilty when she is accused by an in-law of destroying her husband's life. At a time when the mother desperately needs support, she is instead confronted with hostility. The husband, in turn, is placed in a difficult position, feeling that he needs to be supportive of both his mother and his wife. Furthermore, siblings may view the mounting tensions between their parents and their grandparents, with considerable anxiety. Due to grandparent reactions, siblings may be confused about how they should respond to the new and less-than-perfect addition to the family. In short, hostility between the parents and the extended family may, if not resolved, become a major source of continuing intergenerational conflict.

Perhaps the intergenerational family interaction that is discussed most in the literature is that between the mother and the child's paternal grandmother (Farber & Ryckman, 1965; Holt, 1958; Kahana & Kahana, 1970). As in Pieper's situation, paternal grandmothers can blame the mother for the child's disability. Furthermore, Waisbren (1980) found that the father's relationship with his parents is more important than any other relationship among support sources. Waisbren reports that fathers who perceive their parents as highly supportive engage in more activities with their disabled child, feel more positive about that child, and are better able or more willing to plan for the future than fathers with unsupportive parents. She further found that mothers who perceive their in-laws as supportive feel more positive about their disabled child. Farber (1959) reports that frequent contact between the child's mother and her own mother promotes higher marital integration; on the other hand, frequent contact with her mother-in-law tends to be a negative influence. This research suggests that grandparents may have much more influence on how parents respond to their disabled child than originally believed.

Although resentment, guilt, and anger can be destructive, such feelings must be viewed in context. Anger should probably be expected and accepted, especially early on. To discourage family members from expressing their pain through anger is to encourage its expression in subtle ways; thus major underlying issues that are never directly confronted may affect the lives of family members in more camouflaged ways. At any rate, just as professionals must understand and be accepting of the parents' anger, so, too, must they accept similar feelings from grandparents. One grandmother comments:

> Anger and hostility can be destructive forces to live with. Will anger and hostility be all this child will ever mean to me, I wondered. I suffered for him—for what he might have been, should have been. I resented what his birth had done to my lovely daughter.
>
> I cried a lot and prayed a lot and yelled at God a lot. Then, I said, "So be it. You're sorry for yourself, but look at that child. Just look at him. Not what he might have been, but what he is. Grow up lady." (McPhee, 1982, p. 14)

Although grandparents typically enjoyed their own parenting years, they may have looked forward to the time when the parent role would cease. The birth of a child with a disability can suddenly thrust grandparents back in time, causing them to resume a role they thought had been fulfilled:

> When my own kids were little the chaos just all seemed to go with the territory—spilled milk, scattered cereal, orange peels behind the couch, lost socks, wall-to-wall toys. I cleaned it up a dozen times a day without a second thought. Now, just bending over sometimes sparks that second thought! We don't have the peace and quiet we sometimes think we'd like to have. Sometimes I find myself thinking, "I served my time at this! What am I doing here?" (Click, 1986, p. 3)

We have suggested thus far that grandparents, through their lack of support, can be a source of considerable consternation to the nuclear family of a disabled child. The sense of threat and vulnerability, the loss they experience, the ambiguity the situation holds for them, their denial and lack of acceptance can indeed be burdensome for the family. However, perhaps for most families with a disabled child who have living extended family, the situation may be more positive. Indeed, as Vadasy and Fewell (1986) report, mothers of deaf–blind children ranked grandparents high on their list of supports.

Grandparent contributions to the nuclear family can be many and varied. For example, Vadasy and colleagues (in press) conceive of grandparents as valuable resources to their grandchildren and the rest of the family. Due to their experience, grandparents have much to offer in advising about childcare, providing access to community resources, and in sharing coping strategies that helped them in the past. Because they also have time available, they can assist with shopping, errands, and childcare; and any type of respite from the daily chores of caring for a disabled child is welcome. Respite services are not available in some communities, making this a most valuable contribution to the family. Furthermore, because of their community contacts grandparents may be able to provide the family with access to services within the community. For example, as noted by Vadasy and colleagues (in press), through the grandparents' church group, the family might gain access to childcare, special equipment, and other types of support.

Perhaps the most important type of help from the extended family is emotional support. The support of grandparents during the initial diagnostic and "first knowledge" phase and throughout the child's development adds immeasurably to the parents' ability to cope, and it provides excellent role models for siblings as well.

> You think that after you've raised your children you can stop being a parent and become a person again. And then your adult child experiences tragedy

or loss, and your heart aches with the knowledge of your own impotence and how you yearn to go back to the days when a bandaid and a kiss could fix anything. Who are we to try to advise our children? How can we see beyond the moment, how can we diminish their pain or give them our patience and our constancy, and try to keep our own hope alive. (Click, 1986, p. 3)

From the very beginning, there was no question that she was accepted, just like any other child born in our family. I remember how the whole family rallied. They said that she would be fine, and it meant a lot to us to have that family support. They sent us cards and flowers and gifts and did all the things you do when a baby is born. And I think that was so important, because, after all, she was a baby first, and then a baby who had problems. (Vadasy et al., in press)

Grandparents can thus be a source of emotional support and instrumental assistance; but, as noted above, they can also add to the family's burden when they are not accepting of their grandchild and fail to be supportive. The question, then, is how professionals can help those grandparents who wish to be involved and useful as well as those who are struggling with their feelings and, as a result, find it difficult to come to terms with the family's crisis.

Vadasy and colleagues (in press) believe that grandparents have similar needs to those experienced by the parents, namely, support and information. Based on the notion that most grandparents want to be supportive and can potentially be helpful to the family emotionally and instrumentally, Vadasy and colleagues developed the grandparents' workshop model at the University of Washington in Seattle. The Seattle researchers believe that grandparents can add to family stress if they lack adequate information or have unrealistic expectations for their grandchild's potential. Conversely, they believe that access to accurate information can contribute to the grandparents' acceptance and resultant support.

From their research, Vadasy and colleagues (in press) found that grandparents were lacking in a number of areas. For example, they wanted to have more information on available therapies for their grandchild, know more about the child's disability, have some idea of what the child's potential might be, and the like. They often questioned whether they were doing the right thing with their grandchild and expressed concern about the future. Based on these and other concerns, the University of Washington grandparents' workshop model was developed (Meyer & Vadasy, 1986).

Another program sensitive to the needs of the extended family is the Family, Infant, and Toddler Project at Vanderbilt University (Gabel &

Kotsch, 1981). The extended family component consists of bimonthly evening clinics for grandparents and other kin. During the clinics, therapies are explained, educational programs are reviewed, and a portion of the meeting is opened to questions. Gabel and Kotsch report that the relatives are more understanding and helpful after attending the family clinics. Sonnek (1986) reports on a number of localities that have extended their programs for disabled children to include nuclear and extended family members. Although the inclusion of the extended family in existing programs seems to be gaining more acceptance, there is little empirical evidence regarding these individuals' effectiveness in supporting the immediate family.

Based on the belief that grandparents are important resources and that their involvement benefits themselves as well as the nuclear family, we agree with Vadasy and colleagues (in press) when they remark that "all professionals would be wise to look more closely at the extended networks of the families in their programs to appreciate the contributions that extended family members, like grandparents, make, and to recognize and foster their concern for the child and family." Sonnek (1986) also supports this view when she states that "it appears the grandparents, to date, have been an unrecognized and possibly an underutilized resource in the study of the nuclear family" (p. 108).

REFERENCES

Baranowski, M. D. (1982). Grandparent–adolescent relations: Beyond the nuclear family. *Adolescence, 17*, 575–584.

Bowen, M. (1978). *Family therapy in clinical practice.* New York: Aronson.

Bowlby, J. (1951). *Maternal care and mental health.* Geneva: World Health Organization.

Click, J. (1986). Grandparent concerns: Learning to be special. *Sibling Information Network Newsletter, 5*, 3–4.

Cummings, S. (1976). The impact of the child's deficiency on the father: A study of fathers of mentally retarded and of chronically-ill children. *American Journal of Orthopsychiatry, 46*, 246–255.

Darling, R. B. (1979). *Families against society: A study of reactions to children with birth defects.* Beverly Hills, CA: Sage.

Farber, B. (1959). Effects of a severely mentally retarded child on family integration. *Monographs of the Society for Research in Child Development, 24* (Whole No. 71).

Farber, B., & Ryckman, D. B. (1965). Effects of a severely mentally retarded child on family relationships. *Mental Retardation Abstracts, 11*, 1–17.

Freud, S. (1936). *Inhibitions, symptoms and anxiety.* London: Hogarth.

Gabel, H., & Kotsch, L. S. (1981). Extended families and young handicapped children. *Topics in Early Childhood Special Education, 1*, 29–35.

Goldberg, S., Marcovitch, S., MacGregor, & Lojkasek, M. (1986). Family responses to developmentally delayed preschoolers: Etiology and the father's role. *American Journal of Mental Deficiency, 90*, 610–617.

Greenfeld, J. (1978). *A place for Noah.* New York: Pocket Books.

Harris, L., and Associates (1975). *The myth and reality of aging in America.* Washington, DC: National Council on Aging.

Holt, K. S. (1958). Home care of severely retarded children. *Pediatrics, 22*, 744–755.

Hornby, G. (1988). *Fathers of handicapped children.* (Unpublished manuscript), University of Hull, England.

Houser, R. A. (1987). *A comparison of stress and coping by fathers of mentally retarded and non-retarded adolescents.* Unpublished doctoral dissertation; University of Pittsburgh.

Kahana, G., & Kahana, E. (1970). Grandparenthood from the perspective of the developing grandchild. *Developmental Psychology, 3*, 98–105.

Lamb, M. E. (1983). Fathers of exceptional children. In M. Seligman (Ed.), *The family with a handicapped child* (pp. 125–146). Philadelphia: Grune & Stratton.

McPhee, N. (1982, June). A very special magic: A grandparents delight. *The Exceptional Parent*, pp. 13–16.

Meyer, D. J., & Vadasy, P. F. (1986). *Grandparent workshops: How to organize workshops for grandparents of children with handicaps.* Seattle: University of Washington Press.

Meyer, D. J., Vadasy, P. F., Fewell, R. R., & Schell, G. C. (1985). *A handbook for the fathers program.* Seattle: University of Washington Press.

Peck, J. R., & Stephens, W. B. (1960). A study of the relationship between the attitudes and behavior of parents and that of their mentally defective child. *American Journal of Mental Deficiency, 64*, 839–844.

Pieper, E. (1976, April). Grandparents can help. *The Exceptional Parent*, pp. 7–9.

Pruett, K. D. (1987). *The nuturing father.* New York: Warner.

Smith, K. (1981). The influence of the male sex role on discussion groups for fathers of exceptional children. *Michigan Personnel and Guidance Journal, 12*, 11–17.

Sonnek, I. M. (1986). Grandparents and the extended family of handicapped children. In R. R. Fewell & P. F. Vadasy (Eds.), *Families of handicapped children* (pp. 99–120). Austin, TX: Pro-Ed.

Spock, B. M. (1946). *The common sense book of baby and child care.* New York: Duell, Sloan, Pearce.

Spock, B. M. (1957). *Baby and child care.* New York: Pocket Books.

Spock, B. M., & Rothenberg, M. B. (1985). *Baby and child care.* New York: E. P. Dutton.

Stehower, J. (1968). The household and family relations of old people. In E. Shames, D. Townsend, D. Wedderbrunn, H. Friis, P. Michoj, & J. Stehower (Eds.), *Old people in three industrial societies* (pp. 177–226). New York: Atherton.

Vadasy, P. F., & Fewell, R. R. (1986). Mothers of deaf-blind children. In R. R. Fewell & P. F. Vadasy (Eds.), *Families of handicapped children* (pp. 121–148). Austin, TX: Pro-Ed.

Vadasy, P. F., Fewell, R. R., Greenberg, M. T., Desmond N. L., & Meyer, D. J. (1986). Follow-up evaluation of the effects of involvement in the fathers program. *Topics in Early Childhood Education, 6*, 16–31.

Vadasy, P. F., Fewell, R. R., & Meyer, D. J. (in press). Grandparents of children with special needs: Insights into their experiences and concerns. *Journal of the Division for Early Childhood Education.*

Vadasy, P. F., Fewell, R. R., Meyer, D. J., & Greenberg, M. T. (1985). Supporting fathers of handicapped young children: Preliminary findings of program effects. *Analysis and Intervention in Developmental Disabilities, 5,* 125–137.

Waisbren, S. E. (1980). Parents' reactions after the birth of a developmentally disabled child. *American Journal of Mental Deficiency, 84,* 345–351.

Wilcoxon, A. S. (1987). Grandparents and grandchildren: An often neglected relationship between significant others. *Journal of Counseling and Development, 65,* 289–290.

Zinsmeister, K. (1985, September 2). Snapshot of a changing America. *Time,* pp. 16–18.

7

Models of Intervention

This chapter explores various approaches to working with families with disabled children. The interventions that are examined are primarily designed to promote healthy family relationships. Although the goal is to promote family harmony and stability, some of the approaches used to achieve this goal are not necessarily family interventions per se. That is, it is possible to employ individual, marital, or group counseling approaches while keeping the family unit in mind. The key for the professional is to maintain a family systems mindset irrespective of the therapeutic modality employed. Family systems theory (Chapter 1) is the view we believe to be most useful in conceptualizing family structure and interaction.

Therapeutic approaches include interventions that are designed to change families. We preface the remainder of this chapter with the important reminder that *not all families need to be changed.* For too long, professionals in the helping professions have had a pathology orientation and assumed that the birth of a disabled child would necessarily result in pathology in a family's functioning. When families neither need nor desire therapeutic intervention, such approaches as counseling may be more intrusive than helpful. On the other hand, some families *do* express a need for help in this area, either directly or indirectly, and professionals must be able to meet that need when it arises. The reader should keep in mind, then, that the following discussion applies in varying degrees to the families he or she will encounter.

This chapter presents an overview of existing therapeutic modalities and provides references for further reading. Some of the strategies discussed require extensive knowledge and training, and it is our assumption that readers already have or are in the process of acquiring requisite training. We begin our discussion by examining the characteristics of effective helpers.

EFFECTIVE HELPERS AND THE
HELPER–FAMILY RELATIONSHIP

The literature informs us that effective helpers have certain qualities, skills, and values. Indeed, as Ross (1964) points out unequivocally, persons who lack certain characteristics should not work with families with disabled children:

> A student may be able to develop these [characteristics] in the course of closely supervised experience but some people lack these qualities in sufficient measure and these should probably not enter a profession whose central task is helping other people. No amount of exhortation can make a rejecting person accepting, a frigid person warm, or a narrow-minded person understanding. Those charged with the selection, education and training of new members of the helping professions will need to keep in mind that the presence or absence of certain personality characteristics make the difference between a truly helpful professional and one who leaves a trace of misery and confusion in the wake of his activities. (pp. 75–76)

Based on their research at the University of Florida, Combs and Avila (1985) found that effective helpers share certain attributes:

1. Knowledge: To be effective, practitioners must be personally committed to acquiring specialized knowledge in their field. Seligman (1979) agrees and states further that professionals who work with families with disabled children should have at least rudimentary knowledge of family dynamics, disability, and how a child's disability may affect family functioning.

2. People: Effective helpers view people as being able rather than unable, worthy rather than unworthy, internally rather than externally motivated, dependable rather than undependable, and helpful rather than hindering.

3. Self-concept: Effective helpers feel personally adequate, identify readily with others, feel trustworthy, wanted, and worthy.

4. Helping purposes: Successful helpers are freeing rather than controlling, deal with larger rather than smaller issues, are more self-revealing and involved with clients, and are process oriented in helping relationships.

5. Approaches to helping: Effective helpers are more oriented to people than things and are more likely to approach clients subjectively or phenomenologically than objectively or factually.

Others (Carkhuff & Berenson, 1967; Egan, 1986; Ivey & Simek-Downing, 1980; Rogers, 1958) consider the following to be important helper characteristics:

1. Positive regard: Helpers should communicate acceptance of clients as worthwhile persons, regardless of who they are or what they say or do.

2. Empathy: Professionals must be able to communicate that they feel and understand the client's concerns from the client's point of view.

3. Concreteness: Professionals should respond accurately, clearly, specifically, and immediately to clients.

4. Warmth: Professionals should show their concern through verbal and nonverbal expression. This concept appears often in the counseling literature but has not been well defined, yet one "knows" when someone is warm—or cold and distant.

Brammer (1979) and Okun (1987) stress that self-awareness is an essential characteristic for the professional helper. An awareness of one's attitudes toward disabled persons, as well as toward families with disabled children, is essential. We have discussed and will discuss further the rather negative attitudes that the general public *and* professionals hold toward disabled persons (see especially Chapters 4 and 9). These negative attitudes from professionals become manifest in behaviors that communicate coldness, distance, abruptness, and rejection. Such behaviors, in turn, can generate or reinforce and deepen feelings of guilt, depression, and low self-esteem in family members. Therefore, professionals need to examine their attitudes carefully so that they do not interfere with their efforts to be helpful to families.

The evidence to date regarding the quality of relationships families experience with professionals is indeed discouraging. Telford and Sawrey (1977) report that parents of disabled children are almost universally dissatisfied with their experiences with professionals. The authors quote a mother who characterized her contacts with professionals as "a masterful combination of dishonesty, condescension, misinformation and bad manners" (p. 143). Some parents are perceived as problems with which professionals need to contend, while others are blamed for causing or at least not preventing their child's disability (Seligman, 1979). Seligman and Seligman (1980) note that parents are often considered a nuisance rather than a resource and are frequently criticized, analyzed, or made to feel responsible for their child's problems. Furthermore, Rubin and Quinn-Curran (1983) report that it is not unusual to hear of parents being called lazy and stupid, demanding, greedy, conniving, or angry and defensive. Holden and Lewine (reported in Bernheim & Lehman, 1985) found in their research that there are high levels of dissatisfaction with mental health services. In their survey of families in five different locales, families reported that professionals increased their feelings of guilt, confusion, and frustration. The net result was that 74% were dissatisfied with the services received, including: lack of information about diagnosis and treatment, vague and evasive responses, professional avoidance of labeling the illness (which increased their confusion), lack of support during critical periods, lack of help in locating community resources, and little or no advice about how to cope with their child's symptoms or problem behaviors.

Bernheim and Lehman (1985) believe that such negative indicators of professional–family relationships should constitute a strong stimulus for professionals to reexamine how they view and treat families with disabled children. Although professionals must be held responsible for much of the tension between families and themselves, Gargiulo (1985) holds that some of the blame falls on family members. He asserts that families sometimes condemn professionals for not recognizing the disability sooner and occasionally accuse the professional of causing the disability. Some parents, Gargiulo believes, inhibit the growth of their relationship with professionals by withdrawing, while other families prematurely judge professionals to be insensitive, offensive, and incapable of understanding their situation.

We agree with Gargiulo (1985) that the fault for poor parent–professional communication in some measure falls to family members, who must learn to assert themselves in order to receive the services they need and to feel that their views are taken into account. For example, parents can learn to be less timid with professionals and to ask them for fuller and more down-to-earth explanations of medical and psychological concepts. Parents have a right to have accurate and full knowledge of their child's condition—its etiology, prognosis, and implications for the family. Parents can exercise their right to be informed by learning how to act more assertively in the presence of professionals. We will address this issue more fully below.

Ross (1964) raises the question of professional responsibility to families. He takes issue with the many professionals who are attempting to help when the reality may be that the very proliferation of specialists complicates rather than clarifies issues. Furthermore, help should be free from petty professional jealousies that may cause one group to attempt to keep another from giving help.

Another source of difficulty is to be found in the anxieties the child's disability may arouse in the professional (Darling, 1979; Ross, 1964; Seligman & Seligman, 1980). Ross believes that professionals may, due to their anxiety, withdraw from certain families and rationalize that "someone else" will talk with the family about their problems. The difficulty is that other professionals may have similar anxieties, so that in the end the family is not helped by anyone.

There is also the tendency to concentrate on specifics and disregard the whole picture: "All too often the physician will concentrate on the medical aspects, the therapist on rehabilitation, and the teacher on education—each carefully avoiding the problem of the family by focusing on the problem of the child" (Ross, 1964, p. 74).

Moreover, parents may have visited numerous professionals but remain poorly informed about the nature and implications of their child's disability. For many families this problem is not due to their resistance to facts but rather to the failure of the professional to inform the family adequately. As noted above, a parent's lack of knowledge about a child's disability may be attributed to the professional's anxiety and withdrawal from the family.

Another reason for the family's lack of information or confusion may be due to the professional's use of jargon, which renders communication relatively worthless. Professionals need to be concrete with their clients or patients and "check out" their communication when they sense that they are not understood. The use of professional jargon does not generate respect; it causes distance and implies aloofness.

The timing of professional interventions is a key barometer of the success of relationships between professionals and families. Professionals need to be sensitive to a family's receptiveness to a particular intervention. For example, parents may not be ready to explore their feelings about their disabled child and what the disability means to them when they are confused about the practical implications of the child's disability and need to know what services are available to help with some immediate problems. Conversely, when parents need to sort out their feelings about their disabled youngster, professionals, threatened by affective disclosures, should not hide behind a laundry list of agencies and services and avoid discussing emotional responses. The timing of an intervention determines whether family members truly hear what is being said; it also affects their level of trust in the professional and their sense of his/her expertise.

While acknowledging that family members can contribute to tension between themselves and professionals, we would argue that professionals must shoulder most of the responsibility and should (1) gain a thorough understanding of family systems and especially the dynamics of families with a disabled child, (2) be expert in effective interpersonal relationship skills, and (3) acquire extensive experience working with families with children who are disabled.

BARRIERS TO EFFECTIVE HELPING

In any type of helping endeavor it is imperative that professionals interpret parents' circumstances from *the family members* point of view. This means that the professional must listen to them carefully and try to experience what they may be feeling. Empathic listeners have an ability to put their own biases and opinions aside as they try to understand what is being said and felt. Family members intuitively know when they are in the presence of an empathic helper because they feel understood and know that the professional respects their point of view and values their input. Many preparation programs help train professionals to develop empathy skills, and the best way to learn them is to be in the presence of a good professional model. A primary obstacle to good communication skills is graduate school education, where students may be exposed to poor role models. As Yalom (1975) observes: "Pipe-smoking therapists often beget pipe-smoking patients. Patients during psychotherapy may sit, walk, talk and even think like their therapists" (p. 17). Likewise, professional educators often discount the social-modeling effects they have on the people they train.

Professionals in many social service occupations are often stressed because of the nature of the demands placed on them. Stressed and burned-out professionals are often so fatigued psychologically and physically that they are hard-pressed to interact comfortably and productively with family members. Developing a solution to this dilemma is not an easy task, but if we wish to help promote healthier parent–professional relationships we must create less stressful job environments for professionals, who typically begin their careers with energy, high goals, and positive expectations and attitudes toward those they serve.

Preoccupation with personal concerns is another barrier to effective helping. Novice professionals often "think ahead," thereby making it difficult to empathize with clients. Also, preoccupation with personal problems is distracting. Since the lives of professionals resemble those of the people they serve, it is not surprising that personal concerns can occasionally interfere with the professional's effectiveness. The problem is not occasional preoccupation but chronic distraction, which can result in communication impasses. When the latter occurs, it helps to talk with a trustworthy colleague, supervisor, or psychotherapist.

Strong feelings about the family member(s) one is working with are a major barrier to effective listening and rapport building. Angry or anxious feelings toward someone one is trying to help generally limit one's ability to be helpful. In regard to physicians, Darling (1979) provides compelling evidence that some medical practitioners view exceptional families with at least some degree of personal discomfort.

It is remarkable how often professionals allow themselves to be distracted by phone calls or interruptions from secretaries and colleagues. Such behavior conveys a lack of concern and respect, as well as inattentiveness, to family members. Families should be given a predetermined period of time all to themselves. Distractions interrupt and are discourteous. We might reflect on how we feel when our conversation with someone is marked by a series of interruptions.

THE FAMILY'S NEED FOR COUNSELING

Max (1985), a mother of a retarded child and a New Zealand freelance writer, says that "No need is more clearly or more frequently expressed when the parents of the retarded gather than the need to talk to, and be counseled by, an informed, accessible, mature and sympathetic person" (p. 252). She goes on to describe the factors that make counseling necessary and valuable:

1. Figures relating to the incidence of maternal postnatal depression in the population at large support the contention that birth is frequently a time of emotional turmoil, even when no handicap is present.
2. Mothers are in a physical state that makes them even more vulnerable. It is rare to find acknowledgement in a text book of the fact that the woman who is attempting to come to terms with a catastrophic situation may well be suffering postpartum pains, painful breasts and perineal damage. The accompanying discharging and leaking may make her feel messy and uncomfortable. In these circumstances, she must deal competently with often ill-at-ease, usually male professionals.
3. Family disintegration can be initiated or worsened by the birth of an intellectually handicapped baby. Informal observations of families with a handicapped child suggests a rate of friction and desertion that deserves close study, with a view to effective intervention.
4. Grandparents can be the staunchest support of parents of the handicapped yet the birth of an intellectually handicapped child can be the cause of a complete breakdown in the relationship between the generations. Since neighbours and other relatives are not seen as a source of either emotional or practical support it makes sense to facilitate adjustment to the new child together with the grandparents, who are themselves often burdened with outdated fear and shame-laden prejudice.
5. Current concepts of care of the intellectually handicapped are predicated firmly on the basis of a normally functioning family, yet professional neglect of family members is nowhere more grossly in evidence than in the case of siblings. (pp. 252–253)

Throughout the book we have indicated the problems families must contend with in the face of disability, although we acknowledge that many families adapt remarkably well. We have discussed how a major event for one family member reverberates throughout the family unit, leading us to emphasize the wisdom of a systems perspective.

The family must come to terms with their destiny—that of frustrated expectations and thwarted life goals. Depending on the nature and severity of the child's disability, his/her capacity to achieve independence may be limited and therefore not allow the parents to live out a "normal" family life cycle.

Family members experience many and mixed feelings, such as love and hate, joy and sorrow, elation and depression. In addition there are guilt and anger and frustration in dealing with a remarkably complex and difficult service delivery system (Rubin & Quinn-Curran, 1983). There are concerns about the future—about a child's educational and vocational endeavors as well as prospects for independence and possibly marriage. Families will need to confront the stigmatizing attitudes of others in professional, educational, social, and public contexts.

For some parents financial burdens may be the major problem. Medication, special equipment, physical therapy, speech therapy, physician visits, and, perhaps, counseling sessions all reflect potential sources of financial drain. Severe financial problems can, in themselves, create family disharmony.

Harris (1983) discusses *accepting the diagnosis* as a problem families face. Seeking second, third, and fourth opinions regarding a child's diagnosis is to be expected and sometimes encouraged. However, when guilt and denial are present there may be an endless round of visits to professionals for a "cure."

Burnout is another problem experienced by families over time when a child's progress may slow down or plateau. The family's hope for a cure or significant improvement may decline as they begin to accept the chronicity of their child's disability. Not only do family members need to work, study, clean, cook, and find time for leisure and pleasure, but they must also attend to the increasing needs of their disabled family member. When these tasks strain the family's resources, behaviors symptomatic of burnout begin to emerge and threaten the family's ability to cope.

Fatigue, according to Harris, is related to burnout and derives from the many tasks parents must assume, such as feeding, toileting, and managing disruptive and destructive behavior. Fatigued and burned-out families need help from professionals, who need to explore the family dynamics that have contributed to this state of affairs. Professionals must also help families obtain needed services, such as respite care, to help relieve stress.

Harris (1983) notes that families need to know *how to find professional services*:

> One source of frequent frustration for parents is the problem of finding professional services for their child. Locating a pediatrician, neurologist,

dentist, ophthalmologist, audiologist, and other specialists who are good at what they do, who understand the special needs of the developmentally disabled child, and who take time to communicate with parents, is exceedingly difficult. (p. 83)

To help parents locate services and professionals familiar with exceptional families, professionals ought to have the names of competent service providers at hand to pass on to family members.

Some family members may be subject to severe *depression*, while others may be occasionally dispirited. The professional can help parents accept the fact that distress is a reasonable response to a difficult situation. For family members who are seriously depressed, however, psychotherapy may be indicated. As noted earlier, professionals need to be able to distinguish serious clinical depression from temporary and mild "blues" and make appropriate referrals when indicated.

Harris (1983) notes that other feelings, such as *guilt* and *anger*, and other problems, such as *marital dysfunction*, need to be dealt with by the professional. In addition, professionals should be alert to problems that may develop in more peripherally involved family members, such as siblings and grandparents.

INDIVIDUAL INTERVENTIONS

Opirhory and Peters Model

Opirhory and Peters (1982), employing a stage model, provide a useful guide to interventions with parents of disabled newborns. Stage theory holds that parents generally follow a fairly predictable series of feelings and actions after a child's diagnosis has been communicated. Opirhory and Peters (1982) believe that these stages or phases are useful general benchmarks for considering appropriate interventions.

During the *denial* stage, professionals should gently provide an honest evaluation of the situation the parents are confronting. They should simply describe the child objectively and indicate the care that is needed. They should not remove the parents' hope or interfere with their coping style unless it is inappropriate or dysfunctional to their family.

When parents reach the *anger* stage, professionals must create an open and permissive atmosphere so that parents can vent their anger and pain. They must be accepting of the parents' criticism, even if it is directed toward them, without personalizing the parents' remarks or defending other professionals or themselves. It is important to keep in mind that projected anger reflects the parents' own anxiety and stress in the face of a situation that will significantly change their lives. They should be mindful, too, that some parents have been treated so atrociously by professionals that their anger and frustration derive from thoroughly objective circumstances.

Opirhory and Peters recommend that professionals discourage parents from dwelling on a review of the pregnancy during the *bargaining* stage. During this phase, parents feel that they can reverse their child's condition by engaging in certain redemptive activities. The authors advise the professional to point out the child's positive characteristics, encourage involvement, and remain optimistic without giving any guarantees about the child's potential progress. It is also essential that while parents continue to establish a warm and loving relationship with their disabled child they nonetheless balance their lives with personally fulfilling goals and activities. Professionals need to be wary of parents who either fill their lives with a variety of outside activities at the expense of their child or are so involved with the child that their lives become severely restricted and they begin to withdraw from others.

The *depression* stage can be characterized by mild or severe mood swings. Again, the professional needs to be able to distinguish between clinical depression and milder forms of dysphoria. Mild, situational, and time-limited depression is common and liable to emerge at various points in the disabled child's development. Parents need to be reassured that what they are experiencing is normal—not criticized for their feelings of depression. Opirhory and Peters believe that one needs to be especially alert to signs of regression to earlier stages, although we do not necessarily view this with alarm. Anger and mild denial, for example, can resurface and should be considered normal unless these feelings become chronic, excessive, and rigidly held.

During the *acceptance* stage, the professional should continue to reinforce the positive aspects of the parent–child relationship. Because a realistic adjustment to the disabled family member is achieved during this stage, it is typically characterized by fulfilling family relationships. Therefore, the need for professional help and support is unlikely to be crucial, although problems may emerge when the disabled child reaches certain developmental milestones.

Laborde and Seligman Model

Laborde and Seligman (1983) propose a model comprised of three somewhat distinct counseling interventions: educative, facilitative, and personal advocacy counseling. *Educative counseling* is appropriate when families need information about their child's disability. This approach is based on the premise that families know little about disability until they are confronted by it in their own child. As Chapter 2 shows, the parents' need for information tends to be stronger than their need for support early in the infancy period. Especially early on, and particularly relevant to health care professionals, educative counseling can be used to inform parents, to lessen their sense of confusion and ambiguity, and to decrease the stress that is partially a result of not knowing where to turn.

In addition to being informed about their child's disability, its etiology and prognosis, family members may need to know about available services, reading materials germane to their situation, and specialized equipment for their child. Family members should know about their legal rights for service or education as well as about parent organizations, self-help groups, and local professionals who can help with problems of a more psychological nature.

Educative counseling is not just for family members of newborns. Concrete information and guidance is needed at all stages of the child's development as the disabling condition stabilizes, worsens, or improves. After the initial hospital stay, professionals such as social workers and rehabilitation counselors are often in a position to help family members gain access to community resources.

Darling and Darling (1982) argue that psychotherapy is not a substitute for practical help when such help is called for. They cite Australian research reporting that the parents studied were "almost desperate" in their plea for help until a training center for the retarded was established in their community. As a consequence of this resource, parents reported being much happier and more relaxed, and their "neurotic symptoms" virtually disappeared.

Ferhold and Solnit (1978) sound a note of caution regarding a guidance-oriented educative approach when they advise that:

> The counselor is more a facilitator of learning and problem solving than a teacher of facts or an instructor in child-rearing effectiveness. The counselor [should] avoid too many specific directions, even when they appear to be helpful in the short run, because they dilute the process of enabling parents and child to be active on their own behalf—the counselor needs to have faith that parents will make sound choices allowing for some mistakes along the way; when the counselor can no longer accept the parents decisions, he should withdraw. (pp. 160–162)

This brings us to the next element in Laborde and Seligman's (1983) model, *personal advocacy counseling*. We have already established that families need guidance in finding relevant information and in locating appropriate services. Furthermore, we concur with Ferhold and Solnit

(1978) that parents should normally be their own case managers. Parents are, after all, the logical choice to serve as chief coordinators and evaluators of service with the *assistance* of a competent professional. To fill this guidance role adequately the professional must become familiar with general referral procedures and must be knowledgeable about how the various local service agencies operate.

The professional acts as a broker of services by assisting the family in formulating a clear idea of which needs they wish to have met and deciding where to receive services. With information at hand, the professional can help family members develop a plan of action for obtaining needed assistance.

The primary goal of personal advocacy counseling is to help parents experience a sense of control over events in their own and their child's lives. Family members, by experiencing this sense of potency, can act with greater confidence and purpose when confronted with various choices or situations. Personal advocacy counseling can help parents work for their family's welfare in a positive and assertive manner. Family members are encouraged to ask questions of their service providers, to question a provider's responses to inquiries, to seek out second opinions, and to request services they believe they need and are entitled to. In short, parents are given the support and "permission" to obtain the professional help they need without guilt or the feeling that they do not have the right to ask questions. Family members are encouraged to seek out professionals who are knowledgeable and candid yet compassionate and to feel confident enough to dismiss professionals who do not meet these requirements.

There are times when the professional may need to be more active than the family members. For example, when the family first learns of the child's condition they are typically in a state of shock and confusion. The family, at this point, may not be in a position to be their own advocates. A professional, or even another parent, may need to be more active in helping parents sort out the sometimes conflicting and confusing information that can come at them in rapid fire.

Facilitative counseling, the third and final component of Laborde and Seligman's model, resembles relationship counseling or psychotherapy, wherein a professional helps a family member accept or change distressing feelings or behaviors in the context of a trusting relationship.

As noted previously, parents experience a plethora of contradictory emotions when they first learn their child is disabled. The professional should acknowledge to the parents that their dreams and plans for their child may be severely shaken. It is essential that the professional accept these distressing feelings and not encourage the family to deny or repress them. The family requires time to overcome their grief, and the most helpful professional behavior is to be accepting and available, yet not intrusive.

When the parents are ready to move on they can be helped to see that they can still, to a large degree, live normal, productive, and comfortable lives. It is important to encourage the necessary parent–child bonding while also encouraging family members to pursue their own interests and aspirations. If some differentiation between parent and child does not occur, then parents may become angry, resentful, and withdrawn or enmeshed.

While it is important to be accepting of feelings, the professional must also encourage parents to seek help for their child as soon as they feel able. In this regard, Pines (1982) reports that when some Down syndrome children receive adequate infant stimulation, receive appropriate medical intervention, and are monitored for imbalances (such as thyroid deficiency), the child's degree of mental retardation can be minimized.

Parents sometimes blame themselves for their child's disability, but they are rarely at fault (fetal alcoholism syndrome and disabilities resulting from physical abuse of the mother during pregnancy are two exceptions). It is important that the professional help parents understand that their child's condition is not their own doing, although merely telling them that they are not at fault may not alleviate their guilt. Holding on to and being disturbed excessively by guilt feelings may signify a deeper emotional problem.

Unable to shed their guilt feelings, some parents begin an endless and unproductive search for the cause of their child's disorder or for a "cure." Parents may base their feelings on perceived misdeeds, or they may focus on behaviors or even "bad" thoughts that occurred during pregnancy. Professionals need to listen and not pass off such ruminations as unimportant.

Parents may also wish to "make up" for supposed past indiscretions by overprotecting their child, holding the child back from activities that can facilitate his/her growth and independence. Professionals need to help parents explore their guilt, understand its negative effect on the family, and, ideally, curb their overprotective behavior. At the very least, the professional needs to understand that as an overprotective bond develops between a parent and child the other parent and other children are generally adversely affected. The boundaries of the parent–disabled child relationship may become so impermeable that other family members feel abandoned and look to other sources for affiliation and gratification.

In terms of rejection, a professional can help parents separate their confused feelings of anger about becoming the parent of a disabled child from their generally positive feelings toward their child. It is helpful if a parent can find appropriate outlets for expressing anger and rejection so that they are not inappropriately directed toward the disabled child, the other children, or the spouse.

Family members may deeply love the disabled child but find one aspect of the child's condition difficult to accept. Also, feelings of rejection, like other emotions, are cyclical—they come and go over time. It is important for professionals to help family members realize that feelings of anger and occasional or limited rejection are normal and that their expression is acceptable.

Laborde and Seligman's (1983) facilitative counseling model requires professionals to help parents cope with their feelings of shame, which involve the expectation of ridicule or criticism from others. As noted in earlier chapters, some families must deal with community and public attitudes and behaviors that are negative. A useful strategy is to help family members locate peer-support groups, which can reduce feelings of isolation and where they can discover how others cope with negative public attitudes. It is particularly important that families of disabled children reduce their contact with professionals who hold negative attitudes.

Parental denial of a child's disability is a frequently cited phenomenon. It is a defense mechanism that operates on an unconscious level to ward off excessive anxiety (Ross, 1964). Some families approach the mere idea of having a disabled child so fearfully that they submerge the reality of their child's disability. These parents fight unconsciously to keep their situation hidden from their own awareness.

Parental denial is one of the more difficult coping mechanisms for the professional to contend with. A reasonable approach would be to accept the parents' view of their child while gently, when appropriate, pointing out where the child may need special help. A general rule is to never force parents to cast aside a defense mechanism that is rigidly held. The abrupt unveiling of what is being kept from conscious awareness can have a devastating effect, deepen denial, and/or cause shopping for a more "acceptable" view. It is not unusual for parents to seek out appropriate interventions for their child while simultaneously denying the disability. Some parents seem to be able to provide for and deeply love their child while holding onto the unrealistic hope that the child will make dramatic improvements. For most parents, the reality of their child's situation becomes clearer over time.

Shopping behavior, usually attributed to feelings of guilt and rejection and manifested through the coping mechanism of denial, must be carefully evaluated. This behavior may indeed be caused by the threat the disability presents to the family, but alternatively it may reflect a realistic appraisal of the situation due to the nature of the disability and/or the quality of professional assistance available.

Family problems can emerge when one parent begins to realize the implications of the child's disability while the other continues firmly to deny it. Such tensions may specifically reflect the parents' differing views of their child, or they may represent a chronically dysfunctional family dynamic. To intervene successfully, the professional needs to know about family interactional patterns and issues of power and control. A child's disability can serve as a handy vehicle for the acting out of dysfunctional family patterns, and the child can be wrongly identified as the cause of family problems.

Facilitative counseling must also attend to concerns that surface—or resurface—as the child approaches various milestones, such as beginning or completing school. The professional should not be alarmed if parents need to cover "old territory" at different times in their child's development. As noted in earlier chapters, key periods that may trigger the family's anxiety include:

1. When parents first learn about or suspect that the child has a disability.
2. At about age 5 or 6, when a decision must be reached regarding the child's education.
3. When the time has arrived for the child to leave school.
4. When the parents become older and possibly unable to care for the child.

As the child grows into adolescence and young adulthood, parents may have a difficult time giving up their child, either to a residential treatment setting or to independent living. For a number of reasons parents may be so invested in their child that they find it exceedingly difficult to let go. Letting go is especially difficult for overprotective or enmeshed parents, who view their son or daughter's growing independence with apprehension. As the child differentiates from the parents and begins to live a more independent life, professionals can remind parents that independence is in the child's best interest and that contact between them and the child will not cease. Furthermore, for parents who are uneasy about this stage of the family's life cycle, some attempt should be made to help them understand why their child's emerging independence is a threat to them.

Professionals must help family members cope with disturbing thoughts and puzzling, unacceptable feelings. Depressive ruminations, such as wishing the child were dead, may occur and need to be expressed and explored. Professionals can only be effective during such emotionally charged moments if they themselves have come to terms with feelings often condemned by society.

Although disabled children differ from their nondisabled counterparts in some ways, they are similar in other ways—a point the professional may wish to mention to family members. By focusing on such similarities rather than on differences, parents can view their child in a more normal fashion. For example, parents of a physically disabled adolescent can note how typical it is for their child to enjoy rock music, show an interest in the opposite sex, display occasional moodiness, and be more secretive.

In concentrating on normal aspects of a disabled child, the professional must be careful not to inadvertently reinforce denial, which means that his/her decision to follow such a course of action must be based on a careful assessment of the family. A denying family will not be aided by a professional who unrealistically concentrates on a child's normative qualities. Dispirited families, who tend to evaluate their circumstances negatively and need to restructure their thinking along more optimistic and hopeful lines, can find such a focus helpful. These latter families also need to explore how their negative outlook serves unspoken family values or rules.

Ross (1964) argues that professionals who work with families with disabled children need to have an appreciation for ambivalence. We may find it difficult to understand the existence of positive and negative emotions at the same time. Instances of ambivalence occur often in working with families. For example, families may want help but may be unable to ask for it; they may request advice but not follow through on it when it is given; they may agree to certain plans but fail to carry them out; and then there are those who tell us one thing but manifest the opposite by their behavior.

A family's ambivalent behavior can indeed be puzzling and even annoying. However, a deeper appreciation of this behavior along with a greater tolerance of it can be developed by understanding the unconscious motivation that lies behind the behavior we see. What family members verbalize may be what they believe on a conscious level, but what they do is often motivated by unconscious needs that become manifest in the ambivalent behavior they display. It is the professional's task, then, to help family members understand their contradictory behavior, which, incidentally, may be as enigmatic to them as it is to the professional.

BEHAVIORAL PARENT TRAINING

Behavioral parent training (BPT) has been used rather extensively (Harris, 1983; Kaiser & Fox, 1986). BPT has specific applications and tends to be used and recommended by professionals with a strong behavioral bent.

For some families the presenting behavioral problems of their children are so severe and disruptive that parent training is a critical intervention. Focusing on the disruptive behavior of mentally retarded children, Kaiser and Fox (1986) report that parents have been trained successfully to modify diverse behavioral problems and to teach such adaptive abilities as chewing and feeding skills, motor imitation, self-help skills, appropriate play behaviors and social interaction with parents, articulation and vocabulary skills, and compliance behavior.

Effective BPT can decrease some of the stress that parents of disabled children experience (Kaiser & Fox, 1986). With this in mind, we believe that it is important for professionals either to be trained in BPT or to be able to make an appropriate referral to someone in the community who specializes in working with disruptive behavior in children. It is beyond the scope of this chapter to elaborate further on the BPT model; however, an excellent resource for professionals who wish to learn more about individual and group models of BPT is Harris's (1983) book, *Families of the Developmentally Disabled: A Guide to Behavioral Intervention.*

These authors state that studies using BPT with mentally retarded children typically report positive findings. However, a major problem with the BPT model is that some families fail to acquire or maintain newly learned skills. Rose (1974) indicates that some parents "never completed contracts but were either changing the responses to be observed or ineffectively implementing unauthorized procedures" (pp. 138–139). Speculations regarding reasons for parental noncompliance include parents' lack of time to do the training, lack of spouse support, limited materials for teaching, and lack of confidence. Another possible reason for parental noncompliance may be severely disruptive life events, such as death, divorce, illness in the family, or unconscious factors. Some parents may not believe that the program is necessary.

We believe that caution must be exercised in asking parents to engage in "homework" or to act as their child's therapist. Consider the situation of parents who must follow the daily prescriptions of the special education teacher, the speech therapist, the hearing specialist, the vision specialist, the physical therapist, and the doctor. Max (1985) notes that

> the pendulum of fashion might be swinging too far, so that that parents' onerous burden of impotence has been replaced by an equally heavy one of great expectations. As one parent said: "You feel that you have to do it all and it is so exhausting. But if you don't do everything they tell you to do, you feel that you're letting down all these highly qualified people who are giving up their good time to help your child." (p. 255)

GROUP FORMATS

Until World War II, when the necessity of treating war casualties over-whelmed available resources, group interventions were considered a lesser form of therapeutic help. Group formats were considered more efficient, in that they could serve more people, but less effective than existing individual therapies. This early view of groups has changed dramatically. Therapeutic groups are still considered efficient, but the central rationale for their use is that, for certain persons and certain problems, they are more effective.

The decision to recommend group or individual counseling needs to be carefully considered by the practitioner. The suggestion that parents consider some type of group should be based on whether:

1. they feel relatively comfortable in a group context;
2. they are basically mature and emotionally stable but their functioning is temporarily impaired (Ross, 1964);
3. they are not overly self-absorbed and monopolistic (Yalom, 1985);
4. they have pronounced yet well-controlled feelings of hostility (Ross, 1964);
5. they are not overly controlling, masochistic, passive–aggressive, or have psychotic tendencies (Ross, 1964);
6. they have a modicum of empathy for others and are open to others' opinions and guidance.

Group formats vary greatly in that they may be open or closed in membership, gender or disability, homogeneous or heterogeneous, small or large, leader or member led, and so forth. Likewise, the group pur-poses differ in that they may be educational or therapeutic (although some would argue that educational groups are also therapeutic), designed to help parents cope immediately after diagnosis or to consider living and working arrangements and problems of their postschool children, or designed to help siblings and extended family members cope.

In terms of purpose, the major distinction is between providing education and information and providing therapy (Seligman & Meyer-son, 1982). Groups that are primarily *educative* focus on providing fami-lies with information about their child's disabling condition as well as training in effective coping and parenting skills. Educationally oriented groups also inform families about their legal rights and benefits, where to obtain needed services, where to purchase and how to operate special equipment, and the like. This model assumes that family problems arise from deficiencies in skills or information and that families function adaptively to meet their own needs when provided with accurate and relevant information. This view further assumes that parents' emotional reactions are not problematic when they have the resources to perform adequately as parents.

With regard to homogeneity, most groups are composed of parents with children who have a particular disorder. As long as the child's condition falls within a recognized diagnostic category—for example, mental retardation—parents may be invited to join. However, some groups may be composed of parents with children who suffer from a subcategory of a major disorder, for example, Down syndrome. Baus, Letson, and Russell (1958) proposed a group model for parents of epileptic children, but excluded parents whose children also had other problems, such as cerebral palsy, blindness, marked mental retardation, severe hearing loss, or diabetes. The group leaders felt that the group discussions would become too complex if such additional conditions were brought up by the parents. Since many disabling conditions are accompanied by other problems, we would discourage group leaders from using such an exclusionary model.

An early group program with parents of physically disabled children used a heterogeneous model by including parents of children with a variety of disorders and a multitude of handicaps (Milman, 1952). The reports by Baus and colleagues (1958) and by Milman (1952) reflect the diversity of approaches available, but we suspect that the most prevalent model falls somewhere in between, with parents of children with a particular primary disorder invited to join, irrespective of the child's other problems.

In terms of a structured group experience, Baus and colleagues' (1958) description of a time-limited, information-oriented group for parents of epileptic children is a useful model and one that continues to be used. The parents attend five weekly meetings lasting from 1 to 1½ hours. A physician attends the first two sessions and discusses the medical aspects of epilepsy. The next two sessions are led by a psychologist, who discusses management and behavioral issues common with epileptic children. The final session is devoted to the family's emotional response to the child. Questions are encouraged throughout.

This basic model can be expanded and made more flexible by inviting other specialists, such as:

1. a physician to explain more fully the medical implications of a child's condition;
2. a physical therapist to discuss exercise and strengthening regimens that may be helpful;
3. a psychologist or other mental health worker to assist with problems of management and also to help parents understand their emotional reactions;

4. an attorney to elaborate on legal aspects, guardianship, and parent rights as well as to help interpret complicated legislation;
5. a local or state politician to discuss community/state policies regarding disabled persons.

The model can be even further expanded to incorporate a series of more therapeutically oriented sessions regarding parental stress, coping behavior, and emotional responses. It may be advantageous to have several open-ended sessions after the more structured program to allow parents to express feelings and to achieve closure.

Support groups can be led by professionals, led by members, or led by members with professional consultation available (Darling & Darling, 1982; Friedlander & Watkins, 1985). The enormous growth of support groups for almost every type of disability has been well documented (Lieberman, in press). Support groups can benefit their members in several ways:

1. the quick identification with others who are experiencing similar problems;
2. the 24-hour availability of group members to assist during critical periods;
3. the development of a network of friends to help reduce isolation;
4. the lack of costly fees.

One of the more prominent current types of support groups are those for siblings of handicapped children. Although evaluations of the effectiveness of these groups have not been a major priority, clinical reports and personal accounts of the effects of such groups have been promising (see Chapter 5 for more on siblings). At the University of Washington a support group model, which has an educational component, has been established for siblings, fathers, and grandparents (see Chapters 5 and 6 for detailed discussions of these groups).

In addition to educationally oriented groups and peer support groups, Seligman and Meyerson (1982) note that another approach is the *therapy model*, which stresses self-exploration and the disclosure of feelings. Such groups can help parents and other family members gain an awareness of attitudes and behaviors that might bear on the disabled family member. In addition to exploring feelings, family members can examine how the family is coping with the disabled member. Furthermore, group members can explore how they are personally being affected now and how their hopes for future may be affected.

Most parent groups that are reported in the literature combine elements of both education and therapy (Seligman & Meyerson, 1982). At face value this model speaks to the reported needs of families, yet very little research is available to support this or any other approach. Support of the integrated model is based on the premises that group formats should be based on the needs of families and that the family's responses to their disabled child are multidetermined. Group goals should be based on a careful assessment of parent needs and on what professionals have to offer. It is probably true that families need knowledge *and* emotional support in order to cope with the stresses that occur in raising a child with a disability. Families need to know the dimensions of their child's disabling condition and the parameters of his/her growth potential. They need to know what medical, educational, and other services are available within their community. Above all, they need understanding and support for both their wish to raise their child and their need to believe that this task is a hopeful, necessary, and worthwhile commitment.

Parent-to-parent models have become rather popular in the United States (Mott, Jenkins, Justice, & Moon, undated) and elsewhere (Hornby & Murray, 1983). In this model a parent assists another parent on an individual basis, but the success of this approach is predicated on careful screening and group-based training.

A program illustrating this model is reported by Mott and colleagues (undated). Project Hope, which is located in North Carolina, postulates that specific environmental factors are critical in the overall development of the disabled child. Project Hope is based on the premise characteristic of more educationally oriented models; that is, that social support plays a significant role in decreasing the amount of stress experienced by families. Other rationales for Project Hope include the notion that parents may learn more from each other than from professionals; the belief that in-depth understanding of raising a disabled child is best understood by other families; the need to help to alleviate feelings of isolation and promote realization that others experience similar problems, frustrations, and successes; and the desire to help parents express anger, grief, exhaustion, expectations, and hope. A final goal of Project Hope is to be available to families at the point of initial diagnosis *and* throughout the child's life. The project's goals are far-reaching and actually incorporate both educational and therapeutic elements.

Volunteer parents are carefully screened and are selected to participate if they have:

1. positive valuing and acceptance of their disabled child;
2. an interest in and the time to devote to parent-to-parent contacts;
3. a willingness to participate in all parent training sessions;
4. an open mind to other parents' values and feelings that differ from their own;

5. an awareness of family reactions to having a handicapped child;
6. a willingness to help parents whose child has a different disability from their own.

The group leaders who train Project Hope parents must:

1. be familiar with the nature of specific disabilities and their potential impact on the family;
2. have a good working knowledge about services and resources;
3. be able to model empathy skills (this was regarded as most important).

The two days of training for the parents consists of:

1. sensitizing them to the needs of parents whose children have different disabling conditions than their own children;
2. providing them with a basic framework from which to communicate with others in an empathic manner;
3. providing them specific information regarding a variety of conditions and available resource services.

In a personal communication, Hornby, who pioneered a parent-to-parent program in New Zealand and is presently developing similar programs in Great Britain, stated that parents who are accepted in the New Zealand program are closely monitored to be sure that they are performing without major problems. This scrutiny is based on the belief that parents are often under enough stress without the additional burden of coping with another parent also under stress. He notes that on occasion a parent who was initially accepted into the program is terminated due to inadequate interpersonal skills or unresolved emotional problems. Hornby adds that the trained parents come together periodically for additional training and to discuss dilemmas they encounter in their contact with other parents.

As noted in Chapter 1, family and ecological models have properly taken their place as useful conceptual frameworks. Deriving from this, there has emerged a rather singular concern about the welfare of siblings (see Chapter 5). In families in which a disabled child resides, nondisabled siblings sometimes do not receive the parenting accorded to their seemingly more needy disabled brother/sister. As indicated in Chapter 5, some siblings fare well, while others do not. Some group models for siblings have emerged out of the recognition that some siblings cope poorly, while other groups for young siblings have evolved to help prevent future problems.

Groups for siblings have similar goals to groups that presently exist for parents. Not only do siblings need to have a thorough understanding of their brother/sister's condition, its etiology and prognosis, but they also need to know that there are others who have disabled siblings and that they struggle with similar issues. In their groups, siblings explore feelings of love and hate, talk about their fear of developing the same condition, and discuss their concerns about how to handle awkward social situations and how to cope with major anxieties about what the future holds for them. Siblings need a safe place to discuss their feelings of guilt and anger, how they feel their unique situation has affected family life, and how being a sibling of a disabled brother/sister is influencing their choice of a career.

In developing support groups for siblings one should carefully consider:

1. Whether the group will be heterogeneous or homogeneous regarding age: This issue requires careful thought in that children and adolescents vary considerably over 2–3 year spans.

2. Whether the group will be heterogeneous or homogeneous in regard to the type or severity of sibling disability: There is probably little to lose and much to gain from more heterogeneous groups.

3. What activities will reflect the group's goals and purposes: Some view sibling groups as primarily informational and recreational, while others stress feelings and adjustment. There is probably considerable value in *all* of these activities.

4. Practical issues, such as the length of each session (keeping in mind the children's ages and the activities planned) and the long-term duration of the group: Some groups span a relatively brief period of time, with each session well planned, while others meet for longer overall periods with more open-ended sessions.

5. Whether a follow-up meeting is deemed necessary: Sibling groups may stir up feelings beyond the group's life, and it may be beneficial to have one or two follow-up meetings to help siblings achieve closure.

6. Information content: What information would siblings find useful?

7. Leadership: Leaders should be chosen who have had some experience with disabilities and are knowledgeable about both siblings of the disabled and group process.

8. Discussion materials: One may wish to have sibs read certain appropriate materials for discussion purposes. Caution needs to exercised so that books and articles are age appropriate.

A sibling group model developed by Reynolds and Zellmer (1985) is an example of a structure, time-limited group experience. The group was co-led by a social worker and preschool teacher. Six siblings, aged 7–14, participated in the 1-hour per week, six-session experience.

Session I: Participants brought family pictures to the first session to facilitate discussions about themselves and their families.

Session II: "What is a handicap?" was the theme of the second meeting. Siblings explored how every person has some kind of handicap. Medical problems of their handicapped brothers and sisters were also discussed.

Session III: Group members participated in simulated disabilities so that they could empathize with their disabled siblings.

Session IV: This session focused on what it is like to have a handicapped brother or sister. Books and articles authored by siblings can be used to stimulate discussion.

Session V: Siblings discussed ways to deal with their feelings. The notion that all feelings have value and are not necessarily bad was stressed. Role playing of key problematic situations was employed.

Session VI: This wrap-up session was used to discuss unfinished business. The meeting was held in a relaxed social setting with food available.

DYSFUNCTIONAL DYNAMICS

Dysfunctional, tension-filled families are in a poor position to cope with a disabled family member. Although there have been reports that some families have become more cohesive as a result of a child's disability, these families probably had a minimum of existing pathology. Troubled families tend to become more dysfunctional in the face of crises and chronic stressors, while strong ones adapt, cope, and grow in the wake of crisis and stress.

Johnson (in Turk & Kerns, 1985) writes about a family dynamic that may be especially salient in families with a chronically ill child:

> Because chronically ill children are physically vulnerable, the child's illness may encourage overinvolvement by one parent. This parent, usually the mother, then neglects other family members. Her neglect places strain on the marital relationship and also results in feelings of hostility toward the patient by siblings. However, these feelings of resentment are not expressed openly because the patient is not be "upset." The parents' focus on the child's symptoms permit them to avoid their own marital conflicts and consequently the patient's symptoms are reinforced. (p. 239)

Responding to the scenario described above requires a sensitivity to both subtle and obvious family dynamics—hence the need to be well schooled in family systems theory, family dynamics, and family interventions. Below are other potential dysfunctional family reactions:

1. A disabled child can receive excessive attention as the most needy family member. Other family members, such as nondisabled siblings, may experience the resultant lack of attention to themselves as a lack of concern and as a result may feel angry toward the parents and the privileged (disabled) sib. They may also feel resentful and unloved. They may act out their anger in an effort to regain some of the attention they long for. Unfortunately, the method nondisabled children use to receive attention may further alienate them from family members, thus increasing the likelihood of additional disruptive behavior.

2. Grandparents who cannot accept their disabled grandchild's disability add considerably to the parents' burdens. The parents are torn by their natural inclination to accept and love their child and the press they feel from grandparents to shun (and perhaps institutionalize) him/her. This scenario creates tension within both parents (intrapsychic), between them, and between the parents and their own parents and/or in-laws. It is easy to see how parents can be torn by their pain, since they need to make difficult choices regarding whom they wish to align themselves with. Ideally, an astute therapist can help the family resolve this crisis without excessive damage.

3. Family members who experience themselves as significantly stigmatized by their community are in danger of becoming isolated, bitter, and withdrawn. Although the danger comes from outside (of the family), the perception of a hostile community can create major tensions within the family. A major risk factor exists if the family members begin to internalize the perceived negative community evaluations and conclude that they are unworthy.

4. Poor relationships with professionals and the absence of important social services can have devastating effects within the family structure. Families feel unsupported and overburdened, which in turn creates tension and stress in the family.

5. As noted earlier, the birth of a disabled child to a troubled family can exacerbate existing family tension. Fragile families cannot tolerate additional pressures, and the presence of a disabled child is not only an additional burden of some magnitude but also a chronic one.

6. Perhaps the most frequently described situation is the one in which parents, expecting a healthy baby, discover that their newborn is disabled. The potential immediate effects are considerable: shock and the realization that one must make major changes in one's life, one's expectations, and the like.

Drotar, Crawford, and Bush (1984) acknowledge that the presence of a chronic illness has a profound effect on family life. Until recently, professionals have attended to the ill child rather than to the family unit. The focus on children has advanced our knowledge of how children with a chronic affliction cope, but the neglect of the family in its interaction with the disabled child has produced some undesirable consequences. For example, a narrow, child-centered focus fails to recognize the family as a powerful context for socialization and support of the ill child. The nature and quality of intrafamiliar coping is important to assess because children learn their methods of adaptation from their parents. What these children learn from their parents affects their ability to negotiate the stressful demands of their disability. Being knowledgeable about the family's dynamics helps us understand how the family's culture promotes both healthy and unhealthy responses to stress. Furthermore, an analysis of the family can help determine how the family facilitates illness and disability behaviors (e.g., dependency) or how it encourages adaptation and healthy independence.

In the case of physical disabilites, day-to-day treatment regimens require parents to consider their respective contributions to the care of their child (Drotar et al., 1984). Parental roles and responsibilities must be negotiated, and there is a compelling need to reconcile career versus family demands. Furthermore, parental involvement in the physical treatment of their children can violate customary psychological boundaries between parent and child.

Chronic childhood illnesses can intersect with family and individual developmental issues. A disabled child can be a considerable burden to a newly married couple who are trying to establish a family identity. Developmental transitions of the child and of family members can create tension as the family is confronted by changes. For example, the decision on the part of a disabled adolescent to live in a college dormitory can be disturbing to a close-knit, overprotective family. Other developmental milestones, such as when a disabled child begins school or reaches adolescence, may create family tension.

Drotar and colleagues (1984) note that parents may have difficulty maintaining appropriate boundaries concerning their children's privacy and that they can find it difficult to support each other, especially in the area of how best to manage a child with a chronic illness. In general, according to Drotar and colleagues, although a child's chronic illness can cause family strain, it is not necessarily the cause of marital dysfunction. In this regard, Venter (1980, reported in Drotar et al., 1984) suggests that the parents' ability to construct meaning from the child's chronic illness may help the family's ability to cope.

Despite the many publications about disabled children and their families, there have been few attempts to describe family intervention models. Bailey and colleagues (1986) have, however, proposed a model, referred to as family-focused intervention. This model involves assessing family needs, planning goals, providing services for families, and evaluating outcomes. The intervention rests on the assumption that services for families must be individualized. Another key assumption of the family-focused intervention is that although the disabled child is an essential concern, the family is also viewed as a target client. The interested reader can consult Bailey and colleagues (1986) for a detailed discussion of this comprehensive model of family intervention.

Drotar and colleagues (1984) also focus on the family as the client. These authors assert that in working with chronically physically ill children, families should be involved immediately after the child's diagnosis is known. They embrace a structural family systems model, which focuses on observable patterns through which family members relate to one another to carry out important roles and functions.

Another essential concept is the family's subsystems, such as the parent and sibling subsystem (see Chapter 1 for a fuller discussion of this concept). Attention to subsystems allows the professional to evaluate and intervene in the smaller unit within the family that is most dysfunctional, although one cannot lose sight of how the subsystem (e.g., a parent and the disabled child) can influence the whole family. As already noted, the concept of *boundary* is especially relevant for those who work with chronically ill children and their families. The concepts of boundaries and subsystems go hand-in-hand, since families need to negotiate appropriate space between subsystems.

One of the chief contributors to dysfunctional families is the consistent violation of boundaries by the intrusion of family members into functions that are the domains of other family members. An example of this phenomenon is an overprotective, controlling mother's thwarting of the father's involvement with his disabled son, thereby violating his parent role. Another illustration is the parents' violation of the sibling subsystem when they interfere with the siblings' methods of solving conflicts among themselves.

The professional's contact with a family should begin at the point of the child's diagnosis (Bailey et al., 1986; Drotar et al., 1984). These initial contacts often may give unintended yet powerful messages to families. For example, if the professional's initial contact is with the mother only, the family may interpret this as an indication that she should be involved in subsequent contacts. It may further be interpreted to mean that the mother should be the primary caregiver, rather than that caregiving should be shared. These early interactions between professional staff and the mother can isolate the father and other children from the mother–disabled child dyad. A more adaptive model is to involve as many family members as possible, especially at the point of initial diagnosis.

The inclusion of family members in educational sessions enables them to be supportive of each other and may bring out family strengths that would not otherwise be known (Drotar et al., 1984). Drotar and colleagues mention that phone contacts with families of chronically ill children are important, especially after the diagnostic phase, because family members may have to carry out unfamiliar tasks outside of the protective environment of the hospital. Phone contacts can be supportive of families as well as educational.

Siblings can be the source of considerable support to a disabled brother/sister. However, it is difficult for them to be supportive and to feel a part of the family if they are not included in what the parents are experiencing and if they are not informed about their ill sibling's disability or involved, to some extent, in his/her care. Sibling involvement can be beneficial to the family and can help the sibling feel useful, helpful, and a part of the family that is presently coping with a crisis. However, as noted earlier, sibling involvement can be a double-edged sword.

An important element of family-centered care is the family's involvement in decision making. Especially where a disabled child is involved and where there may be numerous decisions to be made, all salient family members (and this may include grandparents) should be allowed to voice an opinion, so that certain members don't take over while others feel left out.

Resnick, Reiss, Eyler, and Schauble (1988) describe a family-oriented multidisciplinary program in the School of Medicine at the University of Florida. This family-focused approach was designed to prevent developmental delay in premature infants and infants of low birth weight. Professionals from several disciplines are involved with the at-risk infant and the family immediately after diagnosis. Supportive counseling is offered during the initial crisis. Also, while the baby is in intensive care, staff teach such skills to family members as coping with stressful emotions, communication skills, crisis management techniques, and so forth. Instruction in developmental activities is provided to the family as well, so that they can be involved in the care and development of the child.

Staff members are involved with the family during the infant's hospital stay and help prepare them for the transition to the home environment. A pediatric nurse visits the family to help prepare them for the infant's homecoming. Also, twice a month staff from the Early Childhood Education Program at the hospital visit the child's home to help family members learn appropriate interaction activities and to teach other activities and exercises from a detailed curriculum. This service continues until the child is 3 years old or is eligible for nursery school.

A particularly innovative aspect of the program reported by Resnick and colleagues is the attention paid to the professional staff. Professionals often experience their own grief, guilt, and vulnerability (similar to parents) when an infant fails to thrive, but they tend to suppress their feelings so that they can continue to provide competent care to the infant and the family. Over time, however, such suppressed feelings may lead to personal distress, withdrawal, and depression. As a result, group meetings are scheduled to help the professional staff air their feelings and concerns. The meetings provide an important safety valve for dealing with personal stress and other volatile issues.

The aspect of professional burnout may need to be addressed more seriously in settings where providing services to disabled children and their families is stressful. In Chapter 9 we discuss the adversarial relationship that sometimes exists between families and professionals. Chronic stress and burnout certainly contribute to strained relationships. It is conceivable that in some encounters family members are experiencing stress as they attempt to cope with their situation, while at the same time professionals may be anxious and stressed because of their demanding work with families and their stressful work environments. This potentially explosive situation needs to be acknowledged and addressed.

A family-oriented approach can rectify the counterproductive view that the disabled child should be the sole focus of concern. When the family is considered the client, one must necessarily keep in mind that families differ in terms of culture, ethnicity, and lifestyle. In addition, as structural changes in family life occur over the years, professionals must be cognizant of the special needs of divorced and reconstituted families. And finally, one must keep in mind that some disabled children live in fragmented and highly chaotic situations that do not provide a nurturing environment. In working with families, all of these considerations must be kept in mind.

Finally, one cannot assume that professionals have a right to intervene in families simply because those families have a disabled child. One parent has written:

> No one ever seemed to examine professionals' reactions . . . *parents* are turned into patients and are endlessly analyzed, scrutinized, and finally packaged into neat stages as if they were one-celled animals going through mitosis. . . . Although parents and people with disabilities do have obligations and responsibilities, they must not be victimized by their status. (Pieper in Darling & Darling, 1982, p. viii)

Parents must be active participants in determining what kinds of help they need and how much help is needed. When families agree that therapeutic intervention would be beneficial, professionals trained in a family systems perspective can be tremendously helpful to them.

REFERENCES

Bailey, D. B., Simeonsson, R. J., Winton, P. J., Huntington, G. S., Comfort, M., Isbell, P., O'Donnell, K. J., & Helm, J. M. (1986). Family-focused intervention: A functional model for planning, implementing, and evaluating individualized family services in early intervention. *Journal of the Division of Early Childhood, 10,* 156–171.

Baus, G. J., Letson, L., & Russell, E. (1958). Group sessions for parents of children with epilepsy. *Journal of Pediatrics, 52,* 270–273.

Bernheim, K. F., & Lehman, A. (1985). *Working with families of the mentally ill.* New York: Norton.

Brammer, L. (1979). *The helping relationship* (2nd ed.). Englewood Cliffs, NJ: Prentice-Hall.

Carkhuff, R. R., & Berenson, B. G. (1967). *Beyond counseling and therapy.* New York: Holt, Rinehart & Winston.

Combs, A. W., & Avila, D. L. (1985). *Helping relationships: Basic concepts for the helping professions* (3rd ed.). Boston: Allyn & Bacon.

Darling, R. B. (1979). *Families against society: A study of reactions to children with birth defects.* Beverly Hills, CA: Sage.

Darling, R. B., & Darling, J. (1982). *Children who are different: Meeting the challenge of birth defects in society.* St. Louis: Mosby.

Drotar, D., Crawford, P., & Bush, M. (1984). The family context of childhood chronic illness. In M. G. Eisenberg, L. C. Sutkin, & M. A. Jansen (Eds.), *Chronic illness and disability through the life span* (pp. 103–129). New York: Springer.

Egan, G. (1986). *The skilled helper* (3rd ed.). Monterey, CA: Brooks/Cole.

Ferhold, J. B., & Solnit, A. (1978). Counseling parents of mentally retarded and learning disordered children. In E. Arnold (Ed.), *Helping parents help their children* (pp. 157–163). New York: Brunner/Maze.

Friedlander, S. R., & Watkins, C. E. (1985). Therapeutic aspects of support groups for parents of the mentally retarded. *International Journal of Group Psychotherapy, 35,* 65–78.

Gargiulo, R. M. (1985). *Working with parents of exceptional children.* Boston: Houghton Mifflin.

Harris, S. L. (1983). *Families of the developmentally disabled: A guide to behavioral intervention.* New York: Pergamon.

Hornby, G., & Murray, R. (1983). Group programmes for parents of children with various handicaps. *Child Care Health and Development, 9,* 185–198.

Ivey, A. E., & Simek-Downing, B. (1980). *Counseling and psychotherapy: Theories and practice.* Englewood Cliffs, NJ: Prentice-Hall.

Kaiser, A. P., & Fox, J. J. (1986). Behavioral parent training research. In J. J. Gallagher & P. M. Vietze (Eds.), *Families of handicapped persons* (pp. 219–235). Baltimore: Brooks.

Laborde, P. R., & Seligman, M. (1983). Individual counseling with parents of handicapped children: Rationale and strategies. In M. Seligman (Ed.), *The family with a handicapped child* (pp. 261–284).

Lieberman, M. (in press). Self help groups. In M. Seligman & L. Marshak (Eds.), *Group psychotherapy: A guide to interventions with special populations.* San Antonio, TX: Psychological Corporation.

Max, L. (1985). Parents' view of provisions, services, and research. In N. N. Singh & K. M. Wilton (Eds.), *Mental retardation in New Zealand* (pp. 250–262). Christchurch, New Zealand: Whitoculls.

Meyerson, R. C. (1983). Family and parent group therapy. In M. Seligman (Ed.), *The family with a handicapped child* (pp. 285–305). Philadelphia: Grune & Stratton.

Milman, D. H. (1952). Group therapy with parents: An approach to the rehabilitation of physically disabled children. *Journal of Pediatrics, 41,* 113–116.

Mott, D. W., Jenkins, V. L., Justice, E. F., & Moon, R. M. (undated). *Project Hope.* Family, Infant and Preschool Program, Western Carolina Center, Morganton, NC.

Okun, B. F. (1987). *Effective helping* (3rd ed.). Monterey, CA: Brooks/Cole.

Opirhory, G., & Peters, G. A. (1982). Counseling intervention strategies for families with the less than perfect newborn. *Personnel and Guidance Journal, 60,* 451–455.

Pines, M. (1982). Infant-stim: It's changing the lives of handicapped kids. *Psychology Today, 16,* 48–53.

Resnick, M. D., Reiss, J., Eyler, F. D., & Schauble, P. (1988). Childrens developmental services: A multidisciplinary program of psychological and educational services for neonatal internal care. *Journal of Counseling and Development, 66,* 279–282.

Reynolds, T., & Zellmer, D. D. (1985). Group for siblings of preschool age children with handicaps. *Sibling Information Network Newsletter, 4,* 2.

Rogers, C. R. (1957). The necessary and sufficient conditions of therapeutic personality change. *Journal of Consulting Psychology, 21,* 95–103.

Rogers, C. R. (1958). The characteristics of a helping relationship. *Personnel and Guidance Journal, 37,* 6–16.

Rose, S. (1974). Training parents in groups as behavior modifiers of their mentally retarded children. *Journal of Behavior Therapy and Experimental Psychiatry, 5,* 135–140.

Ross, A. O. (1964). *The exceptional child in the family.* New York: Grune & Stratton.

Rubin, S., & Quinn-Curran, N. (1983). Lost, then found: Parent's journey through the community service maze. In M. Seligman (Ed.), *The family with a handicapped child* (pp. 63–94). Philadelphia: Grune & Stratton.

Seligman, M. (1979). *Strategies for helping parents of exceptional children.* New York: Free Press

Seligman, M., & Meyerson, R. (1982). Group approaches for parents of exceptional children. In M. Seligman (Ed.), *Group psychotherapy and counseling with special populations* (pp. 99–116). Baltimore: University Park Press.

Seligman, M., & Seligman, P. A. (1980). The professional's dilemma: Learning to work with parents. *The Exceptional Parent, 10,* 511–513.

Telford, C. W., & Sawrey, J. M. (1977). *The exceptional individual* (3rd ed.). Englewood Cliffs, NJ: Prentice-Hall.

Turk, D. C., & Kerns, R. D. (1985). *Health, illness, and families.* New York: Wiley.

Venter, M. (1980). *Chronic childhood illness/disability and familial coping.* Unpublished doctoral dissertation, University of Minnesota, Minneapolis.

Yalom, I. (1975). *The theory and practice of group psychotherapy* (2nd ed.). New York: Basic Books.

8

Cultural Reactions to Childhood Disability and Subcultural Variation

The birth of a child with a disability has different meanings in various societies throughout the world. Even within a single complex society, this event can have a variety of meanings that are shaped by subcultural values and beliefs. In this chapter, we briefly review some of the cross-cultural diversity in reactions to childhood disability and look more closely at the variety of meanings that are attached to disability in American society.

CROSS-CULTURAL DIVERSITY

Values attached to disability have varied both geographically and historically. In ancient Sparta, malformed babies were thrown over a precipice; yet in some societies the disabled are believed to have supernatural powers and are held in high esteem. Safilios-Rothschild (1970) suggests that prejudice toward the disabled varies by (1) level of development and rate of unemployment, (2) beliefs about the role of government in alleviating social problems, (3) beliefs about individual "responsibility" (sin) for disability, (4) cultural values attached to different physical conditions, (5) disability-connected factors, including visibility, contagiousness, part of body affected, physical versus mental nature of disability, and severity of functional impairment, (6) effectiveness of public-relations efforts, and (7) importance of activities that carry a high risk of disability—for example, war. Chesler (1965) suggests that the higher the stage of a society's industrialization and socioeconomic development, the greater the tendency to value high intelligence and achievement. The most highly industrialized societies generally have little tolerance for deviance from behavioral norms.

A sampling of variant reactions to disability in different cultures throughout the world illustrates the role of cultural values in shaping attitudes. Obesity in women is greatly admired in most African tribes yet stigmatized in the American middle class (Chesler, 1965). Among Middle Eastern Muslims, the term *saint* is applied to the mentally retarded, and they are given benevolent and protective treatment (Edgerton, 1970). "Among the Wogeo, a New Guinea tribe, children with obvious deformities are buried alive at birth, but children crippled in later life are looked after with loving care. . . . Among the Palaung, an Eastern clan, 'it is lucky to have extra fingers or toes, and extremely lucky to be born with a hare-lip.'" (Wright, 1983). DeCaro, Dowaliby, and Maruggi (1983) found no difference between English and Italian samples in career expectations for deaf children.

Dybwad (1970) has argued that level of technological development is insufficient to explain varying values toward mental retardation. He notes that infanticide of the retarded exists in both primitive and industrialized societies, as does a belief in the divinity of the retarded. Positive attitudes toward the retarded can be found both in the primitive Truk Islands and in modern Denmark. He quotes an Indonesian report that could as easily have been written about a Western country: "the trainable child presents its problem. The child is mostly hidden. The parents are twisted by the conflict of guilt and shame" (p. 563).

Groce (1987) has suggested that disability issues in developing countries are different from those in the Western world. She writes:

> High tech, hospital-based, rehabilitative approaches to care, urban-based educational facilities, and even support groups, do little to reach the majority of the Developing World's disabled people, the vast majority of whom are poor and an estimated 80% of whom live in rural areas. (p. 2)

Many of the disabilities found in these areas are preventable, and those that are not worsen because of a lack of early intervention and rehabilitative services. The difficulties faced by families as a result of a lack of resources, which have been noted throughout this book, are likely to be grossly magnified in the developing world.

HISTORICAL CONTEXT

Newman (1987) has suggested that attitudes and social policies with respect to disabled persons have resulted from historical processes. He argues that these processes have been guided by philosophies of utilitarianism, humanitarianism, and human rights. These philosophies have been a part of Western culture since primitive times and continue to shape attitudes and policy today.

Lazerson (1975) writes that the 19th century saw a shift in American society from home care of the disabled child to institutionalization. He attributes this shift to the fears early and mid-nineteenth century Americans had about social disorder. The creation of institutions paralleled the influx of large numbers of immigrants into the United States. As families became more transient, institutions outside of the family began to assume certain welfare functions. Concurrently, any deviance from social norms, including disability, came to be defined as a social problem, not merely a family problem.

A common justification for residential care suggested that institutional services were better than those available in the community. A 1914 study (reported in Sollenberger, 1974) illustrates this thinking:

> We have no hesitancy in advocating the creation of a state hospital for crippled children in every state of the union. In no other way can the multitudes of crippled children outside of the large cities be reached. . . .
> That the family home is the best place for well children is now generally recognized. But crippled children are conceded to be a special class, requiring in many cases surgical operations and in many cases very close physical supervision for months, often years. . . . Some surgeons insist that parents cannot be trusted to adjust a child's brace or even to bring him to the dispensary at the time ordered by the doctor. (pp. 8, 22)

Lazerson attributes the shift away from institutions that has taken place in the 20th century to the special-education movement, which places the responsibility for educating children with disabilities in community schools. In addition, inhumane conditions were found to exist in some large institutions. The success of some early efforts to provide family-based services to children led to the creation of more such programs. The success of community-based early intervention programs in particular began to be reported widely in the literature in the 1960s, resulting in the large-scale growth of these programs throughout the country. The availability of community resources, coupled with the spread of the ideology of normalization, has once again made the family the locus of care for disabled children in America today.

MODERN AMERICAN SOCIETY

As noted in earlier chapters, the most pervasive attitude toward disability in modern American society is stigma. As Goffman (1963) and others have written, individuals with disabilities have commonly been discredited and relegated to a morally inferior status in American society. Stereotypes are also prevalent. Gottlieb (1975) has noted, for example, that most people think of mentally retarded persons as organically different, "Mongoloid"-looking, and physically handicapped or mentally ill. Safilios-Rothschild (1970) suggests that the disabled are a minority group in American society and share the following characteristics with other minority groups:

1. They are relegated to a separate place in society (encouraged to interact with their "own kind").
2. They are considered by the majority to be inferior.
3. Their segregation is rationalized as being "better for them."
4. They are evaluated on the basis of their categorical membership rather than their individual characteristics.

English (1971) reports the existence of such negative attitudes toward the physically disabled in over half of the able-bodied population, although, as the rest of this chapter will show, variations exist according to such subcultural factors as age, sex, and socioeconomic status. Variations also exist according to the nature of the disability, with the mentally disabled tending to be more stigmatized than the physically disabled.

Although stigma continues to shape much of the interaction between the disabled and nondisabled in American society, attitudes may be slowly changing. The disability-rights movement has had an impact in reducing some stereotypic thinking, and legislation such as the Education for All Handicapped Children Act has placed individuals with disabilities in the societal mainstream. In the remainder of this chapter, we look at variations in attitude toward childhood disability that exist within this larger, still negative, but evolving framework of society as a whole.

As we have just indicated, attitudes toward disabled children vary considerably from one culture to another. In a pluralistic society, various groups within a culture may also hold divergent views of these children. Although sharing some of the aspects of the culture of the larger society, these subcultures also have their own beliefs, values, attitudes, and norms, which are learned through interaction among their members. Most of the literature on families with disabled children has ignored subcultural variation. Theories of stages of parental adaptation, for example, seem to imply that all parents pass through similar stages regardless of socioeconomic status, race, or ethnicity. In the following pages, we examine the idea that families' views are in fact shaped by the segment of society within which they live.

Societies are stratified along a number of different dimensions, which are not mutually exclusive. Probably the most important dimension is socioeconomic status (SES), or social class. Although SES has a number of components, the most important are occupation, education, and income. Socioeconomic levels have been grouped in various ways, but a five-class system has been commonly used (see, e.g., Hollingshead & Redlich, 1958). In addition to socioeconomic stratification, subcultural groups also form along racial and ethnic lines. Religious and regional variation also exist. Members of these groups are more likely to interact with others like themselves than with members of other groups. Attitudes and behavior are thus shaped by the subculture.

We explore the relationship between subculture and families with disabled children for four major subcultural categories: (1) social class (2) race/ethnicity, (3) religion, and (4) region. We also consider the interactional difficulties that occur when professionals and the families they serve have different subcultural backgrounds.

THE BASIS FOR SUBCULTURAL VARIABILITY

Some subcultural differences appear to be innate. Freedman (1981) notes that even as young infants Caucasian and Chinese babies respond differently to stimuli. Differences have also been found between Navajo and Caucasian newborns. Mother–child interaction also varies among these groups, with Caucasian mothers vocalizing more to their infants than the others. Although parent vocalizations are certainly culturally conditioned, they may also be increased or inhibited through interaction with a naturally active or quiet baby.

A disabled infant who was less responsive than most might thus be less alarming to an Oriental or Native American mother whose experience had been with relatively quiet infants. Conversely, a disability resulting in an increased irritability or activity level might be more difficult for such a mother.

Responses to illness and disability are also subculturally patterned through experience and learning. Kleinman, Eisenberg, and Good (1978) and others have noted the difference between illness and disease. Disease is a physiological condition, whereas illness refers to the patient's perception of disease. Illness is a product of social learning, which determines meanings, expectations, values, treatment-seeking behavior, experience of symptoms, and other characteristics that we associate with disease.

As we have said, disability, like illness, is viewed in many different ways by different cultures throughout the world. Subcultural learning can be equally powerful in shaping views toward disability within a society. Richardson, Goodman, Hastorf, and Dornbusch (1961, 1963), for example, found that in American society, children learn at an early age to devalue disability and show the same preferential pattern for various types of disabilities as adults. However, an Italian subgroup ranked facial disfigurement less negatively than the general sample, and a Jewish subgroup ranked both facial disfigurement and obesity less negatively than the general sample.

Chigier and Chigier (1968) replicated the Richardson study in Israel and found that socioeconomic status was a significant factor in determining attitudes. Children of low SES tended to rank cosmetic disability less negatively than physical disability, and children of high SES ranked physical disability less negatively than cosmetic disability. The authors suggest that physical prowess is generally highly valued in lower-class communities and that middle-class children are more likely to be socialized to value appearance. Middle-class children probably also learn to value education and mental ability more highly than physical skill.

Another Israeli study (Shurka & Florian, 1983) looked at parental perceptions of their disabled children. The authors note that earlier studies had shown that Israeli families of Oriental origin had significantly more negative attitudes toward disabled family members than those of European origin. In this study, Arab parents perceived their disabled young adult children as needing more help, and Jewish parents perceived their children as more independent and capable of work. This finding is attributed to differences between the Arab and Jewish family systems. The Arab system is described as encouraging dependence on the parents and extended family.

In American culture, too, subcultural socialization shapes family reactions to disability. Marion (1980) has noted that minority-group parents are often not nearly as overwhelmed by the birth of a disabled child as are parents in the cultural mainstream. Feelings of protection and acceptance of the disabled child may be more common in these groups than the shock, disbelief, guilt, and depression that have been attributed to mainstream parents by many writers.

THE INFLUENCE OF SOCIAL CLASS

Families with disabled children come from all social classes. Professionals, on the other hand, are more likely to come from middle- and upper-class backgrounds. As a result, professionals and the families they serve may have highly divergent views of disability and its treatment. Perhaps the greatest conflict in this area has occurred in the field of mental retardation, especially in the mild ranges of retardation. Although parents and professionals from middle- and upper-class backgrounds may regard mild mental retardation as a devastating condition, lower-class parents may not even define it as a disability.

In a study of institutionalized retarded children, Mercer (1965) found that the children who were discharged generally came from low-status families. High-status families were more likely to concur with official definitions of mental retardation and the need for institutionalization. The low-status families, who were not as achievement oriented, were able to envision their children's playing normal adult roles. Downey (1963) found, similarly, that more educated families tended to show less interest in their institutionalized children because the children were unable to conform to the family's career expectations.

Lower-class families may have a higher tolerance for deviance in general than middle-class families. Guttmacher and Elinson (1971) found, for example, that upper-class respondents are more likely than lower-class respondents to define a series of deviant behaviors as illness. Middle- and upper-class families tend to share the professional's perspective of mental illness, whereas the lower classes may see such behaviors as normal variants. Children with disabilities that result in nonnormative behaviors may be less accepted in middle- and upper-class families as a result.

As Hess (1970), Kohn (1969), and others have noted, middle-class parents expect independent behavior and achievement from their children. They have higher educational and occupational aspirations for their children and higher expectations that those aspirations will be attained. Socially appropriate behavior is also likely to be viewed by these parents as necessary for achievement. Holt (1958) has written about families with retarded children:

> The families that managed best were not those in the upper classes. These parents were ambitious for their children and never overcame their frustration and disappointment. The ideal parents were those who . . . did not have great ambitions. . . . They looked upon the child as a gift for which to be thankful whatever his condition. (p. 753)

This class-based pattern does not seem to occur as clearly in the case of physical disability. Dow (1966) found no correlation between social class and parental acceptance of their disabled children and notes that parents of all classes tend to have optimistic attitudes. These favorable attitudes are maintained by depreciating the importance of physique.

In working with families of different social classes, professionals should be aware of differences in lifestyle or in parent–child interaction that may affect compliance with treatment or reactions to the professional. Professionals working in home-based programs that use parents as teachers need to be especially aware of the varying teaching strategies employed by parents of different social-class backgrounds. Laosa (1978) found, for example, that in a group of Chicano families, mothers with more formal education tend to use inquiry and praise in teaching their children and mothers with less education are more likely to use modeling as a teaching strategy. Another study of mothers of mildly retarded, low-SES preschoolers (Wilton & Barbour, 1978) found that they show less encouragement of their children's activities than comparison mothers. Attempting to get such parents to use more "middle-class" techniques could result in lack of compliance with a treatment program.

Lower-class parents are also likely to have less time and money to spend on their children's disabilities than their middle-class counterparts. Resources such as transportation, employment opportunities, adequate or appropriate housing, and access to good medical care are limited in the lower classes. When the necessities of life are scarce, a child's disability may not be a family's number-one priority. The disability may be only one of the many problems faced by the family, which could also result in lack of compliance with professional recommendations.

Dunst, Trivette, and Cross (in press) found that low-SES families of disabled children have less family support and more physical, emotional, and financial problems than a higher SES group. Without a strong support network to share the burden, such families are likely to experience considerable stress in managing their children's disabilities, regardless of their level of acceptance. Colón (1980) has suggested that the multiproblem poor family has a truncated life cycle, with a greater loss of family members and greater shortening of life stages than the middle-class family and that the mother is commonly the organizing force in family life. The support offered by the professional can be important to such families.

Lewis (1959) has written:

> One can speak of the culture of the poor, for it has its own modalities and distinctive social and psychological consequences for its members. . . . The culture of poverty cuts across regional, rural–urban, and even national boundaries. . . . I am impressed by the remarkable similarities in family structure, the nature of kinship ties, the quality of husband–wife and parent–child relations, time orientation, spending patterns, value systems, and the sense of community found in lower-class settlements in London . . . , in Puerto Rico . . . , in Mexico City slums and Mexican villages . . . , and among lower class Negroes in the United States. (p. 16)

Many researchers have questioned Lewis's culture-of-poverty hypothesis, however, especially the tenet that the poor do not share in the value system of the larger society. Many of the poor families with disabled children known to us certainly do identify with much of the "American dream" that they see on television and elsewhere. Yet the day-to-day reality of a chronic shortage of cash does affect life possibilities and outlook. A family that is exhausted by the struggle to survive does not have the luxury of being able to search for the best medical treatment or educational program for their child. They cannot plan for their child's future because even tomorrow is uncertain. Professionals who judge such families by middle-class standards are often unwittingly creating a situation of noncompliance by their unrealistic expectations.

ETHNIC VARIATION

An ethnic group has been defined as "those who conceive of themselves as alike by virtue of their common ancestry, real or fictitious, and who are so regarded by others" (Shibutani & Kwan, reported in McGoldrick, 1982, p. 3). Ethnic identification may be based on race, culture, or national origin. Census data from 1983 indicated that the population of the United States was composed of ethnic groups in the following proportions (Harrison, Serafica, & McAdoo, 1984):

Group	Percentage of population
Afro-Americans	11.6
Hispanics	6.4
Asian, Pacific	1.4
Native Americans	0.6
Whites	80.0

Among the whites are various ethnic identifications, including Irish, Italian, Jewish, and German. Members of some ethnic groups identify very strongly with the group, and others think of themselves more as Americans than as ethnics. Because attitudes toward disability and toward children in general vary by ethnicity, professionals should be aware of the ethnic identification of the clients they serve.

Black Subculture

Much of the literature on black families in America has focused on social class rather than ethnicity. Consequently, many of the patterns that have been uncovered have been socioeconomic. Although black families are disproportionately represented in the lower classes, an Afro-American subculture does appear to exist apart from socioeconomic status and can be found in black middle-class families as well as in the lower classes.

Because so many black families are poor, the incidence of poverty-based disability resulting from poor nutrition and poor prenatal care is disproportionately high in these families. Edelman (1985) has noted that almost one in two black children is poor compared to a poverty rate for American children in general of one in five. Infant mortality and low birth weight, a leading cause of childhood disability, are twice as high for blacks as whites. In addition, three out of five black children under the age of 3 live in single-parent households. Jones and Wilderson (1976) have noted that black children are seven times as likely as white children to be placed in special educable mentally retarded (EMR) classes in school, a consequence of labeling, racism, and socioeconomic status. Moore (1981) notes that black children constitute 45% of EMR enrollment nationally. Poverty also contributes to stress, and Korn, Chess, and Fernandez (1978) found, in one sample of physically handicapped children, that black families are more vulnerable to stress than whites.

Studies of poor black families indicate that teenage pregnancies are common and women tend to start families at early ages (Franklin & Boyd-Franklin, 1985; Schulz, 1969). These young mothers are probably poorly prepared to care for a child with a disability. However, as Dodson (1981), Franklin and Boyd-Franklin (1985), Harrison and colleagues (1984), and others have suggested, childrearing in black families has historically been a communal process, with a high level of involvement by the extended family. Mutual-help patterns are usually strong. Staples (1976) suggests that the "attenuated extended family," consisting of a single adult and her children as well as additional relatives in the home, is a common family form. This family is likely to be surrounded by a large kin network, including fictive kin as well as blood relations. A system of informal adoption also exists (Hines & Boyd-Franklin, 1982).

As Jackson (1981) has noted, in urban black families the mother is usually the person responsible for providing care for a disabled family member. The female role in general in such families is associated with respectability, dependability, family, and home. The male role, on the other hand, is associated with the street and freedom from responsibility at home. The oldest female sibling is also typically recruited to help care for younger children (Schulz, 1969).

Foley (1975) has made a number of recommendations for therapists working with disadvantaged black families. He suggests first that the therapist needs to win the family's confidence by bringing about some immediate success, such as helping the family receive Supplemental Security Income (SSI) payments, better housing, or a clinic appointment.

The therapist also needs to be aware of communication styles, including a high percentage of incomplete messages, speaking in generalities rather than specifics, or relying on nonverbal messages rather than verbal ones. Foley also notes that these families tend to label behavior in negative ways and that the therapist must help them relabel family members so that they may interact with those members more constructively. Pinderhughes (1982) has also cautioned the therapist about not compounding the powerlessness of such families.

A number of studies have looked at black families of all socioeconomic levels and backgrounds, not merely the urban poor. Billingsley (1968) has shown that such a perspective reveals that not all black families are disorganized and headed by females. In another study, Heiss (1981) found that no major difference exists between black and white women on attitudes toward marriage and family. Similarly, Scanzoni (1985) found that socioeconomic status is a more important determinant than race in shaping parental values. Black parents were found to have the same values as whites of the same social class. Thus a black middle-class family might be just as devastated as a similar white family by the birth of a mentally retarded child, for example.

However, some characteristics seem to emerge as distinctive of a black subculture regardless of social class. Boykin (1983) has argued that blacks have a distinctive culture marked by spirituality, harmony, movement, verve, affect, communalism, expressive individualism, orality, and a social time perspective. The importance of the extended family and the church as social supports have also been reported at all socioeconomic levels.

The support of significant others has been shown to be extremely important for families with disabled children. Manns (1981) has noted that blacks of all social levels have more significant others than whites. Blacks tend to have large, extensive kin networks, which support overall survival and coping efforts. When asked to name a significant other, blacks are more likely than whites to name a relative. Sudarkasa (1981) suggests that the roots of the black family system lie in the African principle of consanguinity, which emphasizes the extended family over the conjugal relationship.

In naming nonrelative significant others, half of the respondents in Manns's (1981) study mentioned a black minister. Other studies (Franklin & Boyd-Franklin, 1985; Hines & Boyd-Franklin, 1982) have also mentioned the importance of religion in black family life at all social levels. Hines and Boyd-Franklin (1982) have written:

> In the Baptist church, a Black family finds a complete support system including the minister, deacons, deaconesses, and other church members.

> Numerous activities . . . provide a social life for the entire family, which
> extends far beyond the Sunday services and provides a network of people
> who are available to the family in times of trouble or loss. (p. 96)

The willingness of the religious community to provide emotional support and help in caring for a disabled child can greatly ease the burden on a family.

The roles of black parents and children have also been studied at various socioeconomic levels. Hobbs and Wimbish (1977) found that adjustment to parenthood is more difficult for black than for white couples. If the birth of a healthy child is difficult, certainly the birth of a child with a disability would be even more difficult. The most typical marital role pattern in the black family appears to be egalitarian (Hines & Boyd-Franklin, 1982; Staples, 1976). McAdoo (1981) has argued, however, that black fathers tend to be more authoritarian than white fathers, particularly with respect to their daughters. Bartz and Levine (1978) and Durrett (reported in Williams & Williams, 1979) also found that black parents are authoritative with their children. Studies (Bartz & Levine, 1978; Young, 1970) also suggest that black parents encourage earlier independence training in their children than other parents. Black parents who expect accelerated development and early assumption of responsibility by their children may be disappointed by a disabled child whose development is considerably slower than the norm.

Finally, some studies have looked at black "folk culture." Folk beliefs of blacks and other ethnic groups are dying in urban American society. However, the professional may still encounter individuals who subscribe to such traditional beliefs and practices. Jackson (1981) has noted that some lower-class blacks of rural origin still believe in root medicine and root doctors. Spector (1979) also notes the belief in some black communities that certain individuals have healing powers. The use of alternative healers could create conflict with standard medical treatment of children with disabilities. Another folk belief cited by Spector is the notion that eating clay or starch protects a pregnant woman and her child. Such a belief could give rise to feelings of guilt in a mother who gave birth to a disabled child after failing to take this precaution.

Hispanic Subculture

Hispanics constitute the second-largest ethnic minority in the United States. Although similarities exist among various groups of Hispanic origin, Mexicans, Puerto Ricans, Cubans, and other Latin Americans have separate identities and subcultures. In this section, we consider the disability-related aspects of the Mexican-American (Chicano) and Puerto Rican subcultures, which are common among large population segments in some regions of the United States.

Mexican-Americans

Mexican-Americans tend to be geographically concentrated, with 85% living in five southwestern states (Alvirez & Bean, 1976). Wendeborn (1982) has written of this population:

> Unlike the early European immigrants to America who were cut off from their prior homelands by the vast Atlantic ocean, the Hispanic patient of Mexican heritage still has access to Mexico. Many still have immediate families and other relatives in Mexico. This proximity to Mexico lends itself to retention of the Mexican culture—thus the Hispanic of Mexican heritage is in many ways a bicultural person. (p. 6)

As in the case of black families, a significant proportion of Mexican-Americans live in poverty. As a result, they are prone to a certain amount of labeling by professionals. According to Jones and Wilderson (1976), Mexican-American children are ten times as likely as Anglo children to be placed in EMR classes. Such placements are attributable in part to assessment techniques that discriminate against non-English-speaking children and those whose culture differs from that of the majority. The poor Mexican-American family may also lack access to treatment facilities and consistent care for a disabled child. Guerra (1980) notes that "the case of the chronically ill or handicapped child, who often is seen in many different facilities and receives support from many programs and agencies, represents a very serious deficit in the system" (p. 21). He also points to the difficult transition from the "space age" technology of a neonatal intensive care unit to the "two-room casa" in the *barrio*, or neighborhood, as a situation marked by inadequate outreach to the culturally different family.

In addition to high levels of poverty, Mexican culture is also marked by language and lifestyle differences from the mainstream. As a result, Mexican-American parents may find interactions with professionals difficult and may be uncomfortable in institutional settings. Stein (1983) reports that Hispanic parents do not participate as actively in the development of their children's Individual Education Plans as do white parents or parents in general. Both schools and medical settings tend to be intimidating to these parents. Azziz (1981) notes that to Hispanics, hospitals are places where the sick go to die. Hospital visiting rules, which exclude some family members, are also foreign to them. In addition, the Spanish-speaking patient may have difficulty distinguishing among various hospital personnel and may pay more attention to a technician who speaks Spanish than to a physician who speaks only English. Romaine (1982) notes, too, that time has a different meaning in Mexican culture, and Mexican-Americans may not keep appointments, creating scheduling problems for professionals. Quesada (1976) notes, further, that Mexican-Americans are attuned to short-range therapy, from which they expect immediate results. Consequently, they may not comply with long-term treatment programs. Quesada also mentions the concept of *dignidad*, a kind of reticence, which may result in a paternalistic dependence that is misunderstood by professionals. Differences in acculturation are related to socioeconomic status, and middle-class Mexican-Americans are more likely to speak English and have familiarity with the mainstream culture.

The traditional Mexican family has been characterized as marked by values of familism, male dominance, subordination of young to old, and person orientation rather than goal orientation (Alvirez & Bean, 1976). Guinn (reported in Williams & Williams, 1979) notes a number of additional differences between Mexican-American and Anglo values: Mexicans stress being, and Anglos stress doing; Anglos value material well-being more than Mexicans; Mexicans have a present-time orientation, and Anglos have a future orientation; Anglos value individual action, and Mexicans value group cooperation; Mexicans are fatalistic, whereas Anglos value mastery of the universe. All these values may cause Mexican-American parents to be more accepting of a child's disabilty than Anglo parents.

The importance of the extended family in Mexican culture has been noted by many writers. Heller (reported in Williams & Williams, 1979) states that the web of kinship ties imposes obligations of mutual aid, respect, and affection. Falicov (1982) notes that the family protects the individual and that extended family members may perform many parental functions. Cousins may be as close as siblings. In addition, *compadres*, or godparents, play an important role. In a study of the extended family as an emotional support system, Keefe, Padilla, and Carlos (1979) found that Mexican-Americans consistently rely on relatives more than friends, regardless of geographical proximity. Children are more likely to have close relationships with siblings and cousins than with extrafamilial peers. Both Falicov and Karrer (1980) and Keefe and colleagues (1979) note that Mexican women have a strong tendency to confide in female relatives. The young Mexican mother is likely to rely on her mother for advice and support. The support network provided by the family can be very helpful to parents of disabled children.

The proximity of the extended family can also create problems for parents, however. Falicov and Karrer (1980) explain, for example, that the presence of the extended family puts pressure on members to compare themselves with their relatives. The mother of a child with a disability who is surrounded by sisters, sisters-in-law, and cousins whose children are not disabled may be upset by the constant reminder of her child's "differentness." Keefe and colleagues (1979) also note that their Mexican-American respondents sometimes resent their relatives' intrusion into their personal affairs. Friends who react negatively to a disabled child can be avoided by parents: avoidance of close family is more difficult.

Mexican-American attitudes toward childrearing also differ from those of the cultural mainstream. Falicov (1982) and Falicov and Karrer (1980) note a relaxed attitude toward the achievement of developmental milestones and self-reliance, along with a basic acceptance of the child's individuality. Such an attitude would certainly be favorable for a retarded or physically disabled child whose development proceeded much more slowly than the norm or who was not able to achieve independence from the family. Other childrearing values stress the goal of socializing children to be respectful and well mannered (Castaneda, 1976; Williams & Williams, 1979). Children are also socialized to play sex-specific roles: Girls are trained for the home, and boys are taught to be strong and to dominate the family. A child with a disability that affected behavior could have difficulty fulfilling parental expectations for politeness and respectful conduct. Parents could also be disappointed by a male child whose disability prevented him from playing his traditionally defined role.

Like other ethnic groups, Mexican-Americans, depending on their degree of identification with the traditional culture, have folk beliefs about the nature of disease and disability. Spector (1979) notes, for example, that Chicanos may regard illness as a punishment for wrongdoing. Such beliefs are likely to result in guilt, and, in fact, Wendeborn (1982) has noted the presence of guilt feelings in Mexican parents of children with mental retardation and cerebral palsy.

A social worker in a birth defects evaluation center serving a large number of Mexican-American clients describes several illustrative cases (H. Montalvo, personal communication, 1982):

Case 1: A young native Mexican couple presented to our Birth Defects Evaluation Center with their one month old baby girl. She had the typical clinical picture of Apert syndrome and the diagnosis was confirmed during the initial clinic visit. Unknown to the clinic staff was the belief that this condition was blamed on a lunar eclipse which had occurred sometime during the pregnancy. . . . Guilt, either implied or direct, is assumed by the mother because it is her obligation to screen herself, and the fetus, by properly warding off the "harmful" rays of the eclipse. Most women normally wear one or several keys on their abdomen during this period. If this is not addressed, and in a manner so as not to impose one's value on a particular couple, it can prolong the deep sense of guilt on both father and mother. Especially the mother who must also then accept her assumed oversight by caring for the defective member.

Case 2: A young couple, legal residents of the United States, arrived at our clinic with their 4 year old son. He was diagnosed as having a classical Schwartz-Jampel (Pinto-DeSouza) syndrome. This very intelligent couple followed our counseling session well and understood the autosomal recessive transmission and the subsequent one in four risk of recurrence for each pregnancy. However, it was not until the mother was alone with the social worker that she intimated she had had a severe "susto" (fright) during her pregnancy. She noted her husband, an activist in their native Mexico, had been jailed over several days with no word available on his release. Mrs. G. was concerned and afraid for her husband's well-being and she felt this fright and anxiety may have infiltrated the fetus and caused a gene mutation. Interestingly then, an articulate woman who capably followed our concise and detailed session on autosomal recessive transmission nevertheless felt a "susto" could also contribute to such a birth defect.

Schreiber and Homiak (1981) also note the belief that children are susceptible to *susto*, even *in utero*, and Prattes (1973) also mentions the use of a metal key around the abdomen to prevent cleft palate caused by a lunar eclipse.

A number of folk beliefs concern illness in children. One folk belief found in the Mexican-American community is *mal ojo*, or evil eye. As Prattes (1973) explains, "the belief is that if a person, especially a woman, admires someone else's child and looks at him without touching him, the child may fall ill of the evil eye" (pp. 131–132). Another common belief is that *caída de mollera* (sunken fontanel) is caused by a fall or the abrupt removal of the nipple from an infant's mouth (Chesney, Thompson, Guevara, Vela, & Schottstaedt, 1980; Martinez & Martin, 1966; Rubel, 1960).

A less common belief among Mexican-Americans suggests that hydrocephalus is caused by a precious rock inside a child's head (Prattes, 1973). Because the rock is believed to be valuable, parents may refuse to give permission for an autopsy if the child dies. They believe that physicians will sell the rock.

Another preventive measure common in this group is the use of mittens on a baby's hands in order to avoid cutting the child's fingernails (Prattes, 1973). Cutting the nails is believed to lead to blindness or nearsightedness (Hill, 1982; Prattes, 1973), and the mittens prevent the baby from scratching his/her face. A parent holding this belief would certainly feel guilty if a child were found to be blind after having his/her fingernails cut.

Those who believe in folk medicine may employ the services of a *curandero* (folk healer) in addition to, or instead of, those of a health care professional. The *curandero/curandera* derives his/her ability to cure from the supernatural (Spector, 1979). Because these healers maintain a close, warm, personalized relationship with the family, they may be preferred over the impersonal medical professional who works in a clinic or hospital setting. Keefe and colleagues (1979) found, however, that among urban Mexican-Americans in one sample, the use of the *curandero* as a means of emotional support is negligible.

Physicians, however, may be even less likely than folk healers to become significant others for parents. Schreiber and Homiak (1981) note that any diagnosis or treatment is likely to be evaluated and accepted or rejected by the patient's family and that Mexican women usually prefer to go home and discuss any proposed treatment with their entire family. When the professional recommendations are not highly valued, the family may seek other consultations. Wendeborn (1982) notes that Hispanic families of children with cerebral palsy have difficulty accepting the fact that the condition cannot be healed completely and may consult with numerous practitioners at considerable expense before accepting the approach of any professional or facility.

Although many Mexican-American families may behave in the ways suggested above when they have children with disabilities, many others exhibit attitudes and behavior that do not differ significantly from those of Anglo or other non-Mexican families. One recent study of poor Mexican mothers (Shapiro & Tittle, 1986) found, for example, that, like their Anglo counterparts, their subjects experience difficulties in the areas of social support, child adjustment, perceived stress, and family functioning as a result of their children's disabilities.

Puerto Ricans

Perhaps even more than other ethnic groups, the Puerto Rican community relies very heavily on the family as a source of strength and support. García-Preto (1982) has written:

> In times of stress Puerto Ricans turn to their families for help. Their cultural expectation is that when a family member is experiencing a crisis or has a problem, others in the family are obligated to help, especially those who are in stable positions. Because Puerto Ricans rely on the family and their extended network of personal relationships, they will make use of social services only as a last resort. (p. 164)

The structure of the Puerto Rican family also differs from the nuclear family model of the larger society. The basic family unit is commonly extended among Puerto Ricans and may consist of *compadres* (godparents) and *hijos de crianza* (children of upbringing) in addition to blood relatives (Mizio, 1974). Although the extended family is the primary source of help and social support, members of the Puerto Rican community may also approach friends, neighbors, or a neighborhood spiritualist. Secondarily, they may approach professionals whom they know well. As Ghali (1977) suggests, Puerto Ricans will not confide in anyone until *confianza*, or a familial-type of trusting relationship, is established. Professionals working with such families must, therefore, work toward establishing a personal bond with their clients.

Another frequently noted aspect of the Puerto Rican subculture is fatalism (see, e.g., Fitzpatrick, 1976; García-Preto, 1982; Ghali, 1977). Submissiveness and acceptance of fate are encouraged, in contrast with the American values of achievement and aggressiveness. As in the Mexican-American subculture, such fatalism may help parents cope with a child's disabilities.

Harwood (1981) and others have also noted a stricter sexual division of labor among Puerto Ricans than among other groups. Women are expected to care for children at home, and men are expected to demonstrate *machismo*. A woman who must work outside the home is likely to experience some conflict as a result. These patterns are reminiscent of those found in other Hispanic groups. In many ways Puerto Ricans are similar to other Hispanics, yet in other ways their subculture is unique. The professional who works with these families must be careful, therefore, when generalizing from one group to another.

Asian-American Subculture

Just as one should not necessarily generalize from one Hispanic group to another, one must be careful in assuming that all Asian subcultures are alike. However, similarities do exist. In this section, we look at two important Asian-American groups: the Japanese and Chinese.

Like other ethnic groups, Asian-Americans value the family very highly. Any problems are likely to be solved within the family. Family problems are regarded as private, and bringing them to the attention of outsiders is shameful (Shon & Ja, 1982). Professionals might have a difficult time attempting to counsel such families. On the other hand, reticence in revealing coping difficulties does not necessarily mean that a family will not accept more "technical" medical or therapeutic services. A Vietnamese family in the early intervention program directed by one of us (R. B. D.) was very receptive to physical therapy and other services offered to their daughter, who has cerebral palsy.

In the Japanese family, the *ie*, or houshold unit, is the most important frame of reference (Kitano & Kikumura, 1976). Although the family is residentially nuclear, close ties to relatives are maintained. Children are expected to be respectful and considerate toward their parents and to have a high degree of self-control. Obligation to the family is also important (Harrison, Serafica & McAdoo, 1984).

Kitano and Kikumura (1976) note that the Japanese are taught to defer to those of higher status, and open confrontation is avoided. As a result, members of this group are unlikely to challenge the professional, even when they do not agree with a recommended course of treatment. Shon and Ja (1982) note, too, that communication tends to be indirect.

Among Chinese-Americans as well, the family—not the individual— is the major unit of society. Huang (1976) notes that Chinese children usually grow up in the midst of adults and are not left with babysitters. Lee (1982) writes that the mother–son relationship is particularly close in this group, even after a son marries. The oldest son usually has more responsibilities than other children in the family. Difficulties could arise in such families if the oldest son were disabled or responsible for the care of younger, disabled siblings.

Like the Japanese, Chinese parents may not show their feelings for fear of "losing face," making interaction with a counselor difficult. Other group values, however, may encourage acceptance of a disabled child. For example, the Chinese tend to be fatalistic and to believe in collective responsibility among kin (Gould-Martin & Ngin, 1981; Lee, 1982). Although the past is more valued than the future, Chinese parents do have high educational aspirations for their children (Huang, 1976; Harrison, et al., 1984). Acceptance of a retarded child could be problematic within such a value orientation, and Yee (1988) has, in fact, noted that denial of a child's disability is common in Asian families. Family counseling, rather than individual counseling, may be especially appropriate for Asian-American families who have a need for counseling.

Native American Subculture

Because of much intertribal variation, Native Americans cannot be regarded as constituting a single subculture. In some ways, however, various tribes seem to be more like each other than like the cultural mainstream. Attneave (1982) and others have noted, for example, that the Native American tends to be stoic and to accept fate. Attneave (1982), Harrison and colleagues (1984), Pepper (1976), and Price (1976), among others, have listed the following differences in values between Native Americans and the American middle class:

Native American	American middle class
Cooperation	Competition
Harmony with nature	Control over nature
Adult centered	Child centered
Present time orientation	Future time orientation
Expression through action	Verbal expression
Short childhood	Extended childhood
Education for knowledge	Education for grades

Because these families are more accepting of fate and less achievement oriented than others in society, they are likely to have less difficulty coping with a disabled child. Attneave (1982) has written: "Since children are considered precious and are accepted for themselves, a handicapped child is usually given all the support needed to reach his or her own level of fulfillment" (p. 81). Locust (1988) has noted that among the Hopi some of the gods are in fact disabled and that the Native American belief system stresses the strengths of individuals rather than their disabilities.

In addition, these families are likely to have help and support in rearing a disabled child. Traditionally among Native Americans, the extended family shares in childrearing duties. Williams and Williams (1979) have also noted that Native American children tend to be treated permissively and to be loved by everyone in the family. Anderson (1988) has suggested that grandparents may be even more important than parents in childrearing among Native Americans.

Professionals involved with these families should be aware of a tendency toward reticence. Interactions may be marked by long silences and little self-disclosure (Attneave, 1982). In addition, some Native American families still make use of traditional healers, such as medicine men and shamans. The professional who desires to win the trust of these families should not belittle the efforts of folk healers. Spector (1979) has also noted that Native Americans may be offended by direct questions or note taking by professionals.

Native Americans, like other ethnic groups, may hold folk beliefs about various childhood disabilities. Kunitz and Levy (1981) have written that among the Navajo, a child's illness is believed to be caused by a taboo broken by the mother during pregnancy. Seizures are called "moth sickness," which is believed to result from a broken incest taboo.

Varying beliefs about cause can result in positive or negative labeling of disability. Seizures, for example, result in stigma among the Navajo. As Kunitz and Levy (1981) note, some congenital malformations, such as cleft palate, are negatively labeled by the Navajo, and others, like extra fingers or toes or hip displacement, are not labeled at all. In fact, these deformities may be regarded as normal variants, and parents may not comply with professionally recommended treatments. More serious physical disabilities, blindness, and deafness may be ignored by the Navajo because of the economic burden of long-term treatment.

Other Ethnic Subcultures

Blacks, Hispanics, Asian-Americans, and Native Americans are all generally regarded as minority groups in American society. Although ethnic variation is also present among the white majority, value differences from the cultural mainstream may not be as pronounced—especially among the third, fourth, and fifth generations. Some ethnic differences in reaction to disability have been noted by various writers, and these are mentioned here briefly.

Italian-Americans

In a classic study, Zborowski (1952) found that Italian-Americans react to pain in an emotional and exaggerated way. Although the tendency to stereotype should be avoided, Italian culture can generally be characterized as valuing emotional expression more than some other American subcultures. Consequently, the reaction of Italian-American parents to the diagnosis of a child's disability may be a strong one.

In describing Italian culture, virtually all writers refer to the central place of the family. Although family ties are strong in many ethnic groups, they are especially strong among Italians. Femminella and Quadagno (1976) have noted that such ties continue to be important even among third-generation Italian-Americans. Rotunno and McGoldrick (1982) have written: "For Italians, the family has been the thread that has provided not only continuity in all situations, but also the training to cope with a difficult world" (p. 340). Italian parents of disabled children are thus likely to have a strong family support system. In addition, as Rotunno and McGoldrick (1982) have noted: "Italians have learned to utilize environmental support effectively and to extract whatever good is possible from a seemingly hopeless situation" (p. 360).

In addition to being supportive, the Italian family is usually large and generally includes godparents as well as true relatives. The identity of the individual is based on the family rather than on education or achievement (Rotunno & McGoldrick, 1982). Such an environment is likely to encourage acceptance of a child whose disability prevents personal success.

Among the folk beliefs held by Italians are superstitions attributing congenital abnormalities to unsatisfied desires for food during pregnancy. Another belief suggests that if a pregnant woman bends or turns her body in certain ways, abnormal fetal development may result (Ragucci, 1981). A third- or fourth-generation Italian-American mother may not accept these beliefs; however, she may have difficulty coping with a grandmother or other relative who does accept them.

Because the family is the primary source of support, Italian-Americans do not make much use of professional support services. Rotunno and McGoldrick (1982) suggest that Italians do not trust professionals. Ragucci (1981) notes that professionals who are *simpatico* (warm, congenial) may be trusted, but that those who are *superbo* (arrogant, unapproachable) are likely to be avoided by members of this group.

Jewish-Americans

In the study mentioned in the previous section, Zborowski (1952) also found Jewish patients to react to pain in an exaggerated and emotional way. Like Italians, Jews are generally noted for being highly verbal and emotional in response to both adverse and joyous occasions. Verbal expressiveness is one of four values of Eastern European Jewish families noted by Herz and Rosen (1982). The other values are centrality of the family; suffering as a shared value; and intellectual achievement and financial success. Generosity is also highly valued.

In contrast with the Italian family, which encourages dependence in children, the Jewish family encourages children to be independent and achieve personal success. Herz and Rosen (1982) write: "Through the child's success, parents are validated; through their defects and wrongdoings parents are disgraced and shamed" (p. 380). Farber, Mindel, and Lazerwitz (1976) note that Jewish children have an obligation to bring *nakhus*, or pride, to their parents.

The high value that Jewish parents place on achievement creates difficulties when a child is disabled. Mentally retarded children, in particular, pose a threat to the value placed on intellectual accomplishment. Saenger (reported in Zuk, 1962) found that, indeed, Jews are more likely to institutionalize their retarded children than members of other ethnic groups. Jewish values as they reflect on other disabilities may also differ from the American cultural norm. One study (Goodman, Dornbusch, Richardson, & Hastorf, 1963) found, for example, that general American samples tend to regard deformity and disfigurement more negatively than functional (orthopedic) impairment, whereas Jewish samples regard fuctional impairment more negatively than facial or bodily aberrations.

In relationships with professionals, Jews tend to be favorably inclined toward reliance on experts, including psychotherapists and counselors of various kinds. However, Jews are also more likely than members of some other groups to question the credentials of professionals (Herz & Rosen, 1982).

RELIGIOUS VARIATION

A number of earlier studies looked at the effect of religion on parental acceptance of disabled children. Zuk (1959) found, for example, that Catholic mothers in one sample were more accepting of their retarded children than Protestants and Jews. On the other hand, Leichman (reported in Zuk, 1962) found no difference in verbalized acceptance between Catholic and Protestant mothers of the retarded. Zuk (1959) argues that Catholics are absolved from guilt by their religious beliefs and that Catholic doctrine insists that every child is a special gift of God. Yet in another study (Boles, 1959), Catholic mothers of children with cerebral palsy were found to have *more* feelings of guilt than Protestants and Jews.

The relationship between any particular religion and acceptance is thus not clear. Parents who regard themselves as more intense in their religious practices—regardless of their religion—may be more accepting, however. Zuk, Miller, Bartram, and Kling (1961) found that mothers rating themselves as intensely religious are slightly more likely to verbalize attitudes judged to be more accepting of their retarded children. This correlation may be a spurious one, though. Parents who are more religious are probably more deeply immersed in a religion-based support network, and social support, rather than religion itself, may be the important variable in determining parental acceptance or coping ability. Additional studies are needed to clarify the relationship between religion and attitudes toward childhood disability.

REGIONAL VARIATION

Virtually no research has been done on variations in family reactions to disabled children according to residential background, whether urban or rural, northern, southern, eastern, or western. As mass culture becomes more widespread, these differences probably become quite minimal; however, no documentation of this trend exists with respect to such families.

One recent study (Dunst et al., in press) compared Appalachian and non-Appalachian families with disabled children and found that, contrary to expectation, non-Appalachian families find their social support systems to be more helpful in caring for their child than Appalachian families. The authors found that socioeconomic status "rather than 'Appalachianness' accounts for differences in informal social support networks." Although they had less social support, the Appalachian families were able to use the support they had quite effectively. In conclusion, the authors note that social support rather than region is the most important variable in reducing the stress associated with rearing a disabled child. Heller, Quesada, Harvey, and Warner (1981) also note differences in family support between urban and rural families.

IMPLICATIONS FOR PROFESSIONALS

Professionals who work with families with disabled children should be aware of subcultural differences. However, the professional must be careful not to stereotype families on the basis of social class or ethnic, religious, or regional identification. Within most subcultures, a considerable amount of *intragroup variation* exists. Professionals should not assume that individual members of a group will share all of the values and beliefs commonly held by the group as a whole. In a study of lower-class black mothers' aspirations for their children, for example, Bell (1965) found aspirations varied *within* a group that was homogeneous in both social class and race.

Intragroup variation was also found in a study of lower-class Anglo, black, and Chicano couples (Cromwell & Cromwell, 1978). No ethnic differences were found among the groups in styles of conflict resolution. Stereotypic characterizations of black matriarchy and Chicano patriarchy were thus not supported. The authors conclude that "categorical labeling of family structure based on ethnic group membership is unwarranted and inappropriate" (p. 757). The value of subcultural studies, then, is in making professionals more aware of *possible* characteristics their clients may exhibit and in helping to explain some of the characteristics they may encounter.

The need for a better understanding of subcultural differences is demonstrated by a number of studies that reveal misunderstandings between professionals and clients of a different cultural background. One study of therapists and their Spanish-speaking patients (Kline, Acosta, Austin, & Johnson, 1980) found that the therapists did not accurately perceive the patients' wants and feelings and instead projected their own wishes onto the patients. Such misperceptions may persist even when interpreters are used. Marcos (1979) found, for example, that clinicians evaluating non-English-speaking patients through an interpreter were faced with "consistent, clinically relevant, interpreter-related distortions, which may give rise to important misconceptions about the patient's mental status" (p. 173).

A number of recommendations emerge to guide professionals who work with culturally different families:

1. *If at all possible, the professional should speak the client's native language.* As Laosa (1974) has suggested, abandonment of one's native language may imply abandonment of one's entire culture. Also, as indicated earlier, much misunderstanding occurs when professional and client do not speak the same language, even when an interpreter is used. Hanson (1981) has also noted the importance of providing written materials in the client's native language.

2. *Indigenous professionals, paraprofessionals, and consultants should be used as much as possible.* Although professionals can learn about their clients' language and culture, they can never acquire the cultural worldview to the same extent as one raised in the culture. Clients also feel more comfortable interacting with their peers. Quesada (1976) thus recommends the use of community representatives as teachers and consultants or the employment of local community representatives at the paraprofessional level.

3. As Marion (1980) has suggested, *professionals must meet the needs of culturally diverse parents for information, belonging, and self-esteem.* These parents are often excluded from advocacy organizations and support groups and feel isolated as a result. They may come from powerless segments of society and have little knowledge of their rights to educational and other services for their children. Professionals must be supportive of their clients' cultural values and work toward integrating these families into support and service networks located in the cultural mainstream.

4. *Scheduling should be flexible.* Families in the early intervention program directed by one of us (R. B. D.) must often travel to the closest large medical center for consultation and treatment. Some of the clinics there schedule only early morning appointments. Because they have no other means of transportation, lower-SES families must rely on a bus to travel to these clinics, and the earliest bus of the day does not arrive until afternoon. As a result, at least one family has had to spend the night at the bus station. Others simply avoid making the trip. Quesada (1976) notes, too, that people working on an hourly basis may not be able to afford to spend entire days at a clinic. He recommends a system of routine call-backs in order to reschedule missed appointments.

5. *Attempts must be made to elicit the family's definition of the situation.* Although important for all professional–family interactions, this

guideline is especially important in the case of the culturally different family. Montalvo (1974) has presented a number of cases of Puerto Rican children who had difficulties at school because well-intentioned school personnel failed to take into account the meanings attached by the family to a child's language or style of dress. Similarly, Anderson (1988) notes that an early intervention program could not be established in a Native American community until the support of the elders was obtained.

In general, the professional must take what Mercer (1965) calls a *social system* (rather than a clinical) *perspective* when working with culturally diverse populations. To the greatest extent possible, the professional must assume the family's point of view. Helping cannot occur without understanding. Before the professional can begin to meet the needs of families with disabled children, he/she must determine how those needs are defined by the family itself within the context of the subcultural world that shapes its daily round of life.

REFERENCES

Alvirez, D., & Bean, F. D. (1976). The Mexican-American family. In C. H. Mindel & R. W. Habenstein (Eds.), *Ethnic families in America: Patterns and variations* (pp. 271–292). New York: Elsevier.

Anderson, P. (1988, June). *Serving culturally diverse populations of infants and toddlers with disabilities.* Paper presented at the meeting of the Society for Disability Studies, Washington, DC.

Attneave, C. (1982). American Indians and Alaska native families: Emigrants in their own homeland. In M. McGoldrick, J. K. Pearce, & J. Giordano (Eds.), *Ethnicity and family therapy* (pp. 55–83). New York: Guilford.

Azziz, R. (1981, July). The Hispanic patient. *Pennsylvania Medicine*, pp. 22–25.

Bartz, K. W., & Levine, E. S. (1978). Childrearing by black parents: A description and comparison to Anglo and Chicano parents. *Journal of Marriage and the Family, 40,* 709–719.

Bell, R. R. (1965). Lower class Negro mothers' aspirations for their children. *Social Forces, 43,* 493–500.

Billingsley, A. (1968). *Black families in white America.* Englewood Cliffs, NJ: Prentice-Hall.

Boles, G. (1959). Personality factors in mothers of cerebral palsied children. *Genetic Psychology Monographs, 59,* 160–218.

Boykin, A. W. (1983). The academic performance of Afro-American children. In J. Spence (Ed.), *Achievement and achievement motives.* San Francisco: Freeman.

Castaneda, A. (1976). Cultural democracy and the educational needs of Mexican-American children. In R. L. Jones (Ed.), *Mainstreaming and the minority child* (pp. 181–194). Reston, VA: Council for Exceptional Children.

Chesler, M. (1965). Ethnocentrism and attitudes toward the physically disabled. *Journal of Personality and Social Psychology, 2,* 877–892.

Chesney, A. P., Thompson, B. L., Guevara, A., Vela, A., & Schottstaedt, M. F. (1980). Mexican-American folk medicine: Implications for the family physician. *The Journal of Family Practice, 11,* 567–574.

Chigier, E., & Chigier, M. (1968). Attitudes to disability of children in the multicultural society of Israel. *Journal of Health and Social Behavior, 9*, 310–317.

Colón, F. (1980). The family life cycle of the multiproblem poor family. In E. A. Carter & M. McGoldrick (Eds.), *The family life cycle: A framework for family therapy* (pp. 343–381). New York: Gardner.

Cromwell, V. L., & Cromwell, R. E. (1978). Perceived dominance in decision-making and conflict resolution among Anglo, black and Chicano couples. *Journal of Marriage and the Family, 19*, 749–759.

DeCaro, J. J., Dowaliby, F. J., & Maruggi, E. A. (1983). A cross-cultural examination of parents' and teachers' expectations for deaf youth regarding careers. *British Journal of Educational Psychology, 53*, 358–363.

Dodson, J. (1981). Conceptualizations of black families. In H. P. McAdoo (Ed.), *Black families* (pp. 23–36). Beverly Hills: Sage.

Dow, T. E., Jr. (1966). Optimism, physique and social class in reaction to disability. *Journal of Health and Social Behavior, 7*, 14–19.

Downey, K. J. (1963). Parental interest in the institutionalized severely mentally retarded child. *Social problems, 11*, 186–193.

Dunst, C. J., Trivette, C. M., & Cross, A. H. (in press). Social support networks of Appalachian and non-Appalachian families with handicapped children: Relationship to personal and family well-being. In S. Keefe (Ed.), *Mental health in Appalachia*. Lexington: University of Kentucky Press.

Dybwad, G. (1970). Treatment of the mentally retarded: A cross-cultural view. In H. C. Haywood (Ed.), *Social-cultural aspects of mental retardation* (pp. 560–572). New York: Appleton-Century-Crofts.

Edelman, M. W. (1985). The sea is so wide and my boat is so small—Problems facing black children today. In H. P. McAdoo & J. L. McAdoo (Eds.), *Black children: Social, educational and parental environments* (pp. 72–82). Beverly Hills: Sage.

Edgerton, R. B. (1970). Mental retardation in non-Western societies: Toward a cross-cultural perspective on incompetence. In H. C. Haywood (Ed.), *Social-cultural aspects of mental retardation* (pp. 532–559). New York: Appleton-Century-Crofts.

English, R. W. (1971). Correlates of stigma towards physically disabled persons. *Rehabilitation Research and Practice Review, 2*, 1–17.

Falicov, C. J. (1982). Mexican families. In M. McGoldrick, J. K. Pearce, & J. Giordano (Eds.), *Ethnicity and family therapy* (pp. 134–163). New York: Guilford.

Falicov, C. J., & Karrer, B. M. (1980). Cultural variations in the family life cycle: The Mexican-American family. In E. A. Carter & M. McGoldrick (Eds.), *The family life cycle: A framework for family therapy* (pp. 383–426). New York: Gardner.

Farber, B., Mindel, C. H., & Lazerwitz, B. (1976). The Jewish American family. In C. H. Mindel & R. W. Habenstein (Eds.), *Ethnic families in America: Patterns and variations* (pp. 347–378). New York: Elsevier.

Femminella, F. X., & Quadagno, J. S. (1976). The Italian-American family. In C. H. Mindel & R. W. Habenstein (Eds.), *Ethnic families in America: Patterns and variations* (pp. 61–88). New York: Elsevier.

Fitzpatrick, J. P. (1976). The Puerto Rican family. In C. H. Mindel & R. W. Habenstein (Eds.), *Ethnic families in America: Patterns and variations* (pp. 192–217). New York: Elsevier.

Foley, V. D. (1975). Family therapy with black disadvantaged families: Some observations on roles, communication and technique. *Journal of Marriage and Family Counseling, 1*, 29–38.

Franklin, A. J., & Boyd-Franklin, N. (1985). A psychoeducational perspective on black parenting. In H. P. McAdoo & J. L. McAdoo (Eds.), *Black children: Social educational and parental environments* (pp. 194–210). Beverly Hills: Sage.

Freedman, D. G. (1981). Ethnic differences in babies. In E. M. Hetherington & R. D. Parke (Eds.), *Contemporary readings in child psychology* (2nd ed.) (pp. 6–12). New York: McGraw-Hill.

García-Preto, N. (1982). Puerto Rican families. In M. McGoldrick, J. K. Pearce, & J. Giordano (Eds.), *Ethnicity and family therapy* (pp. 164–186). New York: Guilford.

Ghali, S. B. (1977). Culture sensitivity and the Puerto Rican client. *Social Casework, 58,* 459–474.

Goffman, E. (1963). *Stigma: Notes on the management of spoiled identity.* Englewood Cliffs, NJ: Prentice-Hall.

Goodman, N., Dornbusch, S. M., Richardson, S. A., & Hastorf, A. H. (1963). Variant reactions to physical disabilities. *American Sociological Review, 28,* 429–435.

Gottlieb, J. (1975). Public, peer and professional attitudes toward mentally retarded persons. In J. J. Begab & S. A. Richardson (Eds.), *The mentally retarded and society: A social science perspective* (pp. 99–125). Baltimore: University Park Press.

Gould-Martin, K., & Ngin, C. (1981). Chinese Americans. In A. Harwood (Ed.), *Ethnicity and medical care* (pp. 130–171). Cambridge, MA: Harvard University Press.

Groce, N. (1987, Summer). Cross-cultural research, current strengths, future needs. *Disability Studies Quarterly,* pp. 1–3.

Guerra, F. A. (1980, September–October). Hispanic child health issues. *Children Today,* pp. 18–22.

Guttmacher, S., & Elinson, J. (1971). Ethno-religious variation in perceptions of illness. *Social Science and Medicine, 5,* 117–125.

Hanson, M. J. (1981). A model for early intervention with culturally diverse single and multiparent families. *Topics in Early Childhood Special Education, 1,* 37–44.

Harrison, A., Serafica, F., & McAdoo, H. (1984). Ethnic families of color. In R. D. Parke (Ed.), *Review of child development research* (Vol. 7) (pp. 329–371). Chicago: University of Chicago Press.

Harwood, A. (1981). Mainland Puerto Ricans. In A. Harwood (Ed.), *Ethnicity and medical care* (pp. 397–481). Cambridge, MA: Harvard University Press.

Heiss, J. (1981). Women's values regarding marriage and the family. In H. P. McAdoo (Ed.), *Black families* (pp. 186–198). Beverly Hills: Sage.

Heller, P. G., Quesada, G. M., Harvey, D. L., & Warner, L. G. (1981). Familism in rural and urban America: Critique and reformulation of a construct. *Rural Sociology, 46,* 446–464.

Herz, F. M., & Rosen, E. J. (1982). Jewish families. In M. McGoldrick, J. K. Pearce, & J. Giordano (Eds.), *Ethnicity and family therapy* (pp. 364–392). New York: Guilford.

Hess, R. D. (1970). Social class and ethnic influences upon socialization. In P. H. Mussen (Ed.), *Carmichael's manual of child psychology* (pp. 457–557). New York: Wiley.

Hill, C. (1982). Our patients have culture. *Clinical Management in Physical Therapy, 2,* 5–10.

Hines, P. M., & Boyd-Franklin, N. (1982). Black families. In M. McGoldrick, J. K. Pearce, & J. Giordano (Eds.), *Ethnicity and family therapy* (pp. 84–107). New York: Guilford.

Hobbs, D. F., Jr., & Wimbish, J. M. (1977). Transition to parenthood by black couples. *Journal of Marriage and the Family, 18,* 677–690.

Hollingshead, A. B., & Redlich, F. C. (1958). *Social class and mental illness: A community study.* New York: Wiley.

Holt, K. S. (1958). The home care of severely retarded children. *Pediatrics, 22,* 744–755.

Huang, L. J. (1976). The Chinese-American family. In C. H. Mindel & R. W. Habenstein (Eds.), *Ethnic families in America: Patterns and variations* (pp. 124–147). New York: Elsevier.

Jackson, J. J. (1981). Urban black Americans. In A. Harwood (Ed.), *Ethnicity and medical care* (pp. 37–129). Cambridge, MA: Harvard University Press.

Jones, R. L., & Wilderson, F. B., Jr. (1976). Mainstreaming and the minority child: An overview of issues and a perspective. In R. L. Jones (Ed.), *Mainstreaming and the minority child* (pp. 1–13). Reston, VA: Council for Exceptional Children.

Keefe, S. E., Padilla, A. M., & Carlos, M. L. (1979). The Mexican-American extended family as an emotional support system. *Human Organization, 38*, 144–152.

Kitano, H. H. L., & Kikumura, A. (1976). The Japanese-American family. In C. H. Mindel & R. W. Habenstein (Eds.), *Ethnic families in America: Patterns and variations* (pp. 41–60). New York: Elsevier.

Kleinman, A., Eisenberg, L., & Good, B. (1978). Culture, illness and care: Clinical lessons from anthropologic and cross-cultural research. *Annals of Internal Medicine, 88*, 251–258.

Kline, F., Acosta, F. X., Austin, W., & Johnson, R. G., Jr. (1980). The misunderstood Spanish-speaking patient. *American Journal of Psychiatry, 137* (12), 1530–1533.

Kohn, M. L. (1969). *Class and conformity: A study in values.* Homewood, IL: Dorsey.

Korn, S. J., Chess, S., & Fernandez, P. (1978). The impact of children's physical handicaps on marital quality and family interaction. In R. M. Lerner & G. B. Spanier (Eds.), *Child influences on marital and family interaction: A life-span perspective.* New York: Academic.

Kunitz, S. J., & Levy, J. E. (1981). Navajos. In A. Harwood (Ed.), *Ethnicity and medical care* (pp. 337–396). Cambridge, MA: Harvard University Press.

Laosa, L. M. (1974). Child care and the culturally different child. *Child Care Quarterly, 3*, 214–224.

Laosa, L. M. (1978). Maternal teaching strategies in Chicano families of varied educational and socioeconomic levels. *Child Development, 49*, 1129–1135.

Lazerson, M. (1975). Educational institutions and mental subnormality: Notes on writing a history. In M. J. Begab & S. A. Richardson (Eds.), *The mentally retarded and society: A social science perspective* (pp. 33–52). Baltimore: University Park Press.

Lee, E. (1982). A social systems approach to assessment and treatment for Chinese American families. In M. McGoldrick, J. K. Pearce, & J. Giordano (Eds.), *Ethnicity and family therapy* (pp. 527–551). New York: Guilford.

Lewis, O. (1959). *Five families: An intimate and objective revelation of family life in Mexico today—A dramatic study of the culture of poverty.* New York: Basic Books.

Locust, C. (1988, June). *Integration of American Indian and scientific concepts of disability: Cross-cultural perspectives.* Paper presented at the meeting of the Society for Disability Studies, Washington, DC.

Manns, W. (1981). Support systems of significant others in black families. In H. P. McAdoo (Ed.), *Black families* (pp. 238–251). Beverly Hills: Sage.

Marcos, L. R. (1979). Effects of interpreters on the evaluation of psychopathology in non-English-speaking patients. *American Journal of Psychiatry, 136* (2), 171–174.

Marion, R. L. (1980). Communicating with parents of culturally diverse exceptional children. *Exceptional Children, 46*, 616–623.

Martinez, C., & Martin, H. W. (1966). Folk diseases among urban Mexican-Americans: Etiology, symptoms, and treatment. *Journal of the American Medical Association, 196*, 161–164.

McAdoo, J. L. (1981). Involvement of fathers in the socialization of black children. In H. P. McAdoo (Ed.), *Black families.* Beverly Hills: Sage.

McGoldrick, M. (1982). Ethnicity and family therapy: An overview. In M. McGoldrick, J. K. Pearce, & J. Giordano (Eds.), *Ethnicity and family therapy* (pp. 3–30). New York: Guilford.

Mercer, J. R. (1965). Social system perspective and clinical perspective: Frames of reference for understanding career patterns of persons labeled as mentally retarded. *Social Problems, 13*, 18–34.

Mizio, E. (1974). Impact of external systems on the Puerto Rican family. *Social Casework, 55*, 76–83.

Montalvo, B. (1974). Home-school conflict and the Puerto Rican child. *Social Casework, 55*, 100–110.

Moore, E. K. (1981). Policies affecting the status of black children and families. In H. P. McAdoo (Ed.), *Black families* (pp. 278–290). Beverly Hills: Sage.

Newman, J. (1987). Background forces in policies for care and treatment of disability. *Marriage and Family Review, 11*, 25–44.

Pepper, F. C. (1976). Teaching the American Indian child in mainstream settings. In R. L. Jones (Ed.), *Mainstreaming and the minority child* (pp. 133–158). Reston, VA: Council for Exceptional Children.

Pinderhughes, E. (1982). Afro-American families and the victim system. In M. McGoldrick, J. K. Pearce, & J. Giordano (Eds.), *Ethnicity and family therapy* (pp. 108–122). New York: Guilford.

Prattes, O. (1973). Section A: Beliefs of the Mexican-American family. In D. Hymovich & M. Barnard (Eds.), *Family health care* (pp. 128–137). New York: McGraw-Hill.

Price, J. A. (1976). North American Indian families. In C. H. Mindel & R. W. Habenstein (Eds.), *Ethnic families in America: Patterns and variations* (pp. 248–270). New York: Elsevier.

Quesada, G. M. (1976). Language and communication barriers for health delivery to a minority group. *Social Science and Medicine, 10*, 323–327.

Ragucci, A. T. (1981). Italian Americans. In A. Harwood (Ed.), *Ethnicity and medical care* (pp. 211–263). Cambridge, MA: Harvard University Press.

Richardson, S. A., Goodman, N., Hastorf, A. H., & Dornbusch, S. M. (1961). Cultural uniformity in reaction to physical disabilities. *American Sociological Review, 26*, 241–247.

Richardson, S. A., Goodman, N., Hastorf, A. H., & Dornbusch, S. M. (1963). Variant reactions to physical disabilities. *American Sociological Review, 28*, 429–435.

Romaine, M. E. (1982). Clinical management of the Spanish-speaking patient: Pleasures and pitfalls. *Clinical Management in Physical Therapy, 2*, 9–10.

Rotunno, M. & McGoldrick, M. (1982). Italian families. In M. McGoldrick, J. K. Pearce & J. Giordano (Eds.), *Ethnicity and family therapy* (pp. 340–363). New York: Guilford.

Rubel, A. J. (1960). Concepts of disease in Mexican-American culture. *American Anthropologist, 62*, 795–816.

Safilios-Rothschild, C. (1970). *The sociology and social psychology of disability and rehabilitation.* New York: Random House.

Scanzoni, J. (1985). Black parental values and expectations of children's occupational and educational success: Theoretical implications. In H. P. McAdoo & J. L. McAdoo (Eds.), *Black children: Social, educational and parental environments* (pp. 113–122). Beverly Hills: Sage.

Schreiber, J. M. & J. P. Homiak. (1981). Mexican Americans. In A. Harwood (Ed.), *Ethnicity and medical care* (pp. 264–336). Cambridge, MA: Harvard University Press.

Schulz, D. A. (1969). *Coming up black: Patterns of ghetto socialization.* Englewood Cliffs, NJ: Prentice-Hall.

Shapiro, J., & Tittle, K. (1986). Psychosocial adjustment of poor Mexican mothers of disabled and nondisabled children. *American Journal of Orthopsychiatry, 56*, 289–302.

Shon, S. P., & Ja, D. Y. (1982). Asian families. In M. McGoldrick, J. K. Pearce, & J. Giordano (Eds.), *Ethnicity and family therapy* (pp. 208–228). New York: Guilford.

Shurka, E., & Florian, V. (1983). A study of Israeli Jewish and Arab parental perceptions of their disabled children. *Journal of Comparative Family Studies, 14*, 367–375.

Sollenberger, E. R. (1974). *Care and education of crippled children in the United States.* New York: Arno.

Spector, R. E. (1979). *Cultural diversity in health and illness.* New York: Appleton-Century-Crofts.

Staples, R. (1976). The black American family. In C. H. Mindel & R. W. Habenstein (Eds.), *Ethnic families in America: Patterns and variations* (pp. 221–247). New York: Elsevier.

Stein, R. C. (1983). Hispanic parents' perspectives and participation in their children's special education program: Comparisons by program and race. *Learning Disability Quarterly, 6*, 432–439.

Sudarkasa, N. (1981). Interpreting the African heritage in Afro-American family organization. In H. P. McAdoo (Ed.), *Black families* (pp. 37–53). Beverly Hills: Sage.

Wendeborn, J. D. (1982). Administrative considerations in treating the Hispanic patient. *Clinical Management in Physical Therapy 2*, 6–7.

Williams, H. B., & Williams, E. (1979). Some aspects of childrearing practices in three minority subcultures in the United States. *Journal of Negro Education, 48*, 408–418.

Wilton, K., & Barbour, A. (1978). Mother–child interaction in high-risk and contrast preschoolers of low socioeconomic status. *Child Development, 49*, 1136–1145.

Wright, B. A. (1983). *Physical disability—A psychosocial approach.* New York: Harper & Row.

Yee, L. Y. (1988). Asian children. *Teaching Exceptional Children, 20* (4), 49–50.

Young, V. H. (1970). Family and childhood in a southern Negro community. *American Anthropologist, 40*, 269–288.

Zborowski, M. (1952). Cultural components of response to pain. *Journal of Social Issues, 8*, 16–30.

Zuk, G. H. (1959). The religious factor and the role of guilt in parental acceptance of the retarded child. *American Journal of Mental Deficiency, 64*, 139–147.

Zuk, G. H. (1962). The cultural dilemma and spiritual crisis of the family with a handicapped child. *Exceptional Children, 28*, 405–408.

Zuk, G. H., Miller, R. L., Bartram, J. B., & Kling, F. (1961). Maternal acceptance of retarded children: A questionnaire study of attitudes and religious background. *Child Development, 32*, 525–540.

9

Professional–Family Interaction: Working toward Partnership

Ask any five parents of visually impaired children how they first learned their child had vision problems and you will get five different horror stories . . . We parents try to be grateful that professionals pay any attention to the imperfect children we have produced, but we cannot avoid feelings of betrayal and anger when we are the recipients of misinformation or of the kind of callous treatment that ignores parental expertise.
—Stotland (1984, p. 69)

When I placed Matthew into a strange woman's arms on his first day in the infant program, I didn't know what she hoped to accomplish with my 4-week-old baby. . . . As the weeks and months passed, I sensed my baby's growing attachment to his teacher and his response to her obvious delight whenever he accomplished a new feat. I, too, unconsciously formed my attachment to her. . . . Professionals who work with families in the early months of the child's life can have a profound influence on parents. A mother may hear the first hopeful words about her child from the teacher or therapist. And those words and assurances can become the basis of strong attachments, acknowledged or unrealized, between parents and program staff.
—Moeller (1986, pp. 151–152)

Professionals can evoke strong feelings, both positive and negative, in their interactions with parents. During the early months of the child's life especially, both parents and professionals are highly vulnerable: The professional is charged with conveying the "bad news" of a child's disability to parents but is also in a position to offer badly needed information, hope, and support. The parent, on the other hand, is the recipient of the bad news about the child and looks to the professional as an expert who can provide answers to the many questions raised by the diagnosis. The reactions of professionals during these early months can form the basis for parents' future trust:

> I asked what was wrong with her ears, and they said not to worry about it. . . . I always thought they told you the truth in the hospital and if you wanted to know anything you should ask. I really thought her ears looked funny and I had this funny feeling, so I asked the doctor, "Is there anything wrong," and he looked right at me and said, "No." So I assumed she was O.K., and there was nothing wrong with her. . . . The next morning he told me she was retarded. . . . I was very bitter about it. I think I had the shortest stay in the hospital that anyone ever had. That afternoon I just picked up and left. . . . I had had the same pediatrician for six years, and he had always been truthful. I trusted him. (Darling, 1979, pp. 131–132)

In this chapter, we explore the views that professionals and parents have of each other and examine some of the sources of those views. We also look at the parent–professional encounter from a sociological perspective, as an interaction situation. Finally, we discuss the need for a parent–professional partnership and explore some of the new advocacy roles available to both parents and professionals in their quest for improved services for children and families. Most of the literature in this area deals with physicians and educators; however, our discussion may apply equally well to counselors, social workers, psychologists, and other professionals.

PROFESSIONALS AND PARENTS: HOW DO THEY VIEW EACH OTHER?

Parents' Predispositions toward Professionals

Long before they become the parents of children with disabilities, individuals have various beliefs about and attitudes toward professionals. They have interacted with physicians, nurses, teachers, and possibly therapists, counselors, or social workers in different contexts; they have also been exposed to media images of these professionals. As a result, when their children are born, they have expectations about professional behavior that may or may not be fulfilled by the actual professionals with whom they come into contact. As one mother wrote: "The last thing I wanted was a home visitor. . . . I thought Public Health Nurses were for people who beat their kids and drink too much" (Judge, 1987, p. 20).

Professional Dominance

The most common image associated with physicians and other professionals in our society has been one of *professional dominance* (Freidson, 1970). By virtue of their education and high status in the community, professionals, especially physicians, have been expected to play a dominant role in their interactions with clients or patients. Dominance generally includes elements of paternalism and control: The professional determines "what is best" for the client and provides only as much information to the client as is necessary for the clinical management of the case. Parents who have been exposed to this image may view physicians and other professionals with respect, even awe, and submit to their recommendations without question.

Studies (Barsch; Shapiro, both reported in Seligman, 1979) indicate that parents may be more positively predisposed toward teachers than toward other professionals. On the other hand, as Seligman has noted, parents' perceptions of teachers may be colored by negative experiences *they* had in school. In addition, teachers spend many hours with their pupils and may be regarded as being in competition with parents for their children's time, attention, respect, or affection. Lortie (reported in Seligman, 1979) has also suggested that parents may resent a teacher's control over their children when the teacher's values are different from those of the parent.

A number of studies have indicated that professional dominance in general may be declining somewhat in today's society as part of a trend toward greater consumer control in the marketplace. Gallup and Harris polls (reported in Betz & O'Connell, 1983) indicate that the public's confidence in and respect for physicians has declined markedly since 1950. In 1966, 72% of the public expressed confidence in doctors, but only 43% expressed such confidence in 1975. Betz and O'Connell suggest that the sense of trust is diminished as the physician–patient relationship becomes more specialized, impersonal, and shortlived as a result of population mobility, professionalization, and bureaucratization. Haug and Lavin (1983) suggest further that "in the dialectic of power relations, the increasing monopolization of medical knowledge and medical practice could only call forth a countervailing force in the form of patient consumerism" (p. 16).

Prior to their child's birth, then, parents are likely to have been exposed to both professional dominance and consumerism. Shortly after the birth and initial diagnosis, they are likely to defer to the expertise of the professional. As indicated in Chapter 2, parents are typically in a state of *anomie* when they first realize that their child has a problem. Because they are ill prepared for the birth of a child with a disability, they are likely to rely heavily on the advice of the professionals they encounter at that time. Later, especially in cases in which professionals are not able to provide appropriate information and guidance, parents' awareness of consumerism may lead them to challenge professional authority. Such changes in attitude and behavior toward professionals are discussed later in this chapter.

The Professional Role as an Ideal Type

Professional dominance is one of several images of professionals common in society today. Parsons (1951) classically describes the role of the professional as being characterized by the traits of achievement, universalism, functional specificity, and affective neutrality. Although real professionals only approximate these traits to greater or lesser degrees, the public image of the ideal-typical professional may be a composite of all of them.

The professional role is *achieved* rather than ascribed, that is, to become a professional, one must successfully complete a program of education and training. Professionals who work with families of children with disabilities have *chosen* that specialty. Unlike the parent who has given birth to a child with a disability, the professional works in this field because of interest, altruism, monetary or other reward, or convenience. Parents may resent the professional, who deals with their problems only during working hours, while they deal with them 24 hours a day.

The professional role is also *universalistic*, that is, the professional is expected to be fair. Ideally, all children will receive treatment of the same quality. In reality, though, many parents discover that their children with disabilities are *not* treated like their nondisabled children. These parental reports are illustrative:

> [Our pediatrician] seemed to feel that Brian was an unnecessary burden. . . . He didn't take my complaints seriously. . . . I feel that Brian's sore throat is just as important as [my normal daughter's] sore throat.

> She has a problem with her knee, and we took her to ____ Children's Hospital. . . . They said, "There's nothing we can do with one of *these* children." (Parent of child with Down syndrome)

> Our pediatrician . . . says, "She's retarded, and there's nothing you can do about it. You're wasting your time going to specialists." He blames all of her [medical] problems on retardation instead of treating them. (Darling, 1979, pp. 151, 152)

Such experiences may eventually result in parental challenges to professional authority.

The professional role is also *functionally specific* and continues to become increasingly more specialized. Parents expect teachers to be experts in the field of education but do not expect them to be experts in the field of medicine as well. Teachers, physicians, therapists, and other professionals who work with children and families all have their own areas of expertise. Parents, however, are not always aware of the distinctions among disciplines and may not be sure whether a question about feeding skills, for example, would be more appropriately asked of a pediatrician, speech therapist, occupational therapist, or teacher.

Parents are also interested in the whole child. They see their children playing many roles—child, grandchild, playmate, pupil—as well as "child with a disability." Most parents appreciate physicians who take the time to inquire about how their child is doing in school or teachers who show an interest in their child's medical problems. Likewise, they may come to resent professionals who do not show an interest in the whole child. As one father remarked, "The pediatrician . . . would keep him alive but he wasn't interested in Brian as a *person*" (Darling, 1979, p. 152). Similarly, in describing her daughter's clinic visit, one mother complained that "the doctors treated her like a 'thing' " (Darling, 1979, p. 152).

Finally, professionals are expected to be *affectively neutral* and not become emotionally involved with their clients. Again, the professional role is the antithesis of the parental role in this regard, and regardless of ideal-typical role expectations, many parents appreciate professionals who do become attached to their children. Matthew's mother, quoted at the beginning of the chapter, described a strong bond between her infant program teacher, her child, and herself. Because of the frequency and intensity of contact, parents are more likely to develop such a bond with teachers and therapists in a home-based program than with physicians seen only during brief clinic or office visits.

The Need to be Aware of Parental Expectations

Professionals who work with families, then, should be aware that parents have preconceived notions about the nature of the professional role. The degree to which professionals are able to meet parents' expectations may determine the nature of the relationship they will have with a family. Parents' expectations are shaped both by the views of the larger society and, as the last chapter has shown, by their subculture as well. Attitudes toward professionals differ among the various social classes, and parents may react differently to professionals who are of different ethnic groups. An awareness of these differing parental perceptions and expectations can help professionals improve the services they provide to families.

Professionals' Predispositions toward Children
with Disabilities and Their Families

Stigmatizing Attitudes

Families with children who have disabilities come into contact with a variety of professionals. Some of these professionals, such as pediatric physical therapists, have chosen their specialty because they want to work with this population. Other professionals, such as pediatricians or teachers in mainstream classrooms, may not enjoy working with children with disabilities at all. As one pediatrician said:

> I don't enjoy it. . . . I don't really enjoy a really handicapped child who comes in drooling, can't walk and so forth. . . . Medicine is geared to the perfect human body. Something you can't do anything about challenges the doctor and reminds him of his own inabilities. (Darling, 1979, p. 215)

Like others in society, these professionals have been exposed to stigmatizing attitudes toward individuals with disabilities. Most have not had any direct experience with such individuals either in their training or in their personal lives. As a result, they may not be able to understand the positive aspects of relationships between parents and children with disabilities. They may also feel inadequate in their ability to treat such families. These concerns are evident in this pediatrician's comments:

> There are personal hang-ups. You go home and see three beautiful, perfect children; then you see this "dud." You can relate more easily to those with three beautiful perfect kids. . . . If somebody comes in with a cerebral palsy or a Down's, I'm not comfortable. . . . My inadequacy to the task bothers me. . . .
> I liked problems as a resident but I can't say that I enjoy sick kids anymore. It's hard to find much happiness in this area. The subject of deformed children is depressing. . . . As far as having a Mongoloid child, I can't come up with anything good it does. There's nothing fun or pleasant. It's somebody's tragedy. I can find good things in practically anything—even dying—but birth defects are roaring tragedies. (Darling, 1979, pp. 214–215)

Such professionals may have more negative views of families than families have of themselves. One study (Blackard & Barsh, 1982) found significant differences between parents' and professionals' responses to a questionnaire about the impact of the child on the family. As compared with parents' responses, the professionals tended to overestimate the negative impact of the child on family relationships. The professionals overestimated the extent to which parents reported community rejection and lack of support and underestimated parents' ability to use appropriate teaching and behavior management techniques.

Rousso (1985) has suggested that when nondisabled professionals have difficulty identifying with their disabled clients, their attitudes do not help to promote their clients' self-esteem:

> When, as professionals, we find ourselves feeling too tragic, too despairing about our disabled patients' lives . . . we need to look at our own attitudes and our own history regarding disability. We may be imagining how our lives would be if we were suddenly disabled. . . . But keep in mind that congenitally disabled people are not newly disabled. . . .
>
> Being disabled and being intact at the same time is an extremely difficult notion for non-disabled people to make sense of. I keep thinking of my mother's words: "Why wouldn't you want to walk straight?" Even now, it is hard to explain that I may have wanted to walk straight, but I did not want to lose my sense of self in the process. . . . Fostering self-esteem in our congenitally disabled children and clients means helping them reconnect and reclaim these scattered pieces of their identities and once again feel whole, as they deserve. (p. 12)

In some cases, professionals have recommended institutionalization of children with disabilities, more because of *their* negative views of these children than because of parents' inability to cope (MacKeith, 1973). These professionals may project their negative views onto parents without knowing with certainty how the parents perceive their situation. This pediatrician's comments are illustrative:

> Most likely, I recommend institutionalization. I have yet to see a mother who has not been adversely affected by having a Mongoloid child in the house. *Despite the fact that women protest and act in a good, competent way,* I really feel that it's affected their lives in a way that robs their being a better person. . . . Seeing these people over the years . . . the look in their eyes, their demeanor—it's compensatory, not fulfilling. (Darling, 1979, p. 216, emphasis added)

In the well-publicized "Baby Doe" cases, physicians' negative attitudes may have contributed to their recommending against treatment (United States Commission on Civil Rights, 1986). When such decisions are made shortly after a child's birth, most parents, like most physicians, have been exposed only to society's stigmatizing attitudes toward the disabled. They have not had any of the positive experiences reported by families who have lived with disability for any length of time. In addition, parents are vulnerable in the immediate postpartum period and likely to accept the advice of an authority figure or expert. A physician's recommendation, then, about whether or not an infant with a disability should receive life-saving treatment, may strongly influence the parents' decision. Consequently, physicians and other professionals who may be involved in these situations have an obligation to be as fully informed as possible about the consequences—*both positive and negative*—of such decisions for families.

Apart from a child's disability, professionals may have negative attitudes toward parents because of their ethnicity, race, sex, or social class. Like others in society, professionals may have stereotypic views of various minority groups and have difficulty relating to families from those groups. In general, professionals feel most comfortable with families from middle- or upper-class backgrounds who share their own values.

The nature of a child's disability may also affect the attitudes of professionals toward the family. Some professionals may have more negative views of mental retardation than of physical disability, for example. Certain disabilities appear to be more stigmatizing than others. Wasow and Wikler (1983) found, for example, that professionals tended to react more positively toward parents of mentally retarded children than toward parents of children who were mentally ill. Whereas parents of retarded children were viewed as part of the treatment team, parents of mentally ill children were seen as part of the problem, even though chronic mental illness is recognized to be largely organic in etiology. The attitudes of professionals in this case are an example of victim blaming, which is discussed further in the next section.

The Clinical Perspective: Blaming the Victim

In addition to their exposure to stigmatizing attitudes in everyday life, professionals may in fact be *trained* to have negative views of individuals with disabilities and their families as part of their professional education. As Seligman and Seligman (1980) have noted, much of the early professional literature in this field characterized both children with disabilities and their parents as deficient.

Many social workers, psychologists, and other professionals have been trained in a psychoanalytic perspective, which locates the source of human problems within the psyche of the client (or the client's parents) rather than in the structure of the social system. When seen from this perspective, parents' concerns about their children are interpreted as indications of parental pathology. In much of the literature, this pathology is traced to parental guilt over having given birth to an "imperfect" child (see, e.g., Forrer, 1959; Powell, 1975; Zuk, 1959). When such an interpretive framework is used, expressions of parental love may be defined as "idealization" and treating a child as normal may be seen as "denial." Regardless of whether parents apparently accept or reject their children, their actions are believed in either case to be based on guilt.

Within this perspective, when parents are unable to cope, their failure is blamed on a supposed neurotic inability to accept the child. Real, system-based needs for financial aid, help with childcare, or medical or educational services tend to be discounted and attributed to parental inadequacy rather than to a lack of societal resources. Although some parents certainly do have neurotic tendencies, the victim-blaming model is inadequate to explain the many problems faced by parents of children with disabilities. Because society is structured largely to meet the needs of the nondisabled, goods and services for those with disabilities are often difficult, if not impossible, to find. Yet many textbooks in the field persist in stressing guilt-based theories of parental behavior, and as a result, professionals may complete their education with the belief that parents of children with disabilities are responsible for their own problems.

Gliedman and Roth (1980) argue that the nature of the parent–professional encounter encourages the professional to see the parent, in addition to the child, as the patient. They suggest that parents are expected to play the classic "sick role," that is, to be passive, cooperative, and in agreement with the decisions of the "experts." When parents disagree, they are sometimes treated like recalcitrant children and efforts are made to convert them to the "correct" position. Victim blaming and professional dominance can combine to render the parent powerless. "As for the parent . . . he finds himself in a double bind: either submit to professional dominance (and be operationally defined as a patient) or stand up for one's rights and risk being labeled emotionally maladjusted (and therefore patientlike)" (Gliedman & Roth, 1980, p. 150). When such views prevail in a treatment institution, newly trained professionals who join the staff may accept them.

As a result of their training and experience, then, professionals may come to adopt a *clinical* perspective. Mercer (1965, pp. 18–20) suggests that this perspective has the following components:

- The development of a diagnostic nomenclature.
- The creation of diagnostic instruments.
- The professionalization of the diagnostic function.
- [The] assumption that the official definition is somehow the 'right' definition. If persons in other social systems, especially the family, do not concur with official findings . . . , the clinical perspective assumes that they are either unenlightened or are evidencing psychological denial.

- Finally, . . . social action tends to center upon changing the individual. . . . Seldom considered [is] the alternative . . . of . . . modifying the norms of the social system or of attempting to locate the individual in the structure of social systems which will not perceive his behavior as pathological.

Mercer suggests an alternative *social system perspective*, which "attempts to see the definition of an individual's behavior as a function of the values of the social system within which he is being evaluated" (p. 20).

The clinical perspective has persisted in services to families with disabled children for a number of reasons, including professional socialization, transdisciplinary understanding, rewards for the clinician, ease of intervention, and the maintenance of professional dominance. Each of these will be considered in turn.

Professional Socialization. As indicated earlier, the clinical perspective continues to be part of professional training in schools of medicine, education, and social work, as well as in courses in psychology and other related fields. Courses in sociology or a social system perspective have not always been included in curricula used in training professionals in these fields.

Transdisciplinary Understanding. Most intervention programs in medical and educational settings employ a team of professionals. A variety of individuals, including a pediatrician, speech therapist, physical therapist, occupational therapist, and social worker, for example, work together to provide services to each child and family. All of these professionals tend to share the clinical perspective as a result of their training and are consequently able to communicate with one another fairly easily. At case conferences, each is able to discuss a particular aspect of the child and family, whether it be the child's speech or the parent–child relationship, and as a result of the discussion, a course of action is developed. Although the instruments of each specialty vary, they all use some sort of assessment tool to measure the child's or family's dysfunction. A course of remediation involves changing the child or family to meet professionally defined goals.

Rewards for the Clinician. The clinical perspective tends to quantify its concepts. Children can be placed at a specific point along a developmental scale; even family coping skills can be quantified. As a result, progress in a treatment program can be readily measured. When a child or family makes measurable progress, the professional feels rewarded. Social system variables (the availability of financial resources, for example) are not as easy to control, and methods for their measurement are not widely taught in professional schools.

Ease of Intervention. A consideration of all of the systems within which a family interacts complicates the intervention process. Treating the family in isolation is easier for the clinician and allows for more variables to be controlled. The system of categorical labels associated with the clinical perspective also facilitates intervention. Once a family is labeled, a known treatment method can be applied.

Maintenance of Professional Dominance. If they recognized the family's perspective as valid, professionals would have to yield some of their dominance. Many clinicians believe that their dominant status is justified because of their education and clinical experience.

In some cases, professionals may actually fear parents because of the threat they pose to the professionals' dominance. Lortie (reported in Seligman, 1979) notes that teachers, in particular, experience a sense of vulnerability because of parents' rights in the educational realm. Other professionals, such as physicians, may feel more secure, but those in private practice must always be sensitive to the need to please the client.

Limitations of the Clinical Perspective

The clinical perspective is limited in its value as a holistic approach to the treatment of children and their families. By extracting the child and family from their situational context and evaluating them using professionally constructed instruments, the clinician may be attaching meanings to their situation that are different from those attached to it by the family members themselves. When clinicians place children and families in diagnostic categories, they lose some of the uniqueness of any particular family. When the child and family are the primary focus of attention, social system–created problems, whose causes are external to the family system, may be overlooked.

The interaction between parents, children, and professionals is only one of many interaction situations encountered by families. While their child is in a treatment program, parents continue to interact with relatives, friends, strangers, and other professionals. In some cases, the demands of a program may even conflict with the family's pursuit of a normalized lifestyle in other areas. The professional in such a program cannot understand a family's failure to cooperate without an understanding of that family's competing needs. The following quote from the mother of four disabled teenagers illustrates the gap that sometimes exists between parent and professional:

> I'm seeing [a new psychologist] now. He's kind of giving me the blame for the way I am: "It's your fault you feel the way you do about things." I don't *want* to feel this way. . . . He says, "You create your own problems." My problem is that I have four handicapped children, and that has nothing to do with the fact that I had an unhappy childhood. . . . I'm nervous because I

have reason to be nervous. . . . That very night we were supposed to go someplace, and the van at the CP Center broke down, so suddenly we had four kids to worry about. . . . We had to change our plans. . . . That's the problem with these professionals. . . . They have a job. . . . They don't live with the parents 24 hours a day. What sounds nice at the office just doesn't work in real life (Darling, 1979, pp. 179–180).

Parents' priorities may be different from those of professionals, and, as a result, professionals often have little success when they try to intervene in these cases. As one professional who became a parent remarked: "Before I had Peter I gave out [physical therapy] programs that would have taken all day. I don't know when I expected mothers to change diapers, sort laundry, or buy groceries" (Featherstone, 1980, p. 57).

The following anecdote was related by the parent of a disabled child:

One parent . . . told me of her initial clinic visit where the social worker assured her that guilt in a parent was natural and that she shouldn't feel bad about it. . . . Stunned, she allowed the social worker to go on at some length before informing her that the child, in fact, was adopted (Pieper, in Darling & Darling, 1982, p. viii).

Although this anecdotal example is extreme, professionals can overlook important individual and contextual differences by making parents and children fit into clinical categories. Each family's situation is unique and derives from that family's particular place in society. A preconceived diagnostic nomenclature tends to prevent the clinician from seeing the client in a new or creative way.

When families are seen outside of their situational context in a school, clinic, or treatment center, the cause of their problems is more likely to be sought within the family itself. When the family's situation is not completely understood, parents' neurotic symptoms may be attributed to their inability to cope with the disabled child rather than to some external cause. As earlier chapters have shown, however, such symptoms are as likely to result from lack of social support or community resources as from the child's disability. Parents are expected to *accept* and *adjust* to their situation, and the professional role is perceived as one of helping parents cope. This view assumes that the family's situation cannot or should not be changed.

In fact, sometimes the situation *can* be changed. The child can be placed in a more appropriate program; respite care can be provided; financial aid may be available. Parenting a disabled child is expensive and exhausting because society does not have sufficient resources available to help ease the burden for parents. Society's lack of resources is not the parents' fault. Learning to cope may not be a more appropriate response than learning to work to bring about social change. In an early study of 50 Australian families who did not have access to any kind of program for their retarded children, Schonell and Watts (1956) found that the parents were "almost desperate." After a training center was established in the city, however, the parents' "neurotic symptoms" virtually disappeared (Schonell & Rourke, 1960).

Gliedman and Roth (1980) remind us that professionals exist to serve their clients:

> The parents' rights over the child take precedence over the professional's personal moral views. To put it bluntly, the professional exists to further the parent's vision of the handicapped child's future. Should the professional disagree, he has every right to try to *persuade* the parent to adopt a different view. . . . But except in the most extreme cases of parental incompetence and brutality, such as child abuse, the professional has no right to use his immense moral and practical power to intimidate or to manipulate the parent. (p. 145)

Some newer approaches in this field have taken a social system, rather than a clinical, perspective. The family-focused intervention model promulgated by Bailey and colleagues (1986), for example, suggests a "goodness-of-fit" concept for designing early intervention services to reflect family needs. Changing service models are discussed more fully later in the chapter.

THE PARENT-PROFESSIONAL ENCOUNTER: ROLE TAKING AND ROLE PLAYING

Both parents and professionals, then, bring preconceived ideas and views with them when they interact for the first time. Because of their differing life experiences, parents and professionals tend to view children with disabilities differently. The parenting experience is a powerful means of socialization and, as earlier chapters have shown, may shape parents' perceptions and definitions in unique ways. A professional who is not a parent cannot readily "understand" parenthood in the same way as a parent. The divergent views of parents and professionals sometimes result in strained interaction between them. As Freidson (1961) has written, "the separate worlds of experience and reference of the layman and the professional worker are always in potential conflict with each other" (p. 175).

The Setting

Although a number of treatment programs operate in the homes of the clients they serve, most parent–professional encounters take place in clinics, hospitals, offices, schools, and treatment centers, which are natural habitats for professionals but not for parents. Many parents are intimidated by such settings. They may recall prior experiences in schools or hospitals that made them feel uncomfortable during their own childhood or at some other time in their lives. They may also feel powerless because the setting is professionally controlled. Large treatment facilities also tend to have a bureaucratic atmosphere, which depersonalizes families and their problems.

Presentation of Self

Goffman (1959) and other sociologists have looked at how people attempt to create images of themselves in the course of interaction with others. Individuals act in a manner they believe will convey a desired impression. Parents and professionals also engage in self-presentation in their interactions with each other.

One of us (R. B. D.) once made an unscheduled home visit to a family in her early intervention program to find the usually neat and clean home in complete disarray. Toys were strewn about the floor, and dirty dishes filled the kitchen. The mother was extremely embarrassed and uneasy throughout the visit. The interventionist realized, as a result of this experience, that all of her previous scheduled visits had been preceded by much house cleaning and preparation by the family. Activities such as cleaning the house, dressing the child for the visit, and reporting about having worked on therapeutic or educational programs are all forms of self-presentation. Parents' awareness of such presentation is variable, although, as the following parental statement suggests, parents may deliberately and consciously attempt to convey a certain impression to the professional:

> I was conscious of the need to make these doctors identify with us as strongly and as quickly as possible. . . . I made sure that Julian and I dressed in a way that we imagined the doctor's family might dress. We were meticulous about showing up for appointments, at least 15 minutes early, to prove that we were concerned, responsible parents. We paid our bills promptly at the end of each visit. I tried to elicit personal comments from the doctor by referring to topics that might interest him. . . . Finally, I worked with David to make sure he was a cooperative and likable patient. (Stotland, 1984, p. 72)

The need to have the professional see them as "good" parents may be very stressful to some.

Professionals also engage in self-presentation in their interactions with parents. They may want to be perceived as authority figures, or as friends, or as sympathetic listeners. Self-presentation is learned in the course of professional training and experience. Professionals should try to become more aware of the images they are creating and of those they wish to create.

Role-Taking

The concept of role-taking ability suggests that people are able to see a situation from another person's perspective in the course of interaction. As the above discussion has indicated, our definitions of any situation are products of our unique life experiences. As a result, professionals may have difficulty "taking the role" of the parent, and parents likewise may have difficulty understanding the professional's point of view. This difficulty is summarized by Dembo (1984): "the professionals frequently appear to be insensitive to the parents because the professionals' position and values as outsiders stand in opposition to the position and values of the parents as insiders" (p. 93).

The Diagnostic Encounter

The literature suggests that the situation of first informing parents of a child's disability is commonly characterized by the poor role-taking ability of professionals. As Chapter 2 indicated, professionals tend to delay in providing such information to parents because they do not want to be bearers of bad news. These delays are also attributable, in part, to the perception by professionals that parents do not want to receive this information shortly after a child's birth. These pediatricians' quotes are illustrative:

> Birth is a traumatic experience. For 24 to 48 hours after birth the mother has not returned to a normal psychological state, so I just say everything is O.K., even if it isn't.

> I give them a lot of information on the physical aspects but I hold back on prognosis.

> I don't go through all the possibilities. That's cruel.

> It's not wise to go into all sorts of possibilities. I don't want to raise anxiety. Emotionally, they're in shock. They're really not listening. (Darling, 1979, p. 205)

Studies (Berg, Gilderdale, & Way, 1969; Carr, 1970; Drillien & Wilkinson, 1964; Gayton & Walker, 1974; McMichael, 1971) have indicated, however, that most parents *do* want diagnostic information as soon as possible. In a study of mothers of Down syndrome infants, for example, Carr (1970) found that half of those told within the first week would have liked to have been told even sooner; and in another study of Down syndrome parents (Gayton & Walker, 1974) 90% recommended in retrospect being told during the first week. Similarly, Berg and colleagues (1969) note that 43 of the 44 mothers they interviewed who were dissatisfied with the timing of the information they received thought they should have been told sooner. The main reason given for their dissatisfaction was that "the grave news was all the harder to bear if they had had time to build false hopes for the affected child" (p. 1195).

Parents' reactions to lack of information resulting from poor role-taking by professionals are illustrated by this mother's story:

> On our third visit, the neurologist said, "I think I know what's wrong with your son but I'm not going to tell you because I don't want to frighten you." Well, I think that's about the worst thing anyone could say. . . . We didn't go back to him. . . . We insisted that [our pediatrician] refer us to _____ Children's Hospital. He said, "He's little. Why don't you wait—you don't need to take him there yet." I have a feeling that he knew what the diagnosis was going to be and he didn't really think that we needed to know yet. . . . The chief of pediatrics at _____ Children's Hospital told us he was retarded. . . . That was the first person we talked to that we really felt we could trust. . . . Everyone was pablum-feeding us, and we wanted the truth. (Story related by the parent of a 6-year-old mentally retarded child with cerebral palsy)

During the past few years, programs have been developed in medical schools to aid physicians in role-taking during the diagnostic encounter. Perhaps as a result of such training, a more recent study (McDonald, Carson, Palmer, & Slay, 1982) found that 88% of physicians surveyed stated that they presented diagnostic information to both parents immediately after birth. Professionals must continue to be made aware of parents' needs for information as early as possible.

Other Encounters

Examples of poor role-taking can also be found in later encounters between parents and professionals, after a diagnosis has been established. Misperceptions of parents' desires for information continue to occur, primarily in interactions involving physicians. Raimbault, Cachin, Limal, Eliacheff, and Rappaport (1975) report, for example, that in a study of interactions between pediatric endocrinologists and parents of children with Turner syndrome, the physicians tended to avoid concerns raised by parents. Instead, they offered quasi-scientific explanations that parents did not understand.

Studies of the doctor–patient relationship in general have indicated that misconceptions of patients' needs for information are common. Waitzkin (1985) found, for example, in an analysis of 336 outpatient encounters, that physicians overestimated the time they spent in inforation giving and underestimated patients' desires for information. Class-based patterns tended to predominate, with patients of upper socio-economic status (SES) getting more information. Patients' *desires* for information were comparable in all social classes, however. In a recent British study (Boulton, Tuckett, Olson, & Williams, 1986), on the other hand, similar proportions of working and middle-class patients received explanations in general practice consultations.

Another area of misperception involves parents' psychosocial concerns and needs for emotional support. One study of mothers seeking care in private pediatric offices (Hickson, Altemeier, & O'Connor, 1983) found that only 30% of the mothers were most worried about their child's physical health; the others were more concerned with parenting, behavior, developmental, or psychosocial issues. Yet most parent–physician communication involved only health issues. Mothers were not aware that pediatricians could help them with these concerns or believed that pediatricians were not interested in helping them. Pediatricians, on the other hand, assumed incorrectly that mothers who did not raise such issues were not concerned about them. Lack of physician interest was also a barrier to communication leading some mothers to "cloak psychosocial worries in physical terms to gain the attention of the physician" (Hickson et al., 1983, p. 623). In another study (Cadman et al., reported in Bailey & Simeonsson, 1984), clinicians rated family interactions as the most important outcomes of intervention, whereas families rated these as next to least important.

Role Playing

The behavior, or role playing, of parents and professionals is based on their role-taking ability. They will act in a manner they believe will evoke the desired response on the part of the other. Role playing is based not only on preexisting perceptions but also on what actually happens in the course of a conversation. Both parents and professionals constantly adjust their behavior as they engage in an ongoing process of redefinition of the situation.

With regard to the parent–professional encounter, Gliedman and Roth (1980) have written: "Most people adjust their behavior unconsciously to reflect the prevailing structural asymmetries in a relationship" (p. 170). When parents perceive a difference in status between themselves and professionals, they may defer to the expertise of the professional and not express some of their questions or concerns. As Strong (1979) notes in a study of two hospital outpatient departments:

> Many parents disagreed strongly with the doctors' verdict at one time or another. Nevertheless all but a handful made no direct challenge to their authority. Most maintained an outward pose of agreement with what they were told, even though they might say rather different things to ancillary staff such as therapists or social workers. (p. 87)

Studies in the medical sociology literature reveal a rather high rate of noncompliance with doctors' orders among patients who do not openly express any disagreement while they are in the doctors' offices.

Noncompliance with medical advice appears to be related, at least in part, to lack of satisfaction during the parent–physician encounter. Francis, Korsch, and Morris (1968) found in a study of outpatient visits to a childrens's hospital that the extent to which parents' expectations were not met, lack of warmth in the physician–parent relation, and failure to receive a diagnostic explanation were key factors in noncompliance. Compliance was significantly related to parents' satisfaction.

Professional dominance of the parent–professional encounter also varies in response to parental role playing and the degree of professional uncertainty present in the situation. Fox (1959) found that in a situation of medical uncertainty, patients had a more collegial relationship with their physicians, and Sorenson (1974) has noted that in genetic counseling, patients can play an important role in decision making.

Many childhood disabilities also fall within the realm of "physician uncertainty." Diagnosis of mental retardation is very difficult, if not impossible, in very young children with cerebral palsy and other motor disabilities or sensory impairments, such as blindness or deafness. More subtle conditions, such as learning disabilities, are also difficult to diagnose at young ages. In one study of children who appeared to be retarded at 8 months of age (Holden, 1972), great variability in the children's IQ scores at ages 4 and 7 led the author to conclude that mental retardation is not predictable in infancy. In such cases, physicians are likely to communicate their uncertainty to parents and not issue a firm prognosis.

Davis (1960), however, has noted a distinction between *clinical* and *functional* uncertainty, the former a "real" phenomenon and the latter a patient management technique. Davis found that in the case of paralytic polio convalescence, treatment staff tended to be evasive with parents, avoiding the truth even after clinical uncertainty had disappeared. Such avoidance served to prevent emotional confrontations with parents. Functional uncertainty is also apparent in this statement from the medical report of a severely brain-damaged child in one of our (R.B.D.) programs:

> I have discussed the above results with John's parents but have not emphasized his very poor developmental outlook. I feel it is more humane and would be easier for them to accept this child if they observe and come to understand his slow progress for themselves. (Identifying information has been changed for the purpose of insuring anonymity).

Similarly, in a study of a neonatal intensive care unit, Sosnowitz (1984) notes that "the staff wanted a chance to observe how the parents would react to the crisis. When the staff was unable to predict the parents' reactions, they usually gave just enough information to keep the parents involved" (p. 396).

Functional uncertainty is especially characteristic of the diagnostic encounter. As noted earlier, physicians commonly delay in providing complete diagnostic information to parents because they believe that parents "are not ready" to hear the truth. Such delays also have the function of avoiding an emotional confrontation, however. Studies of the process of information giving suggest that four stalling strategies are commonly used: avoidance, hinting, mystification, and passing the buck.

In *avoidance*, the physician or other professional makes no suggestion at all of the existence of a problem and denies any such suggestion by the parent. These initial explanations of spina bifida, a serious birth defect, are illustrative: "There is a small piece of skin missing from his back," "He has a small lump on the spine," "Nothing that a skin graft won't help," "Just a small pimple on her back. . . . Nothing to worry about" (D'Arcy, 1968; Walker, 1971):

Hinting is exemplified in the following pediatrician's quotes:

> The first visit I make a note on the chart. Maybe I make a suggestion to the parent by listening longer to the baby's heart or whatever. By the next visit, parents start to ask.

> You start thinking in your mind as you're examining this child month after month. Here you try to hint. You say, "I'm not really sure. We'll watch it a little longer." . . . When you finally tell them they react pretty well.

> It it's something physical, I say I want to get a particular test or study. If it's developmental, I kind of ease them into it. I talk about milestones and what

they mean. All along I'm working to get them to realize there's a problem in the child's development. I go slowly. I ask them to come back sooner. . . . I don't seek a consultation right away. (Darling, 1979, p. 207)

Mystification involves the use of medical jargon or euphemisms. Although the truth is told, the parent cannot equate the diagnosis with any known (and presumably dreaded) defect. The following pediatrician's explanation is illustrative:

I don't want to worry the parent unnecessarily. I don't use the term, cerebral palsy, very often. . . . I'm hesitant to come out bluntly and use a term like cerebral palsy. I say, "motor delay" or "developmental lag" (Darling, 1979, p. 207)

In a study of diagnostic encounters involving mental retardation, Svarstad and Lipton (1977) found that in 32% of the cases, professionals were vague in describing the child's level of intelligence to parents and sometimes never used the term *mental retardation* at all.

A primary care practitioner can avoid a diagnostic confrontation by *passing the buck* to a specialist:

You suspect this as the child progresses but you don't come right out and say "I think your child has cerebral palsy." You suggest a neurological consultation.

You can't tell them all you know. The specialist can slap them with the facts. (Darling, 1979, p. 207)

As earlier chapters have shown, these techniques can increase rather than alleviate parental anxiety. Svarstad and Lipton (1977) found that parents who received specific, clear, and frank communication were better able to accept a diagnosis of mental retardation in their children than those who received vague or evasive information. Maynard (1983) has shown, too, that parents' responses to diagnostic information are directly related to the style with which the information is presented. Parents' responses, in turn, affect further role playing by professionals.

The variability in parent roles can also be a potential source of conflict between parents and professionals. In many intervention programs, parents are expected to play the role of teacher with their children and are trained for this role by program professionals. As Farber and Lewis (1975) have argued, however, some parents may not *want* to play a pedagogical role, and "such parental training subordinates the uniquely personalized component of the parent–child relationship" (p. 40). In order to be effective in their interactions with families, professionals must develop realistic role expectations for parents that are compatible with parents' expectations for themselves.

THE EMERGENCE OF A PARENT-PROFESSIONAL PARTNERSHIP: NEW ROLES FOR PARENTS AND PROFESSIONALS

Although parent and professional roles have historically been in conflict, some newer directions have been emerging that can help to bring them closer together.

New Roles for Parents: The Emergence of Parent Activism

Ayer (1984) and others have suggested that the failure of professionals to meet family needs has resulted in self-help activities by families. Although most parents begin by acquiescing to professional authority, many come to play an *entrepreneurial* role (Darling, 1979) in order to secure needed services. This role includes (1) seeking information, (2) seeking control, and (3) challenging authority.

As noted earlier in this chapter, parents of children with disabilities, like others in society, have been socialized to accept professional dominance. Haug and Lavin (1983) report that the large majority (72%) of their general population sample had never challenged their physicians in any way. On the other hand, as the consumerist movement has grown, parents and others have become more aware of the *possibility* of challenging professional authority.

Parents' disillusionment with professionals may begin to occur shortly after a child's birth, when professionals fail to provide desired diagnostic or treatment information or deny parents' control over their child's management and care. Parents may come to resent their role as helpless bystanders:

> We were always going back and forth to ＿＿ Children's Hospital. . . . It was a constantly pulling away. We could never be a family. . . . It was always, "We have to go to the hospital." We had to go to doctors, doctors, doctors. . . . We could never get to know our child. . . . We got to the point where we hated doctors, we hated ＿＿ Children's Hospital. (Darling, 1979, p. 154)

On the other hand, some professionals willingly share information with and seek advice from parents:

> The most important aspect of the doctor's presentation was that he involved us as equals in the decision-making process. . . . By involving us in the process and by giving us his professional opinion as an opinion, he returned to us our parental rights of making the important decision that would affect our child's life. *We were in control*, but we were no longer alone. (Stotland, 1984, p. 72, emphasis added)

An encounter with such a professional could be a turning point that would eliminate the need for further parental entrepreneurship.

As noted in earlier chapters, the more parents interact with their children, the more committed they become to their children's welfare. The emotional bond that develops between parent and child is a strong catalyst to parental activism. Pizzo (1983) has suggested that the bond "energizes" parent advocacy. She writes:

> The most universal shared experience we have as parents is the struggle to protect children and to get them the resources they need to develop well. Listening to parent activists describe their work, one soon learns that their organizational activities are not radically different from the basic task we undertake as parents. In self-help and advocacy, parents take the intimate, nurturing vigilance needed for effective child-rearing into a social and political domain. (p. 19)

When parents encounter difficulties in meeting their children's needs, they are likely to continue to search for appropriate services and helpful professionals. Negative experiences with professionals can be a catalyst for further action. Pizzo (1983) argues that parent advocacy derives from "acute, painful experiences,'" and Haug and Lavin (1983) report that the most important variable in consumerist challenges to medical authority is the *experience of medical error*. Such an experience erodes trust in professional authority and may provide the needed turning point to launch parents on a career of activism.

Parents of children with disabilities are more likely to encounter medical error or errors in professional judgement than other people because of the frequency and intensity of their contacts with the many professionals involved in their children's care. They have more opportunities to encounter professional failure. Haug and Lavin (1983) have suggested that, "chronic patients, who live with their conditions for long stretches of time, often learn by their own experience which therapies are helpful and which are not" (p. 33). As one mother of a child with multiple disabilities said:

> In all of her hospitalizations I've been very frustrated by residents who think they know everything. They've given us so much misinformation. . . . Now I

tell them. . . . I find that other parents are too accepting. They don't question their doctors. (Darling, 1979, p. 153)

Through their children's medical treatment or educational programs, most parents meet other parents of disabled children, with whom they exchange stories and thereby learn that their problems are shared. They also learn about the possibilities for activism and advocacy through the relationships they develop in support groups and other disability organizations. When they interact with others, parents learn about techniques that have worked and come to realize that authority can be successfully challenged. As an article about the Parents' Union of Philadelphia noted (Wice & Fernandez, 1984): "Mrs. Thomas was powerful when she was linked to others through an alert advocacy group. . . . Alone, a parent may be tempted to give up. Together, parents have power" (p. 40).

Pizzo (1983) notes that many parents become involved in self-help groups after seeing something in the media. In addition to general newspapers, magazines, and television programs, specialized publications are targeted specifically at parents of children with disabilities. *The Exceptional Parent* magazine, for example, prints success stories about and by parents who have actively challenged professional authority. When Mary Tatro received *The Exceptional Parent* Award of 1984, her merits were described as follows:

> Mrs. Tatro was able to persist more than five years to get the services necessary for her child, although this meant sustaining personal hardship, a prolonged struggle, and an eventual confrontation at the United States Supreme Court. (Related Services and the Supreme Court, 1984, p. 36)

Such stories may inspire other parents to pursue more or better services for their own children.

In addition to opportunities to learn from experience and informal socialization in parent groups, more formalized training in assertiveness and advocacy has become available to parents in recent years. A number of books and manuals have been published that familiarize parents with their legal rights and teach strategies for interacting with professionals and bringing about social change (see, e.g., Biklen, 1974; DesJardins, 1971; Dickman, 1985; Lurie, 1970). Courses are also being offered in activist techniques.

Increasing parent awareness of rights and methods for acting upon those rights is an important step toward the creation of a true parent–professional partnership. Parents and professionals must work together to meet the needs of children with disabilities. The changing roles of professionals are explored in the next section.

New Roles for Professionals:
Advocacy and a Social System Perspective

Developing Role-Taking Ability

In order to be truly effective, the professional must learn to take the role of the parent. The professional exists to help families achieve their goals. To serve that purpose, the professional must understand, as well as possible, the *family's* definition of what its members want and need and must take what Mercer (1965) has called a social system perspective.

Professional awareness of the point of view of families has certainly been increasing in recent years, as evidenced by a growing body of literature in professional journals and books about the family experience. Professional training programs have been using videotapes, trained parents, and other techniques for making professionals more aware of parent perceptions (see, e.g., Guralnick, Bennett, Heiser, & Richardson, 1987; Richardson, Guralnick, & Tupper, 1978; Stillman, Sabers, & Redfield, 1977), and early intervention programs have been designing assessment instruments and curricula based on the expressed needs of families (see, e.g., Bailey et al., 1986). An instrument of this kind is discussed further in Chapter 10.

In order to become more effective in taking the role of the family, professionals must explore their own attitudes, accept their own limitations, and try to experience, through simulation and other techniques, what the families they are trying to help are experiencing. Some practical exercises for increasing role-taking ability are suggested below (adapted from Darling & Darling, 1982, pp. 184–189):

1. *Write a sociological autobiography.* Think about your own background and the experiences that have shaped your attitudes. Try to remember your earliest experiences with disabled children or adults. Do you recall any disabled individuals in your family, your neighborhood, your school, your church, or your Scout troop? What did you think of them. How did you feel in their presence? What did your parents, friends, and other significant others tell you about them?

How have your other group affiliations shaped your attitudes toward disabilities? Do your religious values affect your attitudes? Did your social-class background stress hard work, achievement, and "getting ahead" and deprecate those who were dependent on others for a livelihood? How has your sex-role socialization affected your attitudes? Did you learn that males are supposed to be physically and emotionally strong or that females are supposed to be physically attractive?

Think about the disabled strangers you have seen in public places or on television and those about whom you have read in books or magazines. Have you watched telethons on behalf of various disabilities? As a child did you read *A Christmas Carol, The Prince and the Pauper,* or *Heidi?* Have you seen televised faith healings or read any of the publications of the Christian Science church?

Have you ever deliberately avoided interacting with a person with a disability? Have you walked away from an opportunity to help a blind person cross a street? Have you avoided a friendship with a neighbor who has a retarded child? Why do you think you acted the way you did in these situations?

Make a list of all of your group affiliations and experiences with disability and examine how each has affected your attitudes toward the disabled. Use your list to write an autobiography that traces your experiences and shows how they shaped your present attitudes.

2. *Design and conduct depth interviews with (a) one or more disabled adolescents or adults and (b) one or more parents of disabled children.* Get to know someone with a disability. Make a list of questions that will serve as the basis for an in depth conversation with your respondent. Try to guide the conversation so that your respondents tell you how they feel about their disability. Do they welcome questions about their disability? What kinds of questions are upsetting or offensive? What kinds of questions are helpful?

In interviewing parents, questions should include the following topics: (1) their expectations prior to their child's birth (Did they want their unborn son to be a football player or a doctor?), (2) their experiences during labor and delivery (Did they suspect that something was wrong with the baby?), (3) their reactions to the first information that their child had a disability (How were they told? How did they feel?), (4) their attitudes toward professionals (Which professionals have been helpful to them? Why?), (5) their feelings about their children (What negative and positive effects have they had on their lives?), (6) their experiences with friends, relatives, and strangers (Have grandparents been supportive? How do people react to their children in restaurants; shopping malls?), (7) their perceptions of their child's effect on family relationships (Has their marriage been strengthened or weakened? How have siblings reacted?), and (8) their expectations and hopes for the future (What do they think/hope will happen to their children when they grow up?)

Students and others not currently involved professionally with the disabled can usually find respondents in parent groups affiliated with hospitals, clinics, preschool programs, or organizations such as the Association for Retarded Citizens or the United Cerebral Palsy Association. Adults with disabilities may be found through associations such as Easter Seals, the Spina Bifida Association of America, or United Cerebral Palsy; at sheltered workshops, such as those operated by Goodwill Industries; or through resident managers and houseparents at community-based housing facilities for the disabled. Organized groups for students with disabilities can be found on some college campuses.

These interviews are not intended to provide a complete picture of individuals with disabilities, and you must be careful not to generalize from your respondents to others with similar disabilities. Individuals with disabilities are just as different from one another as individuals without disabilities. This exercise is only intended to make you more aware of how *one person* or *a few people* feel about their situation.

3. *Observe a special situation.* You may want to spend some time observing any or all of the following: meetings of an association of parents of children with disabilities, a preschool center for disabled children, a special-education class in the public schools, a sheltered workshop, a support group for adolescents or adults with disabilities, a residential institution for the retarded, a group home for physically disabled or mentally retarded adults, a day program for mentally retarded adults.

4. *Read some personal accounts written by parents of children with disabilities.* The following are a small sample of such books. Many others are available as well:

Killilea, M. *Karen.* Englewood Cliffs, NJ: Prentice-Hall, 1952. Written by the mother of a child with cerebral palsy.

Pieper, E. *Sticks and Stones.* Syracuse, NY: Human Policy Press, 1977. Written by the mother of a young adult with spina bifida.

Roberts, N. *David.* Richmond, VA: John Knox Press, 1968. Written by the mother of a child with Down syndrome.

Ulrich, S. *Elizabeth.* Ann Arbor: University of Michigan Press, 1972. Written by the mother of a blind preschool child.

5. *Read some literature written from the parents' perspective.* Magazines and newsletters written for parents provide insight into the parents' point of view. See, for example, *The Exceptional Parent,* a magazine written especially for the parents of special children (available from *The Exceptional Parent,* 605 Commonwealth Avenue, Boston, MA 02215). Newsletters such as the National Down Syndrome Society *Update* (141 Fifth Avenue, New York, NY 10010) or the Spina Bifida Association of America *Insights* (1700 Rockville Pike, Suite 540, Rockville, MD 20852) are also valuable.

6. *Participate in simulation experiences or other awareness-promoting programs.* Spend a day in a wheelchair or wearing a blindfold—or spend some time pushing a wheelchair or escorting someone who is blind. Accompany an obviously disabled child to a shopping mall, restaurant, or other public place. Watch the reactions of waitresses, store

clerks, and other customers. (Some individuals with disabilities disagree about the value of simulation experiences.)

Packaged programs are also available. These contain exercises for group instruction or individual use that help to promote awareness of disabilities and the feelings that surround them. Two such programs are:

Everybody Counts! A Workshop Manual to Increase Awareness of Handicapped People. Available from the Council for Exceptional Children, 1920 Association Drive, Reston, VA 22091

Yerxa, E.J. *Human Interaction and Physical Differences: A Program of Instruction for Two Persons.* Available from Concept Media, P.O. Box 19542, Irvine, CA 92714.

7. *Evaluate your goals.* Why have you decided to enter the helping professions? Why have you chosen a field that brings you into contact with families with disabled children? Make a list of your personal professional goals. Evaluate each of your goals in terms of its potential beneficial or negative effect on the client (A goal of "curing," for example, may be counterproductive in working with a family whose child is incurable). Greater insight into your own role can help you to understand your effect on those you serve.

Professionals as Advocates

Traditionally, helping professionals worked to change their *clients*, to cure them, to improve their functional abilities, to make them more comfortable, to aid them in adjusting to their situation. In recent years we have learned that changing the client is not always enough. Sometimes, the client's *social situation* needs to be changed. Because society is designed primarily to meet the needs of those without disabilities, structural barriers exist that prevent those with disabilities from achieving full integration. These include:

- physical barriers, such as curbs, stairs, and narrow doorways
- cultural barriers, such as stigma and prejudice
- social barriers, such as the lack of needed services

These barriers cannot be eliminated without social change to produce access, public awareness, and resources to meet the needs of families with disabled children.

Advocacy involves working to bring about social change. Is advocacy an appropriate part of the professional role? Wolfensburger (reported in Kurtz, 1977) argues that "the advocacy concept demands that advocacy for an impaired person is to be exercised *not* by agencies, and *not* by professionals acting in professional roles, but by *competent and suitable citi-*

zens" (p. 146, emphasis in original). Adams (1973) argues that professional advocacy poses ethical dilemmas. The professional must decide whether to support the rights of the individual or the rights of society when the two are in conflict. Kurtz (1975) has noted that advocacy may produce role conflict, involving the professional's agency of employment, parents, children, and others who may be deprived of services, and Frith (1981) states that "it is becoming increasingly difficult for professionals in the field [of special education] to assume the role of child advocate, while simultaneously attempting to support their employing agency" (p. 487).

Two professional organizations, the Council for Exceptional Children and the Ad Hoc Committee on Advocacy of the National Association of Social Workers, have taken the position that, in the case of advocacy dilemmas, the professional *should act as an advocate for the client.* The Council for Exceptional Children (1981) has issued the following statement:

> The Council for Exceptional Children firmly believes that the role of the professional as an employee should not conflict with the professional's advocate role. Rather, these roles should complement each other. . . . Failing to assume responsibility [as an advocate], the professional can only play the role of participant in whatever injustice may befall the child.

When they become advocates for vulnerable families, professionals become partners with their clients in working toward social change. Unlike the professional dominance that has characterized parent–professional interaction in the past, today's parent–professional partnership must be marked by equality. To be truly effective, professionals must come to understand and respect the point of view of the families they serve and to promote that point of view when conflicts arise. Although we must continue to help families adjust to situations that cannot be changed, we cannot continue to blame families for their problems when society *can* be changed. Social action rather than passive adjustment may be the hallmark of parent–professional interaction in the future. Together, professionals and families can work to eliminate the physical, cultural, and social barriers that prevent families from attaining the best possible quality of life.

REFERENCES

Adams, M. (1973). Science, technology, and some dilemmas of advocacy. *Science, 180,* 840–842.
Ayer, S. (1984). Community care: The failure of professionals to meet family needs. *Child: Health and Development, 10,* 127–140.

Bailey, D. B., Jr., & Simeonsson, R. J. (1984). Critical issues underlying research and intervention with families of young handicapped children. *Journal of the Division for Early Childhood, 9,* 38–48.

Bailey, D. B., Jr., Simeonsson, R. J., Winton, P. J., Huntington, G. S., Comfort, M., Isbell, P., O'Donell, K. J., & Helm, J. M. (1986). Family-focused intervention: A functional model for planning, implementing, and evaluating individualized family services in early intervention. *Journal of the Division for Early Childhood, 10,* 156–171.

Berg, J. M., Gilderdale, S., & Way, J. (1969). On telling parents of the diagnosis of Mongolism. *British Journal of Psychiatry, 115,* 1195–1196.

Betz, M., & O'Connell, L. (1983). Changing doctor–patient relationships and the rise in concern for accountability. *Social Problems, 31,* 84–95.

Biklen, D. (1974). *Let our children go: An organizing manual for advocates and parents.* Syracuse, NY: Human Policy Press.

Blackard, M. K., & Barsch, E.T. (1982). Parents' and professionals' perceptions of the handicapped child's impact on the family. *TASH Journal, 7,* 62–70.

Boulton, M., Tuckett, D., Olson, C., & Williams, A. (1986). Social class and the general practice consultation. *Sociology of Health and Illness, 8,* 325–350.

Carr, J. (1970). Mongolism—Telling the parents. *Developmental Medicine and Child Neurology, 12,* 213.

Council for Exceptional Children. (1981). Editor's note. *Exceptional Children, 47,* 492–493.

D'Arcy, E. (1968). Congenital defects: Mothers' reactions to first information. *British Medical Journal, 3,* 796–798.

Darling, R. B. (1979). *Families against soceity: A study of reactions to children with birth defects.* Beverly Hills: Sage.

Darling R. B., & Darling, J. (1982). *Children who are different: Meeting the challenges of birth defects in society.* St. Louis: Mosby.

Davis, F. (1960). Uncertainty in medical prognosis clinical and functional. *American Journal of Sociology, 66,* 41–47.

Dembo, T. (1984). Sensitivity of one person to another. *Rehabilitation Literature, 45,* 90–95.

DesJardins, C. (1971). *How to organize an effective parent group and move bureaucracies: For parents of handicapped children and their helpers.* Chicago: Coordinating Council for Handicapped Children.

Dickman, I. (1985). *One miracle at a time: How to get help for your disabled child—from the experience of other parents.* New York: Simon & Schuster.

Drillien, C. M., & Wilkinson, E. M. (1964). Mongolism: When should parents be told? *British Medical Journal, 2,* 1306–1307.

Farber, B., & Lewis, M. (1975). The symbolic use of parents: A sociological critique of educational practice. *Journal of Research and Development in Education, 8,* 34–41.

Featherstone, H. (1980). *A difference in the family: Life with a disabled child.* New York: Basic Books.

Forrer, G. R. (1959). The mother of a defective child. *Psychoanalytic Quarterly, 28,* 59–63.

Fox, R. (1959). *Experiment perilous.* Glencoe, IL: Free Press.

Francis, V., Korsch, B. M., & Morris, M. J. (1968). Gaps in doctor–patient communication: Patients' response to medical advice. *New England Journal of Medicine, 280,* 535–540.

Freidson, E. (1961). *Patients' views of medical practice.* New York: Russell Sage Foundation.

Freidson, E. (1970). *Professional dominance.* Chicago: Aldine.

Frith, C. H. (1981). "Advocate" vs. "professional employee": A question of priorities for special educators. *Exceptional Children, 47,* 486–492.

Gayton, W. F., & Walker, L. (1974). Down's syndrome: Informing the parents. *American Journal of Disabled Children, 127,* 510–512.

Gliedman, J., & Roth, W. (1980). *The unexpected minority.* New York: Harcourt Brace Jovanovich.

Goffman, E. (1959). *The presentation of self in everyday life.* Garden City, NY: Doubleday.

Guralnick, M. J., Bennett, F. C., Heiser, K. E., & Richardson, H. B., Jr. (1987). Training future primary care pediatricians to serve handicapped children and their families. *Topics in Early Childhood Special Education, 6,* 1–11.

Haug, M., & Lavin, B. (1983). *Consumerism in medicine: Challenging physician authority.* Beverly Hills: Sage.

Hickson, G. B., Altemeier, W. A., & O'Connor, S. (1983). Concerns of mothers seeking care in private pediatric offices: Opportunities for expanding services. *Pediatrics, 72,* 619–624.

Holden, R. H. (1972). Prediction of mental retardation in infancy. *Mental Retardation, 10,* 28–30.

Judge, G. (1987). Knock, knock . . . It's no joke. *Zero to Three, 8,* 20–21.

Kurtz, R. A. (1975). Advocacy for the mentally retarded: The development of a new social role. In M. J. Begab & S. A. Richardson (Eds.), *The mentally retarded and society: A social science perspective* (pp. 377–394). Baltimore: University Park Press.

Kurtz, R. A. *Social aspects of mental retardation.* Lexington, MA: D. C. Heath.

Lurie, E. (1970). *How to change the schools: A parent's action handbook on how to fight the system.* New York: Vintage.

MacKeith, R. (1973). The feelings and behaviour of parents of handicapped children. *Developmental Medicine and Child Neurology, 15,* 524–527.

Max, L. (1985). Parents' view of provisions, services, and research. In N. N. Singh & K. M. Wilton (Eds.), Mental retardation in New Zealand (pp. 250–262). Christchurch, New Zealand: Whitoculls.

Maynard, D. W. (1983). Notes on the delivery and reception of diagnostic news regarding mental disabilities. In T. Anderson, D. Helms, J. Mehan, & A. Rawls (Eds.), *New directions in sociology.* New York: Irvington.

McDonald, A. C., Carson, K. L., Palmer, D. J., & Slay, T. (1982). Physicians' diagnostic information to parents of handicapped neonates. *Mental Retardation, 20,* 12–14.

McMichael, J. K. (1971). *Handicap: A study of physically handicapped children and their families.* Pittsburgh: University of Pittsburgh Press.

Mercer, J. R. (1965). Social system perspective and clinical perspective: Frames of reference for understanding career patterns of persons labeled as mentally retarded. *Social Problems, 13,* 18–34.

Moeller, C. J. (1986). The effect of professionals on the family of a handicapped child. In R. R. Fewell & P. F. Vadasy (Eds.), *Families of handicapped children* (pp. 149–166). Austin, TX: Pro-Ed.

Parsons, T. (1951). *The social system.* New York: Free Press.

Pizzo, P. (1983). *Parent to parent: Working together for ourselves and our children.* Boston: Beacon.

Powell, J. D. (1975). *Theory of coping systems: Changes in supportive health organizations.* Cambridge, MA: Schenkman.

Raimbault, G., Cachin, O., Limal, J.-M., Eliacheff, C., & Rappaport, R. (1975). Aspects of communication between patients and doctors: An analysis of the discourse in medical interviews. *Pediatrics, 55,* 401–405.

Related Services and the Supreme Court: A Family's Story. (1984, October). *The Exceptional Parent,* pp. 36–41.

Richardson, H. B., Guralnick, M. J., & Tupper, D. B. (1978). Training pediatricians for effective involvement with preschool handicapped children and their families. *Mental Retardation, 16,* 3–7.

Rousso, H. (1985, February). Fostering self-esteem, part II: What parents and professionals can do. *The Exceptional Parent*, pp. 9-12.

Schonell, F. J., & Rorke, M. (1960). A second survey of the effects of a subnormal child on the family unit. *American Journal of Mental Deficiency, 64*, 862-868.

Schonell, F. J., & Watts, B. H. (1956). A first survey of the effects of subnormal child on the family unit. *American Journal of Mental Deficiency, 61*, 210-219.

Seligman, M. (1979). *Strategies for helping parents of exceptional children*. New York: Free Press.

Seligman, M., & Seligman, P. A. (1980, October). The professional's dilemma: Learning to work with parents. *The Exceptional Parent*, pp. S11-S13.

Sorenson, J. (1974). Biomedical innovation, uncertainty, and doctor-patient interaction. *Journal of Health and Social Behavior, 15*, 366-374.

Sosnowitz, B. G. (1984). Managing parents on neonatal intensive care units. *Social Problems, 31*, 390-402.

Stillman, P. L., Sabers, D. L., & Redfield, D. L. (1977). Use of trained mothers to teach interviewing skills to first-year medical students: A follow-up study. *Pediatrics, 60*, 165-169.

Stotland, J. (1984, February). Relationship of parents to professionals: A challenge to professionals. *Journal of Visual Impairment and Blindness*, 69-74.

Strong, P. M. (1979). *The ceremonial order of the clinic: Parents, doctors, and medical bureaucracies*. London: Routledge & Kegan Paul.

Svarstad, B. L., & Lipton, H. L. (1977). Informing parents about mental retardation: A study of professional communication and parent acceptance. *Social Science and Medicine, 11*, 645-651.

United States Commission on Civil Rights. (1986). *Protection of handicapped newborns: Hearing held in Washington, DC, June 26-27, 1986 (vol. II)*. Washington DC: U.S. Government Printing Office.

Waitzkin, H. (1985). Information giving in medical care. *Journal of Health and Social Behavior, 26*. 81-101.

Walker, J. H. (1971). Spina bifida—and the parents. *Developmental Medicine and Child Neurology, 13*, 462-476.

Wasow, M., & Wikler, L. (1983). Reflections on professionals' attitudes toward the severely mentally retarded and the chronically mentally ill: Implications for parents. *Family Therapy, 10*, 299-308.

Wice, B., & Fernandez, H. (1984, October). Meeting the bureaucracy face to face: Parent power in the Philadelphia schools. *The Exceptional Parent*, pp. 36-41.

Zuk, G. H. (1959). The religious factor and the role of guilt in parental acceptance of the retarded child. *American Journal of Mental Deficiency, 64*, 139.

10

Applying a Systems Approach to the Identification of Family Strengths and Needs: The Individualized Family Service Plan and Beyond

As noted repeatedly in this volume, the recognition of the importance of the family as a whole in services to disabled children is a relatively recent development in the history of the field. In the past, medical, educational, and therapeutic services were designed to meet only the needs of the child. The needs of parents and other family members were neglected or left to social workers who had little direct influence on the child's educational or therapeutic program. In recent years, professionals have come to recognize that family needs and child needs are not separate and distinct. This recognition achieved legal acknowledgment with the passage of landmark legislation in 1986, the Education of the Handicapped Act amendments—Public Law 99-457.

Title I of that law, which applies to infants and toddlers with disabilities, recognizes a need "to enhance the capacity of families to meet the special needs of their infants and toddlers with handicaps." Consequently, the law establishes a policy to assist states "to develop and implement a statewide, comprehensive, coordinated, multidisciplinary interagency program of early intervention services for handicapped infants and toddlers *and their families*" (pp. 1–2, emphasis added).

THE INDIVIDUALIZED FAMILY SERVICE PLAN (IFSP)

Services to families of infants and toddlers are to be provided through an Individualized Family Service Plan (IFSP). The IFSP replaces the Individualized Education Plan (IEP), created under P.L. 94-142, the act upon which these amendments are based. The IEP is a document that lists the strengths and needs of special-education students and develops the long-range goals and short-term objectives that will meet those needs. Although the parent may participate in the development of the IEP, the parent's needs, as distinct from the child's needs, are not addressed. With the passage of P.L. 99-457, very young children (under age 3) will not have IEPs at all. Rather, service providers will be forced to take family needs into account in the preparation of IFSPs.

The new law (Education of the Handicapped Act Amendments, 1986) requires that:

> Each handicapped infant or toddler and infant or toddler's family shall receive—(1) a multidisciplinary assessment of unique needs and the identification of services appropriate to meet such needs, and (2) a written individualized family service plan developed by a multidisciplinary team, including the parent or guardian. (p. 6)

The IFSP is to be evaluated once each year, and the family is to be provided with a review of the plan at least every 6 months.

Among other items, the IFSP must include:

- a statement of the child's present developmental levels;
- a statement of the family's strengths and needs relating to enhancing the development of the child;
- a statement of the major outcomes expected to be achieved for the child and the family;
- a statement of specific early intervention services necessary to meet the unique needs of the child and the family and timeframes for these services.

Many standardized evaluation instruments are available for the measurement of young children's developmental levels (see, e.g., Furuno, Inatsuka, O'Reilly, Hosaka, Zeisloft, & Allman, 1984; Glover, Preminger, & Sanford, 1978). Because our focus in this book is on families, we do not attempt to review these instruments here. Rather, we refer the reader to the many texts and journals that are widely available in the fields of child development, psychology, and early childhood special education (e.g.,

Journal of the Division for Early Childhood; Topics in Early Childhood Special Education).

We devote the remainder of this chapter, then, to a discussion of the assessment of family strengths and needs and the development of an IFSP based on this assessment.

THE PARENT NEEDS SURVEY (PNS)

The family needs assessment advocated here is based on the social system perspective (Mercer, 1965) that has been presented throughout this book. To understand families, professionals must accept the statements of parents and other family members as meaningful, regardless of whether they agree with them or think they are true. Intervention must be based on what is real *for the family.* Parents must not themselves become objects of clinical analysis simply because they happen to be the parents of children with disabilities. Parents of nondisabled children are not required to demonstrate a standardized set of "parenting skills"; parents of the disabled should not be subjected to a double standard. Certainly the literature reveals the existence of disordered family relationships in families with disabled children, as well as in families whose children are "normal." Such families may need the assistance of trained counselors or specialized agencies. Unless we have strong evidence to the contrary, however, we should not assume that family relationships are pathologic. Early intervention professionals should limit their intervention to meeting those needs that *families* define as important. The early intervention specialist should help the family help the child and should respect the family's privacy in other areas of family life—unless help is requested in those areas.

The instrument that will be presented here is an example of a tool based on a social system perspective, in that needs are defined by the family rather than by the professional. Other tools have been developed from that perspective as well (see, e.g., Bailey & Simeonsson, in press). The Parent Needs Survey (PNS) has been field-tested for 3 years in a program directed by one of us (R.B.D.) and appears promising as an indicator of family needs that can be used in the development of the IFSP. Figure 10-1 is a sample survey form.

The PNS was developed from an overview of the literature (presented in earlier chapters) on families of young children with disabilities. The literature indicates six major areas of need in this population:

1. *information* about diagnosis, prognosis, and treatment;
2. *treatment* for the child—medical, therapeutic, and educational;

3. *formal support* from public and private agencies;
4. *informal support* from relatives, friends, neighbors, co-workers, and other parents;
5. *material support*, including financial support and access to resources;
6. elimination of *competing family needs*, that is, needs of other family members (parents, siblings, etc.) that may affect the family's ability to attend to the needs of the disabled child.

The PNS contains items that relate to each of these categories of need as follows:

1. information—items #1, 7, 8, 9, 14, 15;
2. treatment—items #6, 8, 9, 11, 14, 15, 19;
3. formal support—items #2, 3, 10, 12, 21;
4. informal support—items #2, 3, 17, 18, 20, 21, 22;
5. material support—items #4, 19, 23;
6. competing needs—items #4, 5, 12, 13, 16, 17, 18, 22, 23, 24, 25, 26.

Field-Test Data

In the early intervention program of one of us (R. B. D.), the PNS is administered upon program entry and at 6-month intervals thereafter, in conjunction with assessments of child development. As of this writing, the instrument has been administered to the families of 107 children at least once and to the families of 49 of these children more than once. The median age of children at entry into the program is 9 months, with a range from newborn to (usually) 30 months of age. Children in the program either have diagnosed developmental disabilities or are at risk for medical or environmental reasons or because they have developmental delays. The population served by the program is both urban and rural and includes one- and two-parent nuclear and extended family units of all socioeconomic strata.

The instrument seems to have validity; it is generally understood and filled out completely by parents of varying literacy levels, and considerable variability exists among items checked by different families. The form is also accompanied by an interview with parents, at least at its first administration, and information revealed during the interview has not differed significantly from what would be expected from the completed survey form. The fact that almost no parents completed the open-ended ("needs we may have forgotten") portion at the end of the form suggests that the previous 26 items are inclusive of the major needs that parents

FIGURE 10-1. Parent needs survey.

Date: _____

Name of Person Completing Form: _____

Relationship to child: _____

    Parents of young children have many different needs. Not all parents need the same kinds of help. For each of the needs listed below, please check (✓) the space that best describes your need or desire for help in that area. Although we may not be able to help you with all your needs, your answers will help us improve our program.

	I really need some help in this area.	I would like some help, but my need is not that great.	I don't need any help in this area.
1. More information about my child's disability.			
2. Someone who can help me feel better about myself.			
3. Help with child care.			
4. More money/financial help.			
5. Someone who can babysit for a day or evening so I can get away.			
6. Better medical care for my child.			
7. More information about child development.			
8. More information about behavior problems.			
9. More information about programs that can help my child.			
10. Counseling to help me cope with my situation.			
11. Better/more frequent teaching or therapy services for my child.			
12. Daycare so I can get a job.			

FIGURE 10-1. (continued)

13. A bigger or better house or apartment.			
14. More information about how I can help my child.			
15. More information about nutrition or feeding.			
16. Learning how to handle my other children's jealousy of their brother or sister.			
17. Problems with in-laws or other relatives.			
18. Problems with friends or neighbors.			
19. Special equipment to meet my child's needs.			
20. More friends who have a child like mine.			
21. Someone to talk to about my problems.			
22. Problems with my husband (wife).			
23. A car or other form of transportation.			
24. Medical care for myself.			
25. More time for myself.			
26. More time to be with my child.			

Please list any needs we have forgotten:

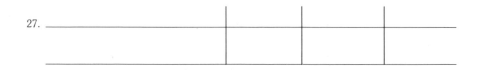

27.

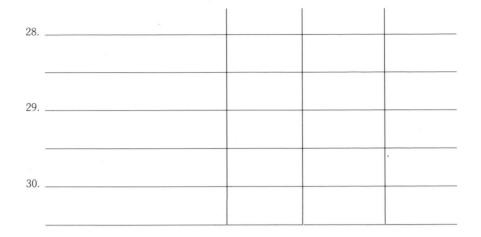

28. _____

29. _____

30. _____

have. Reliability has not been measured directly but is suggested by data from the parents of eight sets of twins indicating no variation at all in parental response between forms completed separately for each twin. Most of the forms have been completed by mothers, and a few by fathers and grandparents.

An analysis of the forms completed by the 49 families who have participated in at least two administrations with the same parent completing the form each time (Table 10-1) lends support to studies indicating that the need for information is paramount in parents of very young children (see, e.g., Carr, 1970; D'Arcy, 1968; Darling, 1979; Gayton & Walker, 1974). At program entry, 58% of parent responses indicated some need in this area. By six months, 40% indicated some need. The 1-year data are less reliable because of the low numbers collected to date (only 24 families). However, only 37% of the 1-year responses indicated any need for information. Responses indicating a *strong* need for information decreased from 22% of the total at intake to 8–9% after 6 months–1 year of service. Presumably the early intervention program, along with other sources of information, was successfully meeting this need.

Needs relating to treatment services are also highest at intake, although not as high as the need for information. Responses indicating a need in this area were 42% at program entry and decreased to 31% at 6 months and at 1 year. Again, the early intervention program probably helped to decrease this need somewhat.

Needs relating to both formal and informal support show a different pattern. Needs in both of these areas were relatively low (17% and 16%

TABLE 10-1. Degree and Type of Need Expressed by Parents during First Year of Participation in an Early Intervention Program as Measured by Number of Responses to Grouped Items on the PNS

	Degree of need								
	Intake ($n = 49$)			6 months ($n = 45$)[a]			1 year ($n = 24$)		
Type of need	High	Low	None	High	Low	None	High	Low	None
Information	58	96	115	22	85	156	12	36	80
	(22%)	(36%)	(43%)	(08%)	(32%)	(59%)	(09%)	(28%)	(63%)
Treatment	51	80	179	28	66	210	11	36	100
	(16%)	(26%)	(58%)	(09%)	(22%)	(69%)	(07%)	(24%)	(68%)
Formal support	13	24	183	16	28	175	8	20	76
	(06%)	(11%)	(83%)	(07%)	(13%)	(80%)	(08%)	(19%)	(73%)
Informal support	15	35	255	18	38	246	11	24	110
	(05%)	(11%)	(84%)	(06%)	(13%)	(81%)	(08%)	(16%)	(75%)
Material support	21	26	89	16	14	100	6	11	44
	(15%)	(19%)	(65%)	(08%)	(11%)	(77%)	(10%)	(18%)	(72%)
Competing needs	39	66	424	43	71	404	21	30	194
	(07%)	(12%)	(80%)	(08%)	(14%)	(78%)	(09%)	(12%)	(79%)

[a]In four cases, the PNS was not administered at 6 months but was administered at 1 year.

respectively) at intake. At 6 months, they increased slightly to 20% and 19% respectively; and at 1 year, they increased to 27% and 24%. This finding does not encourage very early involvement in parent support groups. Parents may not be ready for such groups until they have sufficient information to truly understand their child's disability. On the other hand, professionals should not neglect the parents whose responses indicate some need in this area from the beginning.

Data on competing needs indicate less need in this area than the others and no consistent pattern over time, with 19% of responses showing some need at intake, 22% at 6 months, and 21% at 1 year. Because many competing needs are included in these figures, analysis by individual item is instructive. For example, only nine parents (19%) indicated a need for "more time for myself" at program entry, but 17 (37%) indicated such a need 6 months later. In general, the results from this population suggest some shift over time from concern primarily with the child's disability (needs for information and treatment) to greater concern with some of the parent's own needs, especially for support. However, the need for information continues to be the most salient need at all time periods. This finding supports those of other studies in the literature that were reported earlier in this volume.

Need for material support shows a different pattern, with approximately one-third of responses indicating a need in this area at intake and about one-quarter indicating a need at the later time periods. Interestingly, need for financial support decreases from 52% at intake to 35–37% at 6 months and 1 year. This decreasing financial need is puzzling and may be a peculiarity of this community or simply a recognition by parents that the early intervention program cannot provide much help in meeting this need. An additional indicator of material needs used in the program is the toy checklist section of the HOME Screening Questionnaire (JFK Child Development Center, 1981). The checklist is not scored in any way but provides an additional descriptive assessment of the child-related material resources available in the home.

Based on these data, the range of responses representing any degree of need in the various categories is 16–58% at intake, 19–40% at 6 months, and 21–37% at 1 year. Both degree and range of need do seem to decrease considerably with time, as program involvement continues. However, needs clearly continue to exist, even after a year of receiving early intervention services. An instrument like the PNS can help professionals understand and meet parents' changing needs.

Because these data have been collected from only one program, the reader should not generalize the nature and extent of the needs expressed by this population to those of families elsewhere. In particular, the need for support may be suppressed by the very high level of extended family involvement in this geographic area. In addition, perceived needs may interact with availability of services and consequently may vary by geographic location. The PNS must be field tested by other programs before such generalizations can be made, and such testing is currently underway in additional programs across the country. However, the fact that these preliminary data support the existing literature in the field suggests that the PNS may be a simple instrument that can be used to assess family needs. In addition, because it is a self-administered instrument, staff do not need a high level of training to use it.

Programs may want to assess the needs of mothers, fathers, and other family members separately. The PNS was designed primarily for mothers and fathers. Similar instruments could be developed for siblings and grandparents. As we have noted throughout this book, effective intervention should take the entire family into account.

THE FAMILY INTERVIEW

No checklist type of instrument provides qualitative, in-depth information about families. True understanding of a family's situation can only be obtained by talking with family members about their strengths and needs or through long-term observation. Such observation is probably an invasion of privacy unnecessary for the purposes of providing an early intervention program. A well-constructed depth interview, on the other hand, can be conducted as part of the intake process and will provide valuable information.

The following interview schedule is a suggested model excerpted from a model used in the program discussed in the previous section. The interview should be conducted in a relaxed, conversational style, and follow-up questions may be asked to clarify statements made by parents. The interviewer must be careful to listen empathically and without personal judgment. The interview may be used separately with mothers and fathers, or with other family members, or with both parents present together.

I'd like to ask you some questions about your family to help us understand how we can best meet your needs and help you help your child. If I ask you anything you'd rather not answer, just tell me, and we'll skip that question. Please tell me, too, if there's anything you'd like to talk about that I may forget to ask.

First, it would help me to know a little about your (and your husband's/wife's) background.

Where are you from originally?

Was your family large?

Where did you go to school? What was the last grade in school you completed?

While you were growing up, did you know any children or adults with any kind of disability?

Had you ever heard of (child's disability) before _____ was born?

Do you remember the kinds of things you were thinking before _____ was born? Did you ever think he/she might have a problem of any kind?

Is _____ your first child?

When did you first learn that _____ had a problem? How did you feel when your first heard (or suspected) this?

What kinds of things have you worried about since you first learned about _____'s disability?

Have you told other people—siblings, grandparents, friends, minister/priest/rabbi, neighbors, co-workers? How have they reacted to the news? How have they reacted to the baby?

Do you know any other parents of children with special needs? Would you like to talk to other parents?

How did you learn about this program?

Has it been hard to get information about available services?

Have you been satisfied with your child's medical treatment so far?

How about your health; has it been good?

Has anyone else in the family had any medical problems?

Do you work? (If not) have you worked in the past? What kind of work do you do?

(If not working) would you work if you had someone to take care of _____?

Does your husband/wife help with child care?

Does your family live nearby? Do they help you with anything?

Do any of your other children have any special needs?

Have you had any problems with the baby—with sleeping, feeding, handling, or other areas of care?

Is there anything you need for the baby—furniture, clothing, equipment, toys?

Do you have a car or other means of transportation?

Would you say that you are coping pretty well with your problems right now, or would you like some help with things that are bothering you?

As part of this program, you will be asked to work on some activities with your baby at home. Do you think you will have any difficulty finding enough time to work on these activities? Do you like the idea of being your baby's teacher? Do you think you might have any special experience, skills or feelings that will make you a good teacher for your baby?

Can you think of anything else right now that our program might be able to help you with?

Interviewing skills should be part of the training that professionals in the early intervention field receive. Without such training, they may feel uncomfortable asking personal questions and may not be able to elicit valid responses. We would recommend that a course in social research methods, counseling, or a similar course be included as part of the preprofessional curriculum offered to those planning to enter the early intervention field. An alternative for those already working in the field would be appropriate inservice training. The family interview format included here is intended to serve as a guide and should not generally be used by untrained staff.

Regardless of the level of staff training, data from an initial family interview should be regarded with some caution. The interviewer is a stranger to the family and may not be trusted at the beginning of an intervention program. As a relationship develops between an interventionist and a family, the family is likely to reveal additional information about its needs. Needs also change over time. Consequently, assessment should be an ongoing process, and the interventionist should be sensitive to any changes that occur.

WRITING THE IFSP

After the PNS, family interview, child assessment, and toy checklist or any other assessments have been completed, the interventionist is ready to write the IFSP. Various guidelines exist in the educational literature for writing goals and objectives based on an assessment of the child. In addition to these child-oriented goals, however, the IFSP should contain a "family strengths and needs" section. First, a statement should be made about family strengths in each of the previously identified areas (information; treatment; formal, informal, and material support; and competing needs). The goals of intervention in each area would then be based on identified needs, as illustrated by the following chart:

Examples of Intervention Goals Based on Expressed Family Needs

Area of need	*Suggested goal*
I. Information (e.g., parent wants more information about child's disability)	I. Provide information or make referral to appropriate resource or professional.
II. Treatment (e.g., parent wants a program to help the child learn to talk)	II. Provide speech therapy or make appropriate referral.
III. Formal support (e.g., parent is experiencing incapacitating depression because of child's disability)	III. Provide counseling or make appropriate referral.
IV. Informal support (e.g., parents report that grandparents do not accept their child)	IV. Provide information to grandparents (e.g., "Especially Grandparents" newsletter) and provide or make referral to grandparent support group.
V. Material support (e.g., parents do not have enough money to meet child's needs)	V. Refer to appropriate community resources (e.g., Supplementary Security Income)
VI. Competing needs (e.g., mother wants to resume career but feels that she must stay home to care for child)	VI. Help the family locate appropriate day care.

In some cases, resources may not be readily available in the community to meet identified needs. For example, babysitters trained to care for children who have seizure disorders or who are dependent on highly technical medical equipment may be difficult to locate. In such instances, professionals may wish to explore the possibility of starting new programs or to help parents advocate for the creation of such programs. (The role of the professional as an advocate is discussed further in Chapter 9).

The actual IFSP will also contain timeframes within which goals and objectives are to be met.

The degree to which early intervention programs will be able to meet all of the needs expressed by parents will vary considerably. Programs that employ appropriately trained psychologists may be able to provide family counseling in accordance with the model suggested in Chapter 7. Programs without such resources will need to make referrals to other agencies or professionals. Some needs may not be able to be met at all (e.g., the need for a cure in the case of chronic or terminal illness); in such cases, the interventionist may only be able to help the family cope.

In some situations, then, the IFSP may include a comprehensive clinical treatment plan for parents. Programs must not, however, include such a plan for *all* parents just because there is a psychologist on the staff. Just as all children do not need speech therapy, for example, all parents do not need counseling. The PNS and family interview provide a means for allowing *the family* to define its own needs. An interventionist who is sensitive to the kinds of needs commonly expressed by families may be able to help the family clarify its needs. The interventionist should not assume, however, that the family will fit a particular clinical model of "families of handicapped children." Professionals may try to persuade parents to accept help when obvious needs exist. However, except in extreme cases, such as child abuse, the family's wishes should prevail. The great variability that exists among families must be reflected in IFSPs.

CHILDREN AND FAMILIES: A SUMMARY

Although the IFSP is only required for early intervention programs serving children from birth to age 3, *all* professionals who work with disabled children of any age must recognize the strengths and needs of the family as a whole. Professionals working in medical and educational settings have historically developed a kind of tunnel vision, that is, they have focused exclusively on the child as patient, student, or client and ignored the world within which the child lives. The field of early intervention has become a pioneer in broadening that focus because of the inescapable recognition that infants and their families are clinically inseparable.

In this book, we have tried to show how a child's disability has an impact on mothers, fathers, siblings, grandparents, and all other family members whose lives intersect with the child's life. These family members, in turn, play the most important role in shaping the child's future. Families are circles of interaction, and all of their members have an effect on one another. Professionals who treat children must recognize families and the cultural and subcultural worlds within which those families live.

In review, then, we have looked at childhood disability from the broad perspective of both *family systems* and *social systems.* We have looked at the effect of a child's disability on the family as well as the effects of the family's interaction within a social world of friends, relatives, professionals, and strangers. The family's definition of its situation is the product of all of these interactional experiences. If professionals want to understand families, they must come to understand their interactional worlds.

Specifically, as Chapter 2 suggests, families are located in social worlds long before their children are born. These worlds provide families with definitions of children and of disabilities, and these definitions shape family reactions to a child's birth and diagnosis. Preexisting definitions, however, generally prepare families poorly for the birth of a child with a disability. As a result, families strive to overcome their initial reaction of anomie and reestablish meaning in and control over their lives. Children themselves play an important role in this definitional process as they grow and develop and respond to their families' attempts at interacting with them.

As Chapter 3 indicates, the period of acute anomie usually ends with infancy. After their initial need for information and treatment for their child has been satisfied, most families are able to maintain a normalized lifestyle. As long as the surrounding social system is supportive, families with disabled children can return to the routines of career, household, and recreational pursuits during the years of childhood and adolescence.

For some families, however, normalization remains elusive. When formal and informal sources of support are not available or other family members have overwhelming problems, a child's disability can have a devastating impact on a family's lifestyle. As Chapters 4, 5, and 6 reveal, childhood disability can have both positive and negative effects on mothers, fathers, siblings, grandparents, and other family members. Each of these family members experiences the child's disability in a different way, and professionals need to understand these differences.

When family relationships become inordinately disturbed, intervention by a professional may be necessary. Chapter 7 describes a family systems approach to providing counseling in such situations. In this approach, the interactions among family members become the locus of concern.

In Chapter 8, the reader is once again reminded of the importance of the larger social system in shaping family responses. Reactions to childhood disability vary across ethnic, socioeconomic, and religious groups, and an understanding of a family's location within these groups can help to explain its beliefs, values, and behavior. Attitudes toward disability can also vary within the same cultural group over time.

The first eight chapters, then, further our understanding of the social world of the family. Chapter 9 shows what happens when this world intersects with that of the professional. Professionals have typically been trained to have a clinical worldview, which is different from the perspective of the family. The clinical view tends to define children and families narrowly in terms of a disability category or value-based label. The family, on the other hand, tends to define its situation within the broader parameters of its various interactional contexts. This difference in perspectives can result in conflict when families and professionals interact.

Finally, the present chapter suggests a model for applying the social system perspective developed throughout the book to an actual treatment situation—early intervention programs for infants and toddlers. By using an assessment of family-defined needs rather than a clinical model, the professional can design a treatment program that is system based. The Parent Needs Survey presented here is but one example of a professional tool that does not impose an external interpretation on a family's definition of the situation. We hope that an increasing recognition of and respect for the family's point of view will result in the development of similarly based instruments in all professional disciplines in this field.

Families are our greatest resource. They provide individuals with their earliest emotional and educational experiences. Children from strong families have the opportunity to become strong adults. Professionals cannot help children without the help of families. Only through a professional–family partnership can effective intervention occur. Professionals, then, must work to understand the world in which a child lives— the world of the family.

Families, in turn, reside within larger social structures. They are parts of systems of beliefs, values, and behaviors that shape their thinking and actions. Reactions to disability are social products resulting from a lifetime of interactional experiences. If we truly want to help families, we must do it on their terms, within the context of *their* system of meaning. Only through such a systems perspective can we hope to improve the quality of life for ordinary families who happen to have children with special needs.

REFERENCES

Bailey, D. B., Jr., & Simeonsson, R. J. (in press). Assessing needs of families with handicapped infants. *Journal of Special Education.*

Carr, J. (1970). Mongolism—Telling the parents. *Developmental Medicine and Child Neurology, 12,* 213.

D'Arcy, E. (1968). Congenital defects: Mothers' reactions to first information. *British Medical Journal, 3,* 796–798.

Darling, R. B. (1979). *Families against society: A study of reactions to children with birth defects.* Beverly Hills: Sage.

Education of the Handicapped Act Amendments of 1986, Public Law 99-457. (1987, January 13). (PSBA reprint available from Pennsylvania School Boards Association, 774 Limekiln Road, New Cumberland, PA 17070).

Especially Grandparents: A Newsletter for and about Grandparents of Children with Special Needs. (Available from ARC of King County, 2230 Eighth Avenue, Seattle, WA 98121).

Furuno, S., Inatsuka, T., O'Reilly, K., Hosaka, C., Zeisloft, B., & Allman, T. (1984). *HELP checklist (Hawaii early learning profile).* Palo Alto, CA: VORT Corporation.

Gayton, W. F., & Walker, L. (1974). Down's syndrome: Informing the parents. *American Journal of Disabled Children, 127,* 510–512.

Glover, M. E., Preminger, J. L., & Sanford, A. R. (1978). *E-LAP: The early learning accomplishment profile for developmentally young children.* Winston-Salem, NC: Kaplan Press.

JFK Child Development Center. (1981). *HOME Screening Questionnaire.* Denver, CO: LADOCA Publishing.

Journal of the Division for Early Childhood. Reston, VA: Council for Exceptional Children.

Mercer, J. R. (1965). Social system perspective and clinical perspective: Frames of reference for understanding career patterns of persons labeled as mentally retarded. *Social Problems, 13,* 18–34.

Topics in Early Childhood Special Education. Austin, TX: Pro-Ed.

Index

Please remember that this is a library book,
and that it belongs only temporarily to each
person who uses it. Be considerate. Do
not write in this, or any, library book.